3220 4389

Planning a
New West

◉ *Culture and Environment in the Pacific West*

Series Editor: William L. Lang

Books in this series are intended for general readers and for use in classrooms. They will examine a broad range of historical and contemporary issues about relationships between humans and the larger environment west of the Rockies. The books will be interdisciplinary and focused on issues important to this region.

Planning a
New West

The Columbia River Gorge National Scenic Area

Carl Abbott
Sy Adler
Margery Post Abbott

 **Oregon State University Press**
Corvallis

Cover photograph credits—

front cover: Oregon Tourism Commission
back cover: (top) U.S.D.A. Forest Service; (lower) authors

The paper in this book meets the guidelines for permanence and durability of the Committee on Production Guidelines for Book Longevity of the Council on Library Resources and the minimum requirements of the American National Standard for Permanence of Paper for Printer Library Materials Z39.48-1984.

Library of Congress Cataloging in Publication Data

Abbott, Carl.
Planning a new West : the Columbia River Gorge National Scenic Area / Carl Abbott, Sy Adler, Margery Post Abbott.
    p.   cm. — (Culture & environment in the Pacific West series)
Includes bibliographical references (p.   ) and index.
ISBN 0-87071-392-2 (acid-free paper)
1. Columbia River Gorge National Scenic Area (Or. and Wash.)—History. I. Adler, Sy, 1950- . II. Abbott, Margery Post. III. Title. IV. Series.
F853.A28 1997
979.7—dc21   96-39753
                                                      CIP

Contents

Series Editor's Introduction

The American West in the late twentieth century looks dramatically different than it did a century ago. Most of what has happened to the environment at the behest of an expanding national economy and a technologically ambitious population still lay ahead when the young Frederick Jackson Turner delivered his famous address at the Chicago World's Fair in 1893. Few predicted exactly how important the American West would be in the coming century and even fewer foresaw the potential for environmental crises that so worries this generation of westerners. Prognostications for the coming century by experts in 1893 included everything from recognition of a full range of women's rights and universal access to electricity to the institution of an international currency and 100-mile-per-hour trains. None of the seventy-four futurists at the World's Fair mentioned environmental issues. Yet today that subject is primary to scholars and thinkers about the American West, because of the enormous changes visited on the landscape during this century. And it is a more-than-even bet that the twenty-first century's central conundrums will concern the environment and human activity.

Awareness of contemporary environmental issues and the need to understand the historical relationships between humans and their environment prompts this series in *Culture and Environment in the Pacific West*. Its central focus is what happens when human cultural inventions intersect with the non-human world. Scholars have long agreed that investigations of environmental questions cannot be divorced from the context and ideology that inform and motivate human activity. Likewise, modern thinkers consider it delusionary to attempt explanations of human behavior apart from environmental conditions and places. But explanations of these relationships are nothing if not complex, and the resulting texts often read as very technical and arcane treatises. That is unfortunate, because the issues inherent in studies of human interaction with the environment are important and deserve consideration by a thoughtful public. With that purpose in mind, *Culture and Environment in the Pacific West* will publish books that broadly and creatively investigate the diverse relationships between human communities and their environments in the country west of the Continental Divide, a spectacularly varied and contrapuntal region of aridity and rivers, high plains and coastal slope, canyon lands and seashore.

Cultural diversity among human communities in the Pacific West has matched the region's environmental heterogeneity. From the earliest documented indigenous cultures to the most recent migrants, the Pacific West's people have found their places in the region, sometimes in areas with ready sustenance at hand and sometimes in environments that test human ingenuity. The stories of how they create their places in the larger environment and what that means to their neighbors and subsequent generations are the prime subjects of this series. These narratives are about change in the environment and in the ways people have furthered the human enterprise. The accounts are neither entirely harmonious nor discordant but always revealing about how western people have understood their place. The profound changes that everywhere in the Pacific West seem to signify a crucial reorientation in how people relate to the environment and how they perceive their past is captured in the term "New West," which is generally understood to mean a broad range of new relationships between economic activity and western landscapes, between residents and new settlers, and between orientations that are labeled "Old West" and "New West" is the subject of the inaugural book in the series.

In *Planning a New West,* Carl Abbot, Sy Adler, and Margery Post Abbott investigate the reinvention of a classic western landscape—the Columbia River Gorge. Like some of the stories of conflict in the Old West, which pitted competing users of the land against each other, this narrative describes a contest over the management of an environmental place in the New West. It is a complex and fast-paced story that begins with a land use conflict in 1981, devolves into a cultural tug-of-war between competing visions for a dramatically scenic landscape, and concludes with the creation of an ongoing experiment in regional environmental planning that is unique in the Pacific West.

In this masterful telling, the authors take readers inside one of the most remarkable planning efforts in recent history, perhaps a harbinger of future resolutions of similar environmental disputes. *Planning a New West* is fundamentally about the process of understanding the multifarious connections people have with place and the inescapable conflict when the participants disagree. In the Columbia Gorge, an 28511-acre riverine environment dominated by the powerful Columbia River, breathtaking waterfalls, dense forests, and small communities, the Old West met the New West during the past two decades, when windsurfers discovered the gorge winds, traditional natural resource industries tumbled, and urban emigrants began resettling the place as a recreational area. No single conflict between the new and old residents or between the newer and older economies could be settled, the authors explain, without everyone contending with the environmental power of the gorge itself.

The authors carefully detail how the participants found their way out of an environmental and cultural dilemma by reinventing the place. yet in the reinvention, as *Planning a New West* makes clear, the residents and planners reached back into the earlier visions of the gorge—even to those expressed by Native Americans—to craft a new understanding and foundation for inhabiting the place. The authors draw no hard-edged conclusions about the process and the results, for the heart of their story is in the creative reinvention that makes up the Columbia River Gorge National Scenic Area. If there truly is a New West, it may well be that this book is the first telling of how it will be organized.

William L. Lang

Acknowledgments

This book owes a substantial debt to Sheldon Edner, formerly a colleague in the School of Urban and Public Affairs and now an executive with the U.S. Department of Transportation. In the mid-1980s, Sheldon identified the Scenic Area as a fruitful topic of study, put together a series of colloquia in which we talked with important players in the establishment of the Scenic Area, and helped to plan the organization of the book. His early interest and enthusiasm brought the rest of us into the project, and he graciously passed the torch as his own professional interests changed.

We are indebted to the dozens of individuals who took the time to talk to us during our research. Although some of our informants may disagree with aspects of our interpretation, we have striven for accuracy in depicting their own views. We thank them for their time and interest.

We gratefully acknowledge support from the Faculty Development Fund of Portland State university. Several graduate students including Kathleen Stokes, Fran Tangen, Tracy Allen, and Robert Jones also assisted with the research. In addition, we have benefited from the work of Gordon Euler, whose Ph.D. dissertation in Portland State's Public Administration Policy program explored the process of planning for scenic resources in the gorge.

Columbia River Gorge National Scenic Area

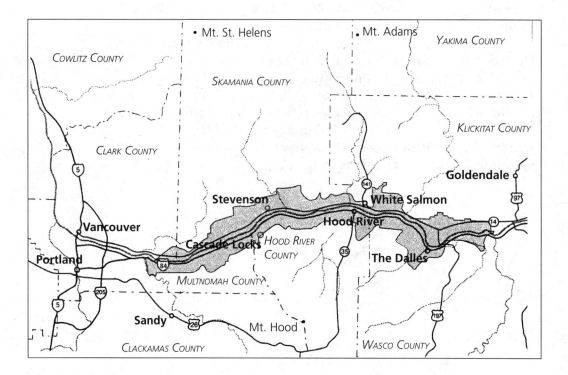

X   *Location map: The Columbia River Gorge National Scenic Area*

Introducing the Columbia River Gorge:
"Magnificent Display and Terrible Grandeur"

"Here wonder, curiosity, and admiration combine to arouse sentiments of awe and delight . . ."
Francis Fuller Victor, 1891

Three stories high, square, and solid as a tan boulder, the Skamania County Courthouse is the most imposing building in the small town of Stevenson, Washington. Set above a sloping park and the town's main drag of State Route 14, the courthouse looks south across the Columbia River to towering bluffs on the Oregon side. On October 16, 1986, however, county workers paid little attention to the view. Their eyes were on cable television coverage of the U.S. House of Representatives as it considered creating a National Scenic Area for the Columbia River Gorge. There was no doubt about sympathies in the courthouse—89 percent of Skamania County voters had agreed with a 1984 ballot measure demanding that the state and federal governments keep their hands off local land management. Nevertheless, the House passed the Scenic Area Act on October 16 and the Senate a day later.

The Skamania County Commission, outgunned in state and national politics, responded with symbolism. For the next week, the American flag fluttered at half-mast in front of the courthouse. No president had died, no national hero was gone, but many residents in the rural communities and small towns of the gorge believed that the new federal law marked the end of a way of life. "It was a statement that it was a funeral, a wake," commented Commissioner H. J. Vandenberg.

Skamania County's official dismay demonstrated the deep division about the proper management and preferred future of the Columbia Gorge. To Scenic Area supporters who broke out the wine and champagne in Portland, Seattle, and Washington, D.C., the legislation represented the success of fifty years of struggle for environmental values; it was a rational way to manage inexorable economic change. To the Stevenson residents who wandered into the offices of the *Skamania County Pioneer* to get the news and shake their heads, the Scenic Area looked like willful murder, a death blow

1

to the old resource economy and those who had shaped their lives around timber and farming.

The full story of the Columbia River Gorge National Scenic Area encapsulates many of the issues and debates that divide the larger Pacific Northwest and nearly every other part of the American West in the waning years of the twentieth century. Who gets to shape and speak for the West? How do national and regional claims interact with local interests? Can old resource regions be planned into prosperity as participants in the networked economy of a New West? Is it worth their while to fight rear-guard actions against change driven by outside forces? From the viewpoint of the far future, will the twentieth century look like one long transition from the pioneer West of the nineteenth century to the globalized West of the twenty-first? Is it inevitable that a New West will replace the Old West?

The Gorge and the River

The backdrop for these debates is the powerful Columbia River itself, for the slopes and valleys of the gorge are a creation of its river. Rising on the western slopes of the Rocky Mountains in Idaho, Wyoming, Montana, and British Columbia, the waters of the Columbia gather as the river loops south through the state of Washington. Melting snows from the mountains of Idaho, Washington, and Oregon feed the major tributary rivers—the Clark Fork, Spokane, Snake, Yakima, John Day, Deschutes. Two hundred miles from the Pacific Ocean, the Columbia nears the great barrier raised by the volcanic peaks and plateaus of the Cascade Range. For seventy-five miles, from the small city of The Dalles to the eastern suburbs of Portland, the river cuts a gorge between the northern flanks of Mount Hood and the southern flanks of Mount Adams. It has carved its passageway through successive uplifts and outflows of lava over millions of years. Towering floods of glacial melt water repeatedly crashed through the gorge between 16,000 and 12,800 years ago to shape its present form.

What we now know as the Columbia Gorge is the only passage near sea level through the Cascade and Sierra Nevada ranges between the United States-Canada border and southern California. Before the arrival of Europeans, the Chinook-speaking peoples of the coast traveled to trade in the future vicinity of The Dalles, where Celilo Falls marked a break

2

Landscape of the eastern gorge: Catherine Creek seen from Oregon.
(Photo: USDA Forest Service)

in navigation and the divide between lush coastal lands and dry interior plateaus. It also divided the distinctive culture of Northwest Coast people from the very different lifeways of inland peoples such as the Shoshonis, Paiutes, and Nez Perce, making the course of the Columbia a natural trade route and the falls a natural marketplace.

The Columbia Gorge has been equally important as a passageway for English-speaking Americans. In November 1805, the Columbia River led Meriwether Lewis and William Clark to the drizzly Pacific shore. Settlers from eastern America followed on their way to the Oregon Country in the 1840s. After mid-century, the gorge became a key link in the regional steamboat system that tied together the American Northwest. Three generations later, the gorge is simultaneously an interstate highway route, an internationally important rail corridor, and a passageway for barge traffic between Portland and the Snake River.

Initially ignored by pioneers seeking the fertile farm lands of the Willamette Valley or the gold fields of Idaho, Montana, and eastern Oregon, the waters and lands along the middle Columbia became themselves major contributors to the resource economy of the Pacific Northwest in the late

3

nineteenth and early twentieth centuries. Salmon fishing peaked between 1883 and 1895, as revolving fishwheels scooped up fish for riverside canneries. Orchards brought prosperity to the Hood River Valley and The Dalles early in the new century. Tall Douglas-fir trees fell to saws and axes as logging railroads zigged up the 3,000-foot mountains that flank the river to reach now-vanished logging camps.

Dramatic alterations in the very appearance of the gorge followed when the Army Corps of Engineers constructed Bonneville Dam (1937) and The Dalles Dam (1957) for hydroelectric power and navigation. The Bonneville pool flooded the narrow mid-gorge rapids and navigation facilities that had given their name to the town of Cascade Locks, Oregon. The Dalles Dam drowned the centuries-old fishing grounds at Celilo Falls, where Native Americans had taken salmon as the fish returned upstream.

Change in the Gorge

This first century and a half of Anglo-American use was part of the construction of the "Old West," the development of which has been central to that of the United States. Investment and settlement of the Old West were tied directly to the production, processing, and shipping of natural resources. The farm communities, cannery towns, and timber camps that overlooked the Columbia shared the larger national assumption that natural resources were to be harvested, transformed, and utilized. Their residents would have been at home in Colorado mining camps, Montana smelter towns, Dakota wheat boom communities, Texas oil fields, or California citrus cities.

During the last century, however, a different economy has gradually emerged in the Northwest in the shadow of resource harvesting. As early as the 1880s, tourism entrepreneurs were praising the "aesthetic enjoyment and hygienic exhilaration" of the scenery to be viewed on an upriver steamboat ride from Portland. The experience was "uninterrupted magnificent display and terrible grandeur," according to the passenger department of the Union Pacific Railway. Completion of the Columbia River Highway from Portland to The Dalles in the 1910s opened the gorge to fuller recreational use. City and state parks, hotels, and auto camps dotted the shoreline. Civilian Conservation Corps workers during the 1930s cut

4

Landscape of the western gorge: Interstate Highway I-84, taken from the old Scenic Highway. (Photo: Oregon State Highway Department)

trails to the waterfalls that crash from the rimming bluffs to the river. In the 1980s, leaders of the booming international windsurfing business discovered the gorge as a prime sailing spot, triggering a new wave of economic change in Hood River and nearby communities and new social tensions between "boardheads" and self-proclaimed "ugly locals." Today, elected officials try to balance the desires of long-term residents and newcomers. Letters to the editor complain about cars with California license plates hogging downtown parking spaces while local merchants feast on the new business.

The identification of the Columbia River Gorge as a distinct natural region rather than a series of separate obstacles is in part a product of this new recreational era. The phrase "Columbia Gorge" does not appear on early nineteenth-century maps. The journals of American explorers and pioneers describe individual features—the "Columbia Rapids" at Celilo, "the Cascades," hills, cliffs—but not as components of a single identified region. Not until the 1880s did regional writers such as Leo Samuel and Francis Fuller Victor identify the gorge as a place where "wonder, curiosity, and admiration combine." A

5

flood of guidebooks and tourist pamphlets that followed in the early twentieth century made "the gorge of the Columbia River" one of the commonly recognized features of the American West.

In the closing decades of the twentieth century, the seeds of tourism have grown into a powerful and diversified force for social and economic change. From New Mexico to Alaska, strong and articulate interests are shaping a New West on the foundations of the Old West. The New West is an archipelago of thriving cities reaching out to "resettle" old and often fading resource regions for recreation and retirement, exurban commuting and telecommuting, and locations for service industries. Las Vegas and Los Alamos, Austin and Aspen, Seattle and Sun Valley—metropolitan centers and their urbanized outliers—are all parts of the New West. So are the hundreds of smaller towns that try to accommodate new and cosmopolitan residents who have few connections to the old economy.

Inside or outside the traditional West, the differences between old and new societies are many: attitudes toward natural resources, orientation to local communities or national networks, sources of livelihood, levels of comfort with large-scale organizations and bureaucratic processes. The Old West depends directly on the production and processing of natural resources. New Westerners tend to value preservation or conservation of those same resources (except, perhaps, for their development into golf courses and ski runs). They also know how to wield credentialed expertise. New Westerners tend to look out their windows and see scenery, not resources, thus modifying the meanings of place. In the most fundamental contrast, the New West is a set of bases for networked lives; the Old West is a set of narrowly focused but deeply embedded communities.

The National Scenic Area

6

In the Columbia River Gorge, creation of a National Scenic Area in 1986 surfaced these differences of goals and life patterns as issues of public policy. Hammered out in a series of meetings among Oregon and Washington lawmakers and then adopted by Congress, P.L. 99-564 declared a national interest in the scenic corridor along the Columbia River from the confluence of the Deschutes River westward to the mouth of the Sandy River just outside Portland. The Columbia River Gorge National Scenic Area runs roughly eighty-three miles along the river and extends two to four miles inland from each bank (see pages 8-9 for a map of the Scenic Area and basic facts on population and ownership).

The Scenic Area is best described as a land use planning program for a region of extra-local importance. The drafters of the legislation drew in part on the experience of parallel planning efforts from the northeastern states and California. They also borrowed ideas from Oregon's statewide land use planning system, from multi-state river compacts, and from the multi-purpose mandates of the Forest Service and Bureau of Land Management. In legal terms, the law provided the consent of Congress for an interstate compact; the consent was contingent on implementation by Oregon and Washington through state legislation establishing the Columbia River Gorge Commission.

The Scenic Area is thus an experiment in American federalism that follows sixty years of sporadic efforts to find a politically acceptable formula for land use and development planning across state boundaries. It is an effort at regional land use planning mandated by the federal government at the instigation of and in partnership with state and local governments. In comparison with similar cases around the country, the Scenic Area involves more jurisdictions than New York's Adirondack Park, New Jersey's Pinelands, or the Cape Cod National Seashore. It aims to avoid the interstate conflicts that have crippled thirty years of bistate management efforts at Lake Tahoe by writing explicit goals into federal law. These goals are:

1. To establish a national scenic area to protect and provide for the enhancement of the scenic, cultural, recreational, and natural resources of the Columbia River Gorge; and
2. To protect and support the economy of the Columbia River Gorge area by encouraging growth to occur in existing urban areas and by allowing future economic development in a manner that is consistent with paragraph 1.

7

By setting these dual purposes and by designating formal management roles for the federal government, two states, six counties, and the Nez Perce, Yakama, Warm Springs, and Umatilla tribes, the legislation internalized permanent tensions between competing visions of the gorge. At its most

continued on page 10

Population and Land Ownership in the Columbia River Gorge

The population of the Scenic Area was estimated at 51,867 in 1987. Fewer than five thousand Scenic Area residents live in Multnomah and Clark counties, leaving 47,000 to 48,000 Scenic Area residents among the 63,500 people of the other four counties.

National Scenic Area Acreage by County		
County	Scenic Area Acreage	Percent of County
Multnomah	39,910	14.7
Hood River	38,620	11.5
Wasco	44,710	2.9
Total Oregon	123,240	5.7
Clark	7,690	1.9
Skamania	87,340	8.1
Klickitat	74,360	6.1
Total Washington	169,390	6.3

Like the rest of the American West, the Columbia River Gorge in the nineteenth and twentieth centuries has been a land of mixed ownership. After the Civil War, private owners began to stake out townsites along the river and its uplands, such as Goldendale in 1879 and Hood River in 1880. The federal government set aside what is now Mount Hood National Forest as Oregon National Forest in 1908, combining the Bull Run Reserve of 1892 and parts of the Cascade Reserve of 1893. What is now Gifford Pinchot National Forest in Washington originated as part of Mount Rainier Forest Reserve in 1897 and was designated as Columbia National Forest in 1908.

At the start of the 1980s, management of lands within the gorge was divided among the multiple-use lands of the U.S.D.A. Forest Service, several National Forest wilderness areas, Oregon and Washington state parks, and private holdings of both rural and urban land. Within Wasco and Klickitat counties were also lands under the control of the Bureau of Land Management. (Portions of the Yakama and Warm Springs Indian Reservations are also located in Klickitat and Wasco counties, but outside the gorge.)

8

The legislation carved the gorge into three management areas:

*The **Special Management Area (SMA)** of 115,100 acres comprises mostly lands in the two national forests. The Forest Service was to prepare a preliminary Management Plan for these.*

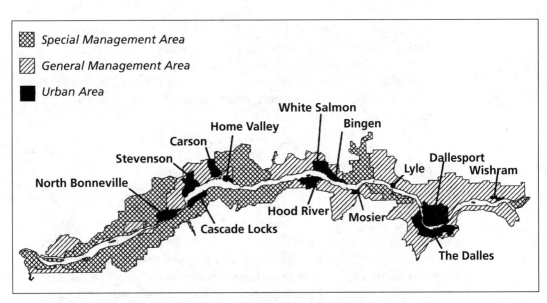

The Columbia River Gorge National Scenic Area

The 149,004 acres of **General Management Area (GMA)** contain a mixture of resource uses and scattered housing on mostly private land. A new bi-state Columbia River Gorge Commission was established to plan for these areas.

Thirteen **Urban Areas** with 28,511 acres were exempted from the Management Plan but invited to receive federal funds by cooperating in implementation. The Urban Areas are North Bonneville, Stevenson, Carson, Home Valley, White Salmon, Bingen, Lyle, Dallesport, and Wishram in Washington and Cascade Locks, Hood River, Mosier, and The Dalles in Oregon. The largest in population in 1990 was The Dalles at 11,000, followed by Hood River at 4,600 and White Salmon at 2,100. The other Urban Areas ranged in population from a few hundred to just over one thousand.

In aggregate, about 70 percent of the land within the National Scenic Area boundaries is privately owned and 30 percent publicly owned. Scenic Area lands range from less than 2 percent of the total area of Clark County to almost 15 percent of the area of Multnomah County.

9

basic, these tensions pit the New West of service industries and globalized cities against the Old West of farming and forestry. The law gives primacy to the presumed interests of city dwellers, but it also tempers these interests by protecting opportunities for economic diversification and growth in the number of locally based jobs.

The Greenline Idea

As an effort to plan for environmentally sensitive economic development, the Scenic Area faces the challenge of balancing very different and sometimes clashing activities within the same small space. In taking on this challenge, the legislation conceives of the gorge as a "greenline park" in the manner of New York's Adirondacks Park and the New Jersey Pinelands. Borrowed from Europe and the United Kingdom, the term comes from the idea of drawing a "green" line on a map to define a district of high scenic or cultural value and devising special land management regulations to sustain its character over time. For example, national parks in the United Kingdom are specially regulated landscapes rather than public reserves in the American style.

The greenline concept is intended for working or living landscapes rather than for wilderness lands. It envisions the conservation of valued regions through special regulations rather than massive land acquisition. Inside the green line, special controls can preserve natural resources, social institutions, and historic landscapes while allowing local residents to continue their previous livelihoods from land-based industries. Senator Mark Hatfield reflected this understanding of the Scenic Area when he told a gorge audience that the legislation "was never intended to dry up those communities in the gorge or to be a blow to the future of those communities."

Implicit in the greenline approach is the recognition that the Scenic Area *is not* an environmental program to save or protect a discrete, measurable, and actively threatened natural resource such as a rare animal species or pure water. By contrast, planning efforts for Lake Tahoe or Chesapeake Bay directly link controls on land use and other human behaviors with measurable effects on resource quality. In the gorge, people have drastically altered the natural environment by logging, fishing, and farming, and by building dams, roads,

10

***Landscape of the western gorge: walking the old Scenic Highway.
(Photo: USDA Forest Service)***

and railroads. We have impounded the river, carved its shores for roads and railroads, and nearly eliminated its salmon runs. No natural resource here exists in anything like its form at the time of Lewis and Clark. Although the legislation and Management Plan include a number of protections for specific environmental systems such as wetlands and tributary rivers, the Scenic Area Act places natural resources on a par with scenic, cultural, and recreational resources. In the gorge, in short, appearance is to be valued and conserved as much as natural systems.

Within the greenline framework, the Scenic Area also attempts to balance and moderate the impacts of tourism. Its regulations limit the expansion of boardsailing sites and facilities and dampen the possibilities of large-scale resort development. By slowing "Aspenization"—the headlong transformation of local economic and social systems that has occurred in many Western recreational hot spots—the legislation may preserve economic opportunities for local entrepreneurs who can serve a limited market but who would be squeezed out by large-scale recreational investment. It meets the interest of Portlanders in maintaining a *regionally*

11

prominent recreation area that balances "cultural tourism" (hiking, looking at waterfalls and wildflowers) with "recreational tourism" (boardsailing, conference centers, golfing) while fending off "entertainment tourism" in the style of Las Vegas or Disneyland.

Old and New in the American West

The Scenic Area thus demands a delicate balancing act among jurisdictions and cultures. Demographic changes and contrasting personal expectations make transitional Old West communities prime candidates for political conflict. The entire American West is becoming increasingly polarized, with a scattering of New West continents (California) and islands (greater Portland, Seattle-Tacoma) set in a thinly populated sea of Old West resource areas. Much of the debate over environmental issues in the region has been a civil war in which the long reach of the urban West has triggered battles over resource policy. Indeed, one of our conclusions is that the Scenic Area represents the steady expansion of Portland's influence over gorge communities. For more than a century, residents of the growing city have staked a complex claim on the gorge as transportation corridor, source of hydroelectric power, and recreation area. Metropolitan outreach is both economic and political. As an economic process it involves capital investment, control of transportation systems, and recreational use. As a political process it involves the mobilization of legislative and regulatory power.

In the midst of rapid regional transformation, the Scenic Area is a vast experiment in mediating between old and new. The intent is to plan and manage the changes that have come piecemeal and sometimes overwhelmingly to other communities and resource regions. It tries to balance the forces of change against the claims of existing social and economic systems, and in so doing mobilizes diverse and divided political constituencies: passionate environmentalists within the gorge, powerfully organized environmentalists in Northwestern cities, fervent defenders of property rights, and gorge political leaders interested in defending their turf. Internal disagreements within the gorge helped to set a context in which those external groups with the best press releases and easiest access to state and federal politicians shaped the legislation. In essence, gorge residents who tag the Scenic Area

12

legislation as an outside job and a backroom deal are correct, although the broader idea of protection for the gorge environment draws on deep local roots.

The Scenic Area land use planning requirements attempt to absorb and dampen competing political interests within an administrative process that produced a Management Plan between 1986 and 1992 and has since enforced that plan. The program requires ranchers and loggers who pride themselves on bluntness to learn the customs of committee work and bureaucracies and simultaneously expects sophisticated interest groups to accept rural communities as partners and agents of change. On both sides, powerful and passionate political constituencies have had to act through the subtle politics of interest group lobbying. Ultimately the Scenic Area and the debates it engenders are about the *possibilities* of sharing the power to make land development decisions.

Planning in Oregon and Washington

In taking on this political challenge, the National Scenic Area has to balance two very different planning regimes in the two states. In Oregon, the passage of Senate Bill 100 in 1973 brought the entire state under a single set of planning goals administered by the Land Conservation and Development Commission. Like those elsewhere in the state, gorge counties and cities are required to adopt local land use plans and implementation tools compatible with statewide goals for the protection of farm and forest land, the containment of urban growth, the development of energy-efficient land use patterns, and the conservation of scenic resources.

Until very recently, in contrast, Washington left land use regulation to the discretion of its localities. Skamania County, in the heart of the gorge, scandalized conservation-minded Oregonians through the 1980s by deciding to live without county zoning or any other basic form of growth management. In the face of rapid growth in the Puget Sound region, the Washington legislature in 1990 and 1991 adopted a strong growth management system that applies to counties of over 50,000 residents, including Clark County but not Skamania or Klickitat counties.

The different institutional systems reflect different political cultures. Land use decisions in Washington emphasize private

13

Planning Styles

Environmental planning efforts can be visualized along two dimensions described by planning theorist Paul Niebanck.

*The first has to do with the conceptual framework for identifying and defining environmental problems. It runs from **targeted action** (specific efforts to solve particular problems) to **principled action** (broad efforts to promote sets of explicit values).*

*The second dimension has to do with responses to these problems. It runs from **rule making** (planning as external regulation and intervention) to **place making** (cooperative community-based management of unique environments in the light of local knowledge).*

We see rule making as an expression of the rationalized modern state. It often draws support from city-based institutions and organizations that are accustomed to influencing abstract processes across multiple locations. Place making can be old-fashioned economic boosterism. It may also be activism by romantic regionalists who work to preserve local differences as a way to resist the homogenizing power of national and international institutions and cultures. It is often rooted in small towns and rural communities where social organizations may have a relatively limited reach and the setting of everyday life is an important contributor to a local sense of identity.

interests in development. State-level politics has revolved around the agenda of economic growth, whether in the entrepreneurial form associated with Republicans or the liberal corporatist form associated with Democrats. As has been true throughout the Old West, the claims of community on individual land development choices have been weak. Oregon land use planning has developed within a framework that is more community-oriented in concept and more bureaucratic in operation. A majority of Oregonians have shared a moralistic approach to the public realm and agreed that civic interests can weigh heavily against private goals. In practice, Oregon planning has been legalistic and procedural, giving an advantage to verbally trained New Westerners. It has also been driven by the needs and concerns of Willamette Valley farmers and cities—concerns that often seem irrelevant in the very different environment of the gorge.

Why Involve the Federal Government?

14 The Columbia River Gorge National Scenic Area originated as a targeted effort to solve the very specific problem of residential subdivision of gorge lands in the state of Washington. The "crisis" that mobilized the Friends of the Columbia River Gorge was the realistic fear that suburban sprawl in Clark County and second-home development in Skamania County would damage environmental systems and create visual blight. It is likely that there would have been no Scenic Area legislation if political leaders on the north side of the river had preempted this triggering issue by regulating growth patterns. Skamania and Clark counties could have derailed the drive for federal regulation by adopting effective land use zoning and growth management plans in the early 1980s instead of waiting to be forced to action in the 1990s.

The argument for a Scenic Area evolved from targeted problem solving to general regulation when advocates of federal intervention tried to broaden their base of support. Activists used scenic photography, media contacts, and sheer power of repetition to define the gorge as a *national* scenic treasure. They could argue that a scenic resource of national merit deserved comprehensive and systematic protection based on national values and standards, and that successful efforts in the gorge could have national and international implications.

The principled arguments that justified federal action to save the Columbia Gorge also implied a preference for rule making rather than place making. Rule making defines particular problems as subsets of broader processes and derives appropriate treatments from general principles. In so doing, it values abstractions and expertise over personal relationships or local knowledge. In influencing the legislation, environmentalists showed their distrust of political leaders within the gorge by pushing successfully for state and federal management and for detailed standards that limit the discretion of officials on the scene. Gorge commissioners frequently lament that they take no end of criticism for actions explicitly required by Congress.

The legislation also invited a role for Portlanders and for national experts who could apply general concepts and principles to managing the gorge and its scenery. By choosing professional staff with state and national expertise, the Gorge Commission helped to structure the politics of gorge planning as a dialogue between locals and "outsiders." Had they been explicitly challenged, the advocates of a federal management role or management standards would have argued that rule making of this kind was the only feasible approach. In the mid-1980s, despite the activities of local gorge activists, there was no *politically effective* constituency for place making that was sensitive to environment and scenery. The alternative to bureaucratic rule making was a continuation of place making by local growth coalitions and networks of pro-growth landowners and politicians.

15

Landscape of the eastern gorge: Horsethief Butte, Washington. (Photo: USDA Forest Service)

Who's in Control?

The issue of "level-of-control" is a hearty perennial in urban and regional planning, where individuals, cities, counties, state agencies, and federal officials all claim rights to make land management decisions. In land use planning, the debate often boils down to how widely advocates of "local control" are willing to draw the boundaries of place. In the world of practical politics, "local" is a variable concept. Many residents within the gorge view Portlanders as outsiders to the Scenic Area, but everyone within the Columbia Basin may see themselves as members of a single region when faced with periodic proposals to divert Columbia River water to California. Much of the political controversy over creation and implementation of the Scenic Area revolves around this question of whether metropolitan Portland and the gorge constitute two distinct places, or parts of a single place.

Gorge residents who define the gorge as distinct from Portland also argue among themselves whether the gorge itself is one place or many, and whether its inhabitants are one people or many. A social geographer mapping the gorge might

16

find at least four distinct social-cultural subregions from west to east: Portland-Vancouver exurbs, a "backwoods" lumbering district, intensely farmed tributary valleys with multiethnic populations, and a fringe of the vast dryland cattle and wheat region of the interior West. The Scenic Area has generated hostility within the gorge in part because it creates the first gorgewide institutions and requires disparate communities to work together.

The limits of the "local community" are defined by time as well as place, further separating residents into insiders and outsiders. Local political establishments and embedded social networks commonly represent residents with two- or three-generation connections to the gorge. As in many Western rural communities, descent from a pioneer or homesteading family confers privileged status. Individuals who have moved to the gorge from a similar resource region also find it easy to fit into leadership roles. Those who have moved from cities find it much harder to shake the status of interloper, even though their commitment to the place may be highly articulate, deliberate, and heartfelt. As Native Americans sometimes discover, however, it is also possible to become an outsider by having a family connection to the gorge that goes back *too many* centuries. In the Columbia Gorge of the 1990s, ten years is not enough time to turn an outsider into an insider, one hundred years is about right, and a thousand years is overdoing it.

What Do We Think?

As planners and historians, we view the Scenic Area as a troubled but worthy undertaking. Fundamentally, we believe that it is better to plan for change than to let it come completely at the whim of outside forces of capital and fashion. The Scenic Area provides opportunities for local residents to take part in a regional planning process and to think explicitly about the future of their communities. This is an advantage that few resource-dependent communities enjoy. In contrast to people in many other regions, gorge residents have a federally sanctioned public forum in which to talk about the fate of their communities. Thoughtful consideration of community futures can perhaps bridge local differences and increase the capacity of local people to shape their own future in a way that business as usual under the direction of a land-owning elite cannot.

17

We also view the rise of the New West as more beneficial than harmful. The decline in world commodity prices and the reduction of federal expenditures on dams, irrigation canals, and alternative fuels in the 1980s knocked the remaining props from under many resource communities. In the later 1990s, the national drive to balance the federal budget by reducing domestic programs is likely to outweigh the developmental effects of weakened environmental regulations. Much of the replacement economy provided by the leisure industry is supported by the modern equivalents of remittance men—in this case retirees living on pensions, Social Security, and Medicare, or students paying tuition and rent with dollars earned elsewhere. Retirees may be explicit about their desire to escape urban problems and prices. Nonetheless, most of them bring values and expectations formed in cities where communication is quick and quality medical care is readily available. Their net impact will raise the quality and variety of community services, further the incorporation of formerly rural communities into metropolitan networks, and expand the range of opportunities for coming generations.

At the same time, we recognize problems with the legislation and its implementation. In some ways the Scenic Area is too big, forcing common solutions on disparate communities and counties that believe they have very distinctive problems. At the same time, the Columbia Gorge may be too small an area for effective comprehensive analysis and planning for either resource development or resource conservation. It is a small fragment of the Columbia River basin, of the Cascade Mountains, and of the Northwest timber region. The legislation ignores the river itself except as a scenic resource and omits essential areas of concern such as energy generation choice, fish habitat, and survival of salmon runs. The Scenic Area regulators are required to respect Native American treaty fishing rights but have no role in their enforcement. The Scenic Area deals, in actuality, with those parts of the gorge above the waterline.

Although we characterize the Scenic Area as an opportunity for residents to take thought for the future, there has been disagreement on the Columbia River Gorge Commission about the direction and quality of that conversation. These disagreements reflect differences among gorge residents and interest groups. Supporters of the Management Plan believe that the commission has met the challenge of thinking broadly and fending off development chaos. Others see a missed opportunity for exploring new models of community-based stewardship as an alternative to rigid regulations.

Outside commission meeting rooms, the Scenic Area has been less effective than hoped at bridging the social gaps among the region's fifty thousand people. It has often been uncomfortable for local supporters of the Scenic Area to voice their views. In the mid-1990s, the national resurgence of individualistic property rights ideologies has revitalized attacks on the Scenic Area as a symbol of government interference and the devaluation of pioneer lifeways.

To the credit of its advocates and framers, Scenic Area planning has formally involved all important actors and interests. But it is troublesome that those who advocate landscape conservation also espouse the regulatory approach to management, while supporters of resource exploitation favor a place-making approach. As a system of planning, the central challenge to the Columbia River Gorge National Scenic Area is to recognize and incorporate local regard for place within the framework of generalizable and legally defensible rules.

It is not yet clear whether it is possible to find such a middle ground within a rapidly changing and deeply divided West. The Scenic Area is a work in progress—a balancing act that can easily tilt off center or collapse. Nevertheless, the Scenic Area may well be as good a chance as Americans are likely to get at crafting a cooperative search for an ethic of place, for it ideally provides a structured opportunity for the region to talk about its future. By examining and explaining the origins and implementation of the Scenic Area, we hope that this book contributes to this dialogue within the gorge and within the larger American West.

Comparing the Scenic Area
Experiments in Regional Environmental Planning

We have chosen four examples of innovative intergovernmental regional planning programs for comparison with the Columbia Gorge National Scenic Area. Each comparison case is described in detail in professional and academic studies.

> *The oldest and smallest is the **Cape Cod National Seashore**, established in 1961 and covering 44,000 total acres.*
>
> *The **Tahoe Regional Planning Agency** is a bistate agency established in 1969 by California and Nevada under federal enabling legislation; the institutional structure for Tahoe regional planning was substantially revised in 1980. The area is a close match to the Columbia Gorge in terms of geographical coverage and year-round population.*
>
> *The **Adirondack Park Agency** (APA) is the only program without federal involvement. New York state legislation in 1971 established the APA to create a comprehensive plan to regulate private as well as public lands within a vast territory that the state had identified as the Adirondack Park in 1892.*
>
> *The **New Jersey Pinelands Commission** was established by a gubernatorial order (1979). This action followed congressional designation of a Pinelands National Reserve and approval of planning and land acquisition funds for a state planning effort.*

Although the New York and New Jersey programs deal with much larger populations and territories than the Scenic Area, many planning and management challenges are similar.

The five programs have important elements in common. Like the Columbia Gorge, the other cases cover resource-producing regions—equivalents of the Old West—that have been gradually transformed by the recreational overspill of major metropolitan areas—Boston, New York, Philadelphia, San Francisco. Scenic preservation is an important goal in every instance. In part because of the implications of this for land development, each program has faced moderate to severe local opposition. Each has tried to deal with opposition by giving substantial authority to an advisory or implementing commission with a mandated mix of local and non-local members. Four of the five programs include the "carrot" of land purchases along with the "stick" of land use regulation; in the exceptional case of the Adirondacks, the state already owned hundreds of thousands of acres. All but the Lake Tahoe program allow local governments to take on regulatory responsibility by adopting ordinances that meet the essential program goals as defined by regional plans.

20

Columbia River Gorge National Scenic Area (CRGNSA) compared with other regional environmental management programs

	Cape Cod	Lake Tahoe	Adirondacks	Pinelands	CRGNSA
Year established	1961	1969/1980	1971	1979	1986
Area (acres)	27,000 land 44,000 total	207,000 land 330,000 total	6,000,000	927,000	293,000
Year-round population	200	52,000	130,000	700,000 in component towns	52,000
Bistate	no	yes	no	no	yes
Federal role in creation	essential	facilitative	none	facilitative	essential
National Park Service role	yes	no	no	yes	no
Forest Service role	no	yes	no	no	yes
Federal involvement in planning	high	low/indirect	none	none	high
Level of local opposition	moderate	severe	severe	moderate	moderate
Regionwide planning with local government buy-in	yes	no	yes	yes	yes
Acceptance of boundaries	yes	yes	yes	some concerns	minor concerns
Land purchase program	yes	added 1980	no	yes	yes, but secondary
Legislatively specified subdivisions of area	no	no	state land/ private land	preservation area/ protection area	GMA/SMA/ Urban Areas
Minimum local membership on governing commission	7 of 10	7 of 10 max. 6 of 14*	5 of 11	7 of 15	8 of 12

* Changed in 1980

continued on page 22 **21**

	Cape Cod	Lake Tahoe	Adirondacks	Pinelands	CRGNSA
Goal salience: scenic preservation	high	high	high	moderate	high
Goal salience: preservation of natural systems	high	high	moderate	high	low
Goal salience: preserving old resource economy	moderate/explicit	low/explicit	moderate/explicit	high	moderate
Importance of old resource economy to area	low	low	high	high	high
Time for preparation of initial plan	11 months from initial NPS regulations	under 2 years	18 months	2 years	2 years for land use designation/3 years for Management Plan
Basic regional plan approach	local zoning under federal oversight	land use & zoning plan	6 land use areas with density levels	8 management areas with density levels	functional zones with development standards
Permitting for new development	local under approved ordinances	local, with regional review of variances & administrative permits	local for small developments, regional commission for large	local permits with regional commission option to review	under approved county ordinance or by bistate commission

CHAPTER 1

Portland's "Private Elysium"

"This is no place for factories."
    Samuel C. Lancaster, 1939

The Columbia River Gorge spans the two great natural provinces of the Pacific Northwest. To travel from The Dalles to Portland and Vancouver is to pass from the dryland country of the great interior basin to the fog and rain belt that lines the Pacific coast from San Francisco to Glacier Bay. Residents know that the climate and environment of the gorge change dramatically in the course of a few miles—from Mosier to Cascade Locks, for example, or North Bonneville to Vancouver.

In equally dramatic fashion, the gorge is an economic and social frontier. In the twentieth century the gorge has become a borderland between the fast-lane West of booming cities and the traditional West of resource industries. The context for understanding the origins and political dynamics of the National Scenic Area is the sharp division and deeply embedded tension between New West and Old West.

In the Columbia Gorge, this division has involved long-standing claims by Portland to control and enjoy the landscape as its own. The gorge has been a destination for Portland-based recreation from steamboat excursions of the 1880s to the phalanx of automobiles that clog the Multnomah Falls parking lot on summer weekends. Portland investors built and managed the gorge's transportation system in its first three generations of settlement, and Portlanders have often led debates over the balance between economic growth and scenic preservation. The Scenic Area legislation thus represents a culmination of Portland's sense that the gorge is its "private Elysium."

The Metropolitan Frontier and the Western Rangebelt

Over the last half-century, growth in the American West has concentrated in a crescent that sweeps from Texas through the Southwest and northward along the Pacific Coast. Western development has built on international trade and immigration, the expansion of the American leisure industries, and electronics and defense manufacturing. Regional growth has turned Dallas and Denver, Phoenix and San Jose, Portland and Seattle into great metropolitan centers. Some experts call this area the Gunbelt in recognition of military spending. Others talk about a Sunbelt West. Whatever the specific terminology, urban growth has made the New West of the late twentieth century a metropolitan frontier—a land of powerful cities and spheres of urban influence.

In contrast are the vast interior spaces of the Rangebelt. These are the states and half-states whose fortunes rise and fall with farming, mining, and ranching. Rangebelters have learned to depend on federal irrigation projects, federal electricity, and the direct use of lands managed by the Bureau of Land Management and Forest Service for grazing and logging. The Rangebelt's core is the Great Plains and northern Rockies: Kansas, Nebraska, South Dakota, North Dakota, Montana, Wyoming, Idaho. It also overlaps into fast-lane states to create a deep tension between metropolitan and rural districts. Officials in Denver see the crest of the Rockies as an economic divide between the prosperous and failing halves of Colorado. Policymakers in Salem worry about the "other Oregon" outside the urbanized Willamette Valley.

In an American West that is ultimately dominated by greater Texas and greater California and their capital cities of Houston, Dallas, Los Angeles, and San Francisco, the Rangebelt has struggled with the booms and busts of a narrow resource economy. Nearly four hundred counties reported fewer than six residents per square mile in 1980—a continuing frontier by anyone's definition. The total population of these empty counties was only 2.2 million—fewer than the number of people *added* to metropolitan Los Angeles in the single decade of the 1980s. Much of this persistent frontier is marked by problems indistinguishable from inner city ghettoes. Educational achievement is relatively low. Access to health care is limited. The rate of violent death among young white males in several Rocky Mountain states has run consistently above the national average.

24

Many Rangebelt communities are mired in deep economic and social crisis. Mining cities have been at the mercy of fluctuating world markets. Timber towns have faced scarcities of cheap trees, competition from the American South, and rivalry from foreign producers. Following the dictates of economic theory, large resource corporations have substituted capital for labor, producing more coal or timber with fewer workers. Young men find it impossible to follow their fathers' footsteps to the mine or mill or to enjoy the accustomed pattern of intensive short-term work at high wages alternating with months off for hunting, fishing, and personal projects. The shift toward a service and tourism economy may also trigger a social upheaval that replaces men working at union rates with women working at low wages as the main family support. For many men over forty-five, a layoff notice often means forced retirement interrupted by short-term jobs. One resident of the lumber mill city of Coos Bay, Oregon, described the effect of mill closures: "Losing their cars, losing their homes. People with their homes almost paid for. No way to finish it. Trying to sell out cheap to get to move somewhere to go to work. . . . Forcing the older people into early retirement, taking a reduced pension. Trying to survive."

At the same time, a number of Rangebelt cities have benefited from a selective rebalancing within the Western economy. During the 1980s, the costs of metropolitan concentration and congestion caused big city businesses to look to smaller communities for cheaper land, low living costs, and inexpensive labor for routine production. Expanding metropolitan commuting and recreation zones are also bringing the world into the heart of the West, incorporating Rangebelt towns and rural communities into city-centered flows of people, goods, and ideas. The transformation of Aspen, Colorado, from a dying mining town in 1948 to a center for intellectual life and a playground for the rich is a much-studied prototype for the changes. In much of the Western high country, resource workers now coexist with tourists, artists, writers, consultants, and other dealers in national information markets. Within the Columbia River basin, towns like Joseph, Oregon, and Sandpoint, Idaho, are examples of Western communities where artists, retirees, high-tech post-hippies, and jet set entrepreneurs live next door to men and women who continue to wrest a living from resource industries.

25

The differences between the two kinds of West have set the stage for a long-lasting contest over resource policy. Although the Sagebrush Rebels of the early 1980s identified the enemy as a national government that seemed like an increasingly alien intrusion, many of the regulations that they and other Old Westerners resent represent the thinking of Western city people as much as easterners. The Endangered Species Act, the Federal Land Policy and Management Act of 1976 (which required multi-use management by the Bureau of Land Management), and similar legislative mandates have strained the close relationship between ranchers, miners, loggers, and the federal land agencies. The cities of California, Colorado, Washington, Oregon, and Montana are the seed beds for a regional environmentalism. Along with Arizona, New Mexico, and Hawaii, these are states that consistently rank high in the proportion of residents with memberships in national environmental organizations.

The expanding commuting and recreation zones of major Western cities have become arenas of regional conflict. Low-density landscapes still separate metropolitan areas, but much of this superficially rural West has been gradually centralized into the daily commuting and weekly recreation orbits of the major cities. Call it an urban shadow or an urban spotlight, this steady expansion of metropolitan reach is continuing to bring the world into the heart of the West. Dollars earned in cities keep the stores open in small towns, employ country lawyers on land deals, turn school teachers into real estate agents, and transform underemployed farmers and miners into instant construction contractors.

This metropolitan incorporation has operated over the course of the twentieth century as Portlanders and official Portland have staked their "claim" on the Columbia Gorge as a recreational zone. Between 1900 and 1930, Portlanders assumed that they were the primary users and beneficiaries of the magnificent scenery of the gorge. Between 1930 and 1970, they extended that interest to assert the *primacy* of scenery as a gorge resource and claimed the right to influence decisions about economic development within the gorge itself. After 1970, these two facets of the Portland agenda—the utilization of scenery and the control of economic development—flowed logically into support for systematic and comprehensive management of Columbia Gorge scenery as a place serving regional—that is, Portland—needs.

Portland Admires the Gorge

Samuel Lancaster

Samuel Christopher Lancaster's book *The Columbia: America's Great Highway through the Cascade Mountains to the Sea* was written in 1915 and republished in 1916 and 1926. Sam Lancaster was the engineering genius behind the construction of the first Columbia River Highway in 1913-15. With tinted photographs and colored plates, his book is a rhapsody to "one of the rarely beautiful places" of the earth. It tells a story of Portland men building a Portland road. The key illustration reproduces a panoramic bird's-eye view painting of the gorge and highway as exhibited at the Panama-Pacific Exposition in San Francisco. Portland lies at the center of the composition—the focal point for roads to the gorge and Mount Hood. The scenery of the Columbia Gorge, says the pictorial map, is reached from and through Portland.

Lancaster's book signaled the transition from one era of gorge tourism to the next. Since the 1880s, Portland had been the base for upriver steamboat journeys to enjoy the "uninterrupted magnificent display and terrible grandeur" of the hills, chasms, and cataracts that flanked the Columbia. A shorter trip took travelers the sixty-five miles to The Cascades and back; the "grand tour" took two days for the round trip to The Dalles. Nineteenth-century travelers in search of "aesthetic enjoyment and hygienic exhilaration" made their trips on working vessels that stopped to take on lumber, shingles, and salmon and to offload merchandise and supplies. By the early twentieth century their successors could choose specially built passenger boats with large public rooms and cabins.

Columbia Gorge tourism in the steamship era was essentially a passive activity that supplemented a tour through the major West Coast cities. Most passengers followed the example of historian Francis Fuller Victor, who described the pleasures of "sitting out upon the steamer's deck, of a summer morning" when "each moment affords a fresh delight to the wondering senses." The gorge was a series of backdrops to be comfortably enjoyed or marveled over, not landscape to be vigorously explored.

Change came with a new generation and a new form of transportation. The national context for understanding the gorge highway and Sam Lancaster's view of its implications for

27

Portland's recreational reach was formed by the rise of middle-class travel and automobile-based recreation. One of the remarkable features of the late nineteenth and early twentieth centuries is the democratization of tourism. Travelers in the American West through the 1870s had needed money and plenty of it for high train fares, expensive resort hotels, and entourages for camping trips that sometimes resembled royal processions. The construction of competing transcontinental railroads, followed by a national economic depression in the 1890s, however, convinced Western rail companies to offer special convention rates and summer excursion fares aimed at families and school teachers. West Coast cities staged international expositions in 1905, 1909, and 1915 to attract mass tourism. In the years between, tourists could take in Denver's Festival of Mountain and Plain, the Fiesta de Los Angeles, or Portland's Rose Festival.

The broadening market for long-distance tourism went hand in hand with the growth of locally based automobile excursions and weekend trips. The good roads movement of the early 1900s drew on both the frustration of farmers who found themselves stuck in the mud with every spring thaw *and* the desire of city people to have someplace outside of town where they could try out their new automobiles. While they waited for state and federal governments to adopt systematic highway programs, residents of Western cities took matters into their own hands by building scenic parkways and improving segments of roadway that would eventually link into a national highway system.

The Columbia River Highway

The movement for an automobile road through the Columbia River gorge began in 1909, when Portland highway enthusiast Lewis Russell funded a preliminary survey out of his own pocket. At the urging of Russell and Portland businessman Henry Wemme, Multnomah County (the county containing Portland) undertook an unsuccessful road-building effort in 1911. The following year, Portland lumber magnate Simon Benson donated $10,000 for an experimental stretch of road between the river and Shellrock Mountain between Hood River and Wyeth, Oregon. Early efforts climaxed in July 1913 under the leadership of Multnomah County commissioner Rufus Holman, who secured the creation of a county Advisory Board on Roads and Highways. The advisory board, which included C. S. Jackson, publisher of the Portland-based *Oregon Journal*, was supported by a Columbia Highway Association, headed by Portland merchant Julius Meier. Over the next three years, Multnomah County supplied the funds which built the Columbia River Highway eastward to Hood River County. Portlanders were also instrumental in convincing Hood River County to join in the project by passing a highway bond issue in 1914 and using the funds for the Columbia River Highway rather than farm-to-market roads to serve the county's fruit industry.

The Portland business community saw a highway through the Columbia Gorge as a way to compete with upstart Seattle, which was benefiting from a newly built road to Mount Rainier. The *Oregon Journal* and *The Oregonian* were strong supporters. The highway, said its advocates, would expand Portland's attractiveness to out-of-state tourists. It would supplement the railroads for transporting agricultural exports and allow residents of eastern Oregon and Washington to patronize Portland stores. In sum, said the *Oregon Journal*, the Columbia River Highway was one of Portland's greatest assets.

Portlanders put themselves center stage at the formal dedication in June 1916, a year after the highway opened between Portland and Hood River. The ceremonies coincided with the city's annual Rose Festival. The Portland Chamber of Commerce and Rose Festival Association sponsored a beautification contest with cash prizes for property owners along the roadway. A quasi-historical pageant at Multnomah Falls featured *Oregon Journal* editor Marshall Dana's impersonation of a highly fictional Chief Multnomah.

The Columbia River Highway individualized access to the gorge and made it Portland's mountain playground. The Portland Auto Club built a clubhouse on the Sandy River at Troutdale, to serve as a starting point for auto touring expeditions eastward through the gorge or toward Mount Hood. Portland attorney Jacob Kanzler, a pillar of business and fraternal organizations, helped to persuade the U. S. Forest Service to set aside fourteen thousand acres as a scenic reserve and public recreation grounds. This "Columbia Gorge Park" paralleled the highway for twenty-three miles between Warrendale and Viento. The next year—1916—the Forest Service constructed its first public campground at Eagle Creek. The agency was soon attracting four thousand campers and three thousand hunters and anglers annually. As more

29

Volunteer workers from the Portland Realty Board and Ad Club helping to build the Columbia River Highway, April 25, 1914. (Photo: Oregon Historical Society, neg. 38744)

and more autoists pushed the capacity of the highway on Sundays and holidays, the Forest Service counted one hundred thousand picnickers a year at Eagle Creek by the start of the 1920s.

Portland's city officials responded by following the lead of Denver, Cleveland, and other cities that were acquiring parks far outside the city limits. The land around Multnomah and Wahkeena falls came by donation from Simon Benson to the city in 1915. Shepperd's Dell came in another donation in the same year. The acquisition of Crown Point and the construction of Vista House followed in 1916-18 with funds raised by Portland businesses. The concerted effort to spread city parks through the gorge continued through the 1920s. In 1921, civic leaders J.C. Ainsworth, A.E. Doyle, and E.B. McNaughton recommended through the city's new streets and parks plan that the city or county should establish a "municipal mountain camp" based on the model camp

30

constructed in the Angeles National Forest by the city of Los Angeles. They suggested that the city of Portland should control a strip of 100 feet on either side of the Columbia River Highway from Troutdale to Hood River and should acquire title to Latourelle Falls, Bridal Veil Falls, Oneonta Gorge, Horsetail Falls, and Larch Mountain. The Forest Service, they proposed, should set aside Lost Lake, Wahtum Lake, and Mount Defiance for park use. The city continued to acquire parcels of gorge property by donation and purchase into the mid-1920s. With considerable ambitions for its string of gorge parks, it also built Multnomah Falls Lodge in 1925.

Private investment paralleled the public incorporation of the gorge and the Columbia River Highway into Portland's weekend recreation zone. The Progressive Business Men's Club of Portland opened negotiations with Crown Columbia Pulp and Paper Company even before the highway opened in hope of obtaining title to the rocky tip of Larch Mountain and permission to build a trail from Multnomah Falls. The Progressive Business Men sold pencils, sponsored a musical comedy and a railway excursion, corralled private contributions, and helped the Forest Service complete a trail in September 1915. Six years later, Simon Benson built the Columbia Gorge Hotel to serve tourists at the end of their scenic tour through the gorge. Sam Lancaster built and operated a rustic resort at Eagle Creek, with furniture hewn from logs and Reed College students as summer staff. Energetic guests could climb to auxiliary camps at Wahtum Lake and Lost Lake. Several prominent Portlanders had already built substantial estates in gorge locations served by the new highway.

For residents of the gorge itself, the Scenic Highway was a practical tool rather than a weekend toy. It offered improved access to Portland doctors and to bargains in Portland department stores. It served small loggers and orchardists as a farm-to-market road that opened the possibility of freedom from rate gouging by the big transportation companies. It reduced the social isolation of families tucked into the small settlements along its route.

Nevertheless, Portland guidebooks in the 1920s claimed the Columbia River Gorge and its Scenic Highway as one of *Portland's* key attractions. The Portland Chamber of Commerce issued a *Tourist's Guide of Portland and Vicinity* that led off with scenic trips on the Columbia River Highway—"generally characterized by the travelling public as the finest

31

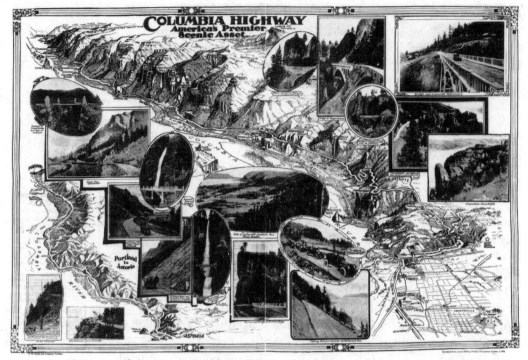

Perspective map of the Scenic Highway. (Photo: Oregon Historical Society, neg. 62621-B)

roadway in America." The Broadway Auto Service in 1925 offered Columbia Highway tours in its Packard twin-six open touring car for only $5. Portland's grandly named Atlantic and Pacific Highway and Electrical Exposition in the same year advertised the city's proximity to the gorge. The prize for purple prose went to Edward S. Jordan, president of the Jordan Motor Car Company. His "Tribute to Portland" (distributed as a pamphlet by the Chamber of Commerce) rhapsodized over "that marvelous blending of the magic of nature and the ideals of commerce which you call the Columbia Highway. . . . No spectacle of nature, anywhere in the world, neither the flames of the western sun, nor the tempest among the palms . . . seem worthy of astonishment to those who have contemplated the nuptials of nature and commerce . . . the inspiring scenery united with commercial purpose of the Columbia Scenic Highway."

32

Portland Plans for the Gorge

The 1930s, of course, were a bad decade for tourism and any other business that depended on discretionary spending. As they scrounged to balance their budget, the Portland city council deeded over their gorge parks to the new state parks department. At the same time, attention began to shift to the new question of the compatibility between industrial development and scenery along the Columbia River.

The context for gorge planning in the 1930s and 1940s was deep national concern about economic survival. Depression was followed by economic mobilization for World War II and by nagging worries about postwar reconversion. The Northwest welcomed public investment to expand primary production and manufacturing, with a list of projects ranging from subsistence homesteads at Longview, Washington, to irrigation projects to hydroelectric dams. In the Columbia River gorge the key action was the construction of Bonneville Dam and the key issue was industrialization.

Setting one side of the issue was a *Columbia River Industrial Site Survey* of 1940. Prepared by the economic development staff of the Bonneville Power Administration, the report mapped nearly the entire gorge riverfront as potential industrial land. The identified parcels amounted to twenty-one square miles in Washington from the Washougal River to Dallesport and twenty-five square miles in Oregon from the Sandy River to The Dalles. The implied vision is clear—a gorge lined with a series of industrial towns at Dodson, Wyeth, Cascade Locks, Mosier, Stevenson, and Home Valley, teeming with prosperous workers, drawing clean hydropower and shipping their manufactured output by rail and barge to the markets of the world.

The question of industrial development in the gorge was one front in the ongoing war between Portland and Seattle for economic dominance in the Pacific Northwest. Port of Portland commissioner John H. Lewis put the situation simply: "[T]hat city of the Northwest which first captures and uses the greatest amount of Columbia River power, will be the largest city. The fight for industrial supremacy will be over when all the Columbia River power is distributed." It was therefore to the economic interest of Puget Sound cities that Bonneville's electricity be available at equal cost in all parts of the region. The expense of long-distance transmission, said the Tacoma Chamber of Commerce, should be covered by all users,

33

Building Bonneville Dam. (Photo: Oregon Historical Society, neg. 65247)

making the new dam a truly regional resource. Sharing the multistate vision was J. D. Ross, the head of Seattle City Light who became the first administrator of the Bonneville Power Administration.

Portland's interest was the opposite. The Portland Chamber of Commerce vigorously argued that Bonneville's power was a local commodity that should not be burdened with the cost of extensive transmission lines. Staffer W. D. B. Dodson worried that Seattle "for so many years has put things over on us through superior effort and energy, often by mere bluffing," that Portland might also lose control of Bonneville. Dodson saw the political maneuvering over Bonneville as a

34

conspiracy to keep Columbia River power at least as expensive as power from Seattle's Skagit River turbines. At his urging, the chamber in 1936 and 1937 was an adamant advocate of the sale of power near the dam site at the direct cost of production. Factories in the heart of the gorge, said the chamber, were unfortunate but necessary for the industrialization of Portland's hinterland; any extra charges for Bonneville power would likely drive new factories to cheaper power in Canada.

On another side of Portland's internal discussion were gorge preservationists. They accepted, indeed welcomed, industrial uses of Bonneville's kilowatts. The question, however, was *where* to put the factories—within the gorge or outside.

The key document on this position was a 1937 report by the Pacific Northwest Regional Planning Commission (PNWRPC) entitled *Columbia Gorge Conservation and Development.* Developed by a Columbia Gorge Committee chaired by Portland architect John B. Yeon, the report represented three years of consideration by recently established state planning boards of Oregon and Washington. In the climate of the 1930s, the report recognized the importance of social and economic development and the likelihood of industrialization tied to Bonneville Dam. At the same time, it urged consideration of the less ponderable but very real economic values involved in recreational facilities and scenery. The report called for larger forest reserves, more state park lands, new game refuges, rural zoning, and a unified general plan to help protect recreational resources. Most immediately, it argued that minimum rates for Bonneville's electricity should be extended beyond the gorge itself to encourage industrialization in near-gorge locations rather than directly adjacent to the dam. Although, on its face, a regional document, the report thus defined a parochial agenda by which Portland could have it both ways: preserving scenery in the gorge *and* building factories.

The Oregonian popularized the position. In 1938, for example, the newspaper painted a possible vision of the gorge if the PNWRPC report were not heeded: "towering factory chimneys belch smoke over the majesty of Beacon Rock; spray from Latourelle Falls spatters off low-lying roofs of galvanized iron; slag heaps block views of Multnomah Falls." Sam Lancaster seemed to share the same fear. "In the development of the great hydro electric plant at Bonneville where a million

35

foaming white horses are being harnessed," he wrote in a dedication of his book in 1939, "may we be able to prevent the spoilation of the gorge by human greed. This is no place for factories."

This stance allowed Portlanders to hope for a beautiful gorge bracketed by new factories at its gateways at the head of navigation at The Dalles and along the Columbia River near Portland. A confidential report to interior secretary Harold Ickes, for example, reported that the liberals of the Oregon Commonwealth Federation "agreed that industry should not be located in the Columbia Gorge, but that if it came in, it should locate between Camas [Washington] and Rainier [Oregon]." Portlanders pointed out the abundance of industrial sites on the North Portland peninsula. Lower power rates along the entire lower Columbia River, said the Portland City Club, would benefit Portland's economy while raising "no danger of marring the scenic or recreational features of the Columbia Gorge by the location of industrial plants." The Oregon State Planning Board, Mayor Joseph Carson, and even Portland's electric utilities all found themselves in basic agreement with urbanist Lewis Mumford, who suggested that the new cheap hydroelectricity be used to build a greenbelt town where the gorge widens out at its west end near the Sandy River.

The results of industrial development after 1940 confirmed this second Portland agenda for gorge conservation. Power was

sold most cheaply within fifteen miles of Bonneville Dam, with a flat rate throughout the rest of the Northwest. However, the requirement that users within the fifteen-mile circle furnish their own electrical transformers and connection facilities negated the advantage. The new wartime aluminum plants that were by far the largest industrial offspring of Bonneville

Dam located just outside the gorge at Troutdale, Oregon, and Vancouver, Washington, and downstream at Longview, Washington. Later industrial development at The Dalles after the construction of The Dalles Dam would again take place outside the scenic zone.

Scenic Preservation vs. Economic Development

As the Northwest settled back after the boom of World War II, the Portland Women's Forum in the early 1950s began to work with the Portland Chamber of Commerce to revive interest in scenic preservation. Their first attempt was for unified management through interstate compact. When this was not quickly accomplished, they turned to the more easily implemented idea of independent Oregon and Washington gorge commissions with members appointed by each governor. The Oregon Columbia River Gorge Commission, established in 1953, faced a mandate that was explicitly contradictory: its responsibilities included "preserving, developing and protecting the recreation, scenic and historic areas" of the gorge. As would soon be apparent, developing recreation and protecting scenery might lead policymakers toward two very different choices about the kinds of recreation appropriate for the gorge.

The Oregon Columbia Gorge Commission was a Portland outfit in operation as well as origins. During its first two decades, it used a Portland office and two of three commissioners were always from the Portland area (most importantly, Gertrude Jensen, who had previously led the Women's Forum effort). The commissions obtained open space designation for segments of the gorge through Multnomah County's initial zoning ordinance in 1958. Portlanders continued to provide the lead even after Washington in 1959 set up a parallel Washington Columbia Gorge Commission with similar responsibilities for education and advocacy.

> ### Scenic Protection in the 1930s
>
> *Several Portland-based initiatives in the 1930s supported the increasingly prominent idea of scenic protection. The Portland City Council in June 1931 called for a joint committee of the city, Multnomah County, and the state highway commission to guard the gorge and its highway against defacement by power lines. The resulting committee worked against unnecessary logging roads in the Multnomah Falls-Larch Mountain area as well as the intrusion of power lines, and encouraged Washingtonians to acquire Beacon Rock as a state park.*

37

Job Growth

Manufacturing jobs outside the wood products industry in Skamania and Klickitat counties in Washington grew from 104 in 1950 to 974 by 1980. Over the same three decades, non-wood products manufacturing in Wasco and Hood River counties in Oregon grew from 594 to 1,839 jobs. Wholesale and retail jobs in the same period grew by 82 percent on the Washington side and 43 percent on the Oregon side, outpacing the growth of local population.

At the same time, increasingly active local efforts at economic development revived the tensions between scenic preservation and economic development. The completion of a high-speed interstate highway in the early 1960s increased the accessibility of the Columbia Gorge to mass tourism. It also opened new possibilities for industrial development utilizing truck transportation. With surplus generating capacity in the 1950s, the Bonneville Power Administration encouraged industrialization; several towns along the river responded by establishing port districts as economic development entities. Regional economic development agencies used federal funds to research topics such as the expansion of active recreation opportunities, potential industrial sites, and industrialization strategies.

One result of the renewed drive for economic diversification was a substantial expansion of the manufacturing base in the four gorge counties. A second result was an emblematic conflict over intrusive tourism in the form of a ten-year debate about aerial tramways to carry sightseers to the rim of the gorge in dangling gondolas. A private proposal in 1964 for a tramway at Munra Point led the Forest Service to evaluate eighteen possible tramway sites. Advocates of elaborate attractions for auto-based tourists lined up against defenders of a management style that preserved "the dominating influence of the features of natural wonder by restricting man's intrusions to simple roads and basic facilities." The Port of Cascade Locks revived the issue in 1968 when it began to plan to use federal Economic Development Administration funds for a tramway to the 3,200-foot rim of the Benson Plateau. The proposal passed through environmental impact statements prepared by Mount Hood National Forest in 1972-73, permitting the port to prepare full construction and operation plans on the expectation that the project might add 345 new jobs and spur economic growth as far away as Parkdale and The Dalles. The Oregon Environmental Council, the Vancouver *Columbian*, and the Portland-based Mazama mountaineering club all opposed the tramway itself and especially the dining and service facilities that would serve visitors at the top. The chance to "wine and dine in the sky," argued the opponents, had to be weighed against need to protect wilderness areas and "quiet recreational activities."

Before the issue was resolved against the tramway in 1974, the debate not only set Portlanders against gorge residents but also defined the increasingly specific character of the "Portland claim" on gorge scenery. From the point of view of local economic development planners who wanted to reverse the population decline of Hood River County, the tramway was "a very legitimate recreational and educational forest use" that would allow visitors to view "various types of forest management practices." To members of the committee on recreation that prepared a background report for a Columbia River Gorge Conference in 1970, in contrast, it was "apparent that mass recreation which depends on intensively developed man-made facilities, is incompatible with the natural scenery. It would be particularly undesirable allow any structures or facilities which would alter the bluffs or cliff-faces of the gorge."

Urban Environmentalism and the Gorge

The contest over the tramway set the stage for the most recent period of debate over the Columbia Gorge.

The background of three generations of Portland interest in the gorge makes the politics of the later 1970s and 1980s seem historically logical, if not necessarily inevitable. In the 1910s and 1920s, Portlanders defined themselves as the prime users of gorge scenery for personal enjoyment and publicized the gorge as an element in the city's tourism package. From the 1930s through the 1960s, Portlanders developed an increasingly exclusive interest in protecting the scenery of the gorge and influenced the direction of local economic development within the gorge.

This history confirms the observations of environmental historians and regional planners about the metropolitan sources of environmental activism. The partially rural fringes of expanding metropolitan areas are the most common sites for battles over land use regulation, and the urban middle class is the major source of support for such regulation. City people put their factories in the country, ship their garbage to the country, vacation in the country, and retire to the country. They also reshape the countryside to their own purposes. In the process, resource regions are put to work meeting the

39

needs of larger and more inclusive metropolitan and regional systems.

The last twenty years have brought what is probably a permanent shift in the balance between Old West and New West in the Columbia Gorge. One key trend, the weakening of the area's resource economy, especially in the timber recession of the 1980s, was caused by factors far beyond scenic preservation, including the fluctuations of international markets, the substitution of machinery for workers, and national environmental legislation. Economic recovery through tourism, the common strategy of the 1990s, explicitly orients the gorge counties to the metropolis. Nearly two-thirds of the bookings for Skamania County's new conference center, partially funded by the Scenic Area legislation, are by Portland area individuals, firms, and organizations. The boardsailing boom that has metropolitanized Hood River and the central gorge since 1985 exploits the renewable resources of wind and water, but its horizons and markets are national and international.

The increasing attachment of segments of the gorge economy to the Portland market has affected the dynamics of local politics. There is now internal disagreement within the gorge over environmental and economic development goals. A second tension arises from competing ideas about how best to promote the public good, often dividing regulatory-minded Oregonians from laissez-faire Washingtonians. There are also differences between Portlanders and gorge residents over both the process and the content of gorge conservation, with the National Scenic Area Act representing a logical next step for Portland's interest and involvement.

The record is clear. In the Columbia Gorge, early efforts at recreational development and later efforts at scenic preservation reflect the desires of Portland's commercial and civic elite. The long-standing debates about economic development policy that began with the construction of Bonneville Dam resulted in explicit efforts to mark out separate territories appropriate for industrial production and private enjoyment. The Scenic Area legislation codified the same sort of distinction by subdividing the gorge into Urban Areas and Management Areas. And the incipient expansion of the Portland exurbs into the gorge during the boom years of the late 1970s triggered the drive for the legislation itself.

40

The National Scenic Area, in short, is far more than a product of the contemporary environmental movement or a simple attempt at land use regulation. Seen in historical context, it is one more entry on the long list of ways in which Portland has made the Columbia River Gorge its own, translating an interest in the scenery of the Columbia River into a claim on influencing the future development of the gorge itself. And in the regional dynamic of the late twentieth century, it is part of the process by which the New West is turning parts of the Old West into new and different sorts of places.

CHAPTER 2

From Trading Posts to Tourism:
The Gorge Economy in Transition

"When I was a kid you either worked in the orchards or fruit processing plant, or you didn't work. Now you have a choice."
Bev Rowland, Hood River County commissioner, 1996

A t first a lot of people, especially the businessmen, were ready to throw in the towel. But now they've taken stock of this thing—and most of them figure we can make a go of it." This newspaper lead is not about an endangered species shutting down logging. Nor is it about passage of the National Scenic Area Act. It is rather a story

Boating at Beacon Rock, ca. 1900.
(Photo: Oregon Historical Society, neg. 4232)

from 1959 about the decision of state and federal officials to reroute U.S. Highway 30 away from the main street of Cascade Locks and over a new high-speed bypass.

The episode is small, but it could be repeated a hundred times. The economy of the Columbia Gorge has been in continual transition since the middle of the nineteenth century. The changes, moreover, have usually been initiated from outside the region. Like the strong gorge winds that are created by air pressure gradients between the Pacific Ocean and the continental interior, economic change has come to the gorge from outside forces. The creation of the Scenic Area, in this perspective, is one more gale.

But the late twentieth century may have brought fresh winds. In what we have identified as the New West, the pressures for change have come from different quarters. The development of industries and activities that are independent of the extraction, processing, and transportation of natural resources adds unprecedented dimensions to the story of economic change.

The Political Economy of the Columbia River Gorge

Patterns of development in the heart of the gorge show the controlling influence of the Columbia River, whose deep cut through the rugged Cascade Mountains has concentrated transportation, population, and economic activity in the narrow riverside "flatlands" and tributary valleys of Skamania, Klickitat, Hood River, and Wasco counties. The spectacular nature of the landscape has simultaneously made dense settlement infeasible and pushed development into highly visible locations.

Like other regions with declining resource industries, the four counties dominated by the gorge have followed an erratic economic course. Unemployment has often been high. Job creation has depended on national and global market cycles rather than local actions; log prices respond to construction demand in both California and Japan. Manufacturing employment in the four counties climbed to 1980, then dropped in response to the national recession of the early 1980s before recovering in the last years of the decade. When workers came back to the job, they found substantially lower wage rates in major regional industries such as aluminum and wood products.

43

Beyond the effects of the natural environment and the business cycle, the gorge economy reflects the reach of Portland as a source of investment capital, corporate control, and customers for gorge industries and products. Portlanders controlled nineteenth- and twentieth-century shipping lines and played major roles in building the first railroad and highway through the gorge. Portland firms dominated the early timber industry. Portland also shaped the emergence of the gorge tourist industry and still provides its largest pool of customers. As the Portland-Vancouver metropolitan area in the 1990s shifts toward new national and international markets and networks, side effects reverberate through the gorge.

The other outside influence on the development of the gorge has been the federal government, which has brought desired investment and unwanted side effects. The government has played an important role in the ongoing transformation of the gorge from the construction of Fort Lee at The Dalles in 1848, through the great dams, to the massive engineering of Interstate 84. The federal government provided cheap land in the nineteenth century and cheap power in the twentieth century. It has changed the natural environment, altered Native American ways of life, moved entire towns, imposed rules on economic activity, disregarded county governments, and created the boardsailing boom by impounding Lake Bonneville. Several local observers believe that a redeeming feature of the Scenic Area Act is to limit the federal government's power within the gorge.

Despite such skepticism, the gorge remains deeply dependent on federal agencies and programs. Federal land and water management agencies are major employers. The post-World War II economy was supported by generous timber sales that outpaced the capacity of National Forests for sustained yield. Federal programs have indirectly subsidized the local economy by improving navigation and highways, bringing light to farmsteads through rural electrification, and supporting a poorly paid agricultural work force with welfare payments and food stamps at rates above the Oregon and **44** Washington averages.

Apart from the federal government and large service employers such as school districts and hospitals, the gorge is a region of small-scale enterprises. In the private sector, big employers in the gorge count their workers in the hundreds. The big five of 1996 all had three to five hundred employees:

two local service employers (Sprint-United Telephone and Mid-Columbia Medical Center) and three employers serving outside customers (SDS Lumber, Northwest Aluminum, and Skamania Lodge). The Scenic Area itself is a land of small businesses and individual entrepreneurs, an economic environment that supports a deep skepticism of public regulations, long-range planning, and sweeping changes like the National Scenic Area. It is a region that has learned to distrust *both* Portland and Washington, D.C., and to resent its economic dependence on them.

Within these constraints, the economic history of the gorge is one of gradual diversification that mirrors the historical development of the broader United States economy from resource extraction through manufacturing to services. This development is compressed, since intensive English-speaking settlement did not start until the mid-nineteenth century. But it is also prolonged, as the area still struggles to salvage the timber industry, protect its agricultural base, and resist dependence on the low-wage jobs associated with tourism.

The evolution of long-distance transportation systems and exploitation of the seemingly limitless fish and timber resources dominated the gorge in the nineteenth century. By 1900, agriculture was gaining a substantial footing and triggered two decades of explosive population growth. The

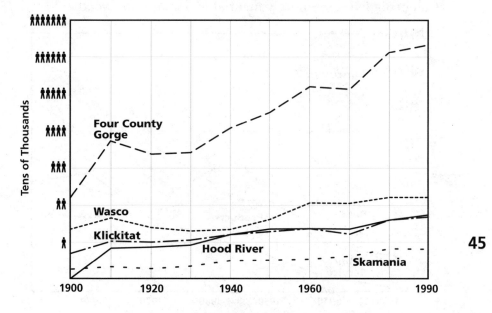

The population of the four Columbia Gorge counties.
(Source: U.S. Census)

45

Population growth in Columbia Gorge counties					
	Hood River	Wasco	Skamania	Klickitat	Total
1900		13,200	1,700	6,400	21,300
1910	8,000	16,300	2,900	10,200	29,400
1920	8,300	13,600	2,400	9,300	33,600
1930	8,900	12,600	2,900	9,800	34,200
1940	11,600	13,100	4,600	11,400	40,700
1950	12,700	15,500	4,800	12,000	45,000
1960	13,400	20,200	5,200	13,500	52,300
1970	13,200	20,100	5,800	12,100	51,200
1980	15,800	21,700	7,900	15,800	61,200
1990	16,900	21,700	8,300	16,600	63,500

Notes: Hood River County was created from Wasco County in 1908. Part of Klickitat County was shifted to Benton County in 1905.

Source: U. S. Census

opening of the Columbia River Highway cracked the door for diversification and expansion of recreational opportunities in the 1920s. Since then, the gorge economy has shifted away from timber and agriculture, although both remain substantial components of the four-county economy. Manufacturing expanded with the availability of federal hydroelectric power in the late 1930s. World War II and the postwar housing boom in California fed a seemingly insatiable demand for wood

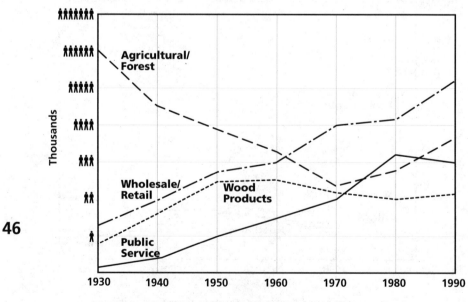

Trends in employment in the four Columbia Gorge counties.
(Source: U.S. Census)

46

products and aluminum that supported slow but steady population growth until a turndown in the 1960s. Agricultural markets expanded and local health care and government services increased, followed by rapid growth in tourism as the economic base broadened in 1970s and 1980s with a third cycle of population growth and stabilization. Even during the slow-growth 1980s, population inched upward in Hood River, Skamania, and Klickitat counties, despite local perceptions to the contrary. The same is true of employment, which jumped sharply in the 1970s and continued to grow in the 1980s. The result of these changes has been to layer New West activities onto an Old West base.

Riverboats and Railroads

A dominant theme of the gorge economy is its role as a pass-through transportation corridor for migration, supply of mining camps, shipments of forest and farm products, tourism, and international trade. The modern gorge is an avenue for exports from eastern Oregon, Washington, Idaho, Montana, and Wyoming to Portland and overseas markets, as well as distributing Asian imports to the central and eastern United States. An observer at mid-gorge would count a through truck every minute, a through freight train every half hour, and a towboat pushing heavily laden barges several times a day. The highways, railroads, and barge traffic obtrude in river level vistas and have permanently altered the character of the gorge as a natural and scenic area.

This commerce has been central to the growth of Portland as a regional metropolis, but though the transportation industry supports motels, gas stations, and shipyards it leaves few other dollars in gorge communities.

The system of high-speed highways, railroads and inland navigation is integral to the character and appearance of the gorge. The interstate highway, in particular, is essential to economic vitality and daily life. At the same time, the transportation system allows travelers and goods to bypass gorge communities. Navigation improvements have removed the break-of-bulk and transhipment functions that originally created Cascade Locks and The Dalles. More than anything, the railroads, barge locks, and highway make the gorge a passageway rather than a destination.

47

Native Traders

Long before the arrival of British and American merchants, the native peoples of the lower Columbia River traded at the future site of The Dalles, where the river narrowed at Celilo Falls to a few dozen yards and created enormously bountiful fisheries. This was the meeting point for settled villagers from the lush raincoast and semi-nomadic peoples from the drier interior. Even before the arrival of the British fur traders, The Dalles was a major trading center, as well as "a general theater of gambling and roguery" in the critical view of one white trader. Hundreds and sometimes thousands of Indians came together among clouds of dust and racks of drying salmon to exchange hides, shells, fish oil, and foodstuffs.

By the early 1800s, the tribes of the lower Columbia were skilled and active trading partners of both American and British fur companies. Indeed, the river peoples considered themselves the rightful custodians of commerce through the gorge, and sometimes harassed or blocked parties of European-American fur traders who ventured upriver. As David Thompson reported in 1811, "they render any service required, but demand high payment and [are] ready to enforce their demands." The balance shifted in the 1820s and 1830s, when diseases devastated lower Columbia towns and the Hudson's Bay Company expanded its use of the river to supply far-flung inland posts.

Lewis and Clark in 1805 and 1806, British fur traders in the 1810s through the 1830s, and settlers from the eastern United States in the 1840s all had to deal with Celilo Falls and with The Cascades—six miles of rapids at the present site of Cascade Locks. Traders portaged small craft around the barriers, with cargo strapped on mules' or men's backs. In the early 1840s, the first immigrants to the Willamette Valley found that the overland Oregon Trail effectively ended at The Dalles. They had little choice but to hire Indian boatmen or to lash together unwieldy rafts, often launching into a rain-swollen river in October or November storms. The last hundred miles to Oregon City could take a month of rain- and river-drenched misery.

Travel conditions improved markedly when the first steamboat service reached The Cascades from Portland in 1850. Soon thereafter, service began from above The Cascades to The Dalles. Passengers and goods could now shuttle between downriver, midriver, and upriver vessels using wagon roads and then short portage railroads around the unnavigable water.

The emerging river transportation system came under unified management in 1860 as the Oregon Steam Navigation Company. This Portland-owned "millionaire-making machine" monopolized river traffic for two decades. Until 1870, the most valuable commodity shipped through the gorge for export from Portland was "treasure"—gold dust and ingots from Idaho and Montana bound for San Francisco. Slowly other products such as boxed apples, barrelled salmon, livestock, and potatoes

48

began to move downstream. The first load of wheat transitted the gorge from Walla Walla to Portland in 1872, signalling the opening of what is still the river's largest volume cargo.

Barges at Bonneville Lock. (Photo: USDA Forest Service)

Railroads challenged the steamboats for through service in 1882 with the completion of a south shore rail line to Portland. The North Bank Railway on the Washington side opened in 1905. Despite new canal and lock systems around The Cascades in 1896 and Celilo Falls in 1915, the early twentieth century belonged to the railroads. By the 1910s, they had forced many of the middle-river steamboats out of service, and the hard-won canals fell into disuse.

Competition between navigation and rail interests still affects freight movement. For half a century (1882-1935), the balance tilted to the Union Pacific and Northern Pacific (now Burlington Northern) railroads. The late 1930s, however, brought diesel-powered tugs and steel barges. The improved equipment coincided with the new lock and dam at Bonneville. The full reemergence of commercial navigation waited for the construction of seven additional dams on the Columbia and Snake rivers between 1957 and 1975. Cargo volumes at Bonneville grew from 100,000 tons annually before 1938 to as much as 10 million tons by the 1980s. In March 1993, a new lock opened at Bonneville Dam; barge tows that can pass through all seven of the larger, newer upriver locks no longer need to be split at Bonneville.

The latest investments in navigation have greater implications for Portland than for the gorge itself. In 1993, 10.8 million tons of cargo moved by river between Vancouver, Washington, and the dam at The Dalles. Of this, more than 7.8 million tons was through cargo, primarily wheat moving downriver to the big elevators at Portland and petroleum

49

I-84 under construction at Mosier, October 1952.
(Photo: Oregon Historical Society, neg. 50138)

products bound upstream. The largest movements originating or ending within the gorge were wood chips, pulp, and paper moving to and from the James River mill at Camas, just outside the Scenic Area.

The situation is similar with land transportation. The high-speed "water-level" highway along the south shore—now I-84—has been a major interstate truck route since the 1950s. The Union Pacific and Burlington Northern railroads are important to a few industries in the gorge, but the volume transported to or from local customers is minuscule in relation to the volume in transit. The rail tracks in the gorge, once thought to link Portland inevitably to its regional hinterland, now provide easy access to the eastern United States for ocean vessels calling in the Pacific Northwest. Double-stack trains carry containers of Asian electronics and auto parts from Seattle, Tacoma, and Portland to U.S. markets. Specially designed rail cars haul automobiles eastward from Portland, others carrying agricultural goods westward, bound for Asia.

The Timber Economy

During the summer, it is impossible to miss the visual contrast of the eastern and western sections of the gorge. Open, browning grasslands dominate Wasco and Klickitat counties. Even in the July and August dry season, however, a westbound traveler can leave the constant blue skies over The Dalles for rain clouds over Cascade Locks or Stevenson. Annual rainfall totals less than 20 inches a year in the eastern end of the Scenic Area, but exceeds 80 inches a year where Douglas-firs march over the crest of the Cascades. This extreme contrast is significant in creating the timber economy to the west and the ranchlands to the east.

Forests dominate the two western counties. In Skamania County, 72 percent of the land is designated as timberland, with the largest portion being the Gifford Pinchot National Forest. Approximately 78 percent of the land in Hood River County is commercial timberland. In the drier east end, forests make up less than 10 percent of Klickitat County and 28 percent of Wasco County.

The first pressure for timber cutting in the gorge was for construction of Native American cedar long-houses, then for immigrant rafts and forts, for home heat, and for the wood-fired boilers of the early steamboats. The latter consumed four

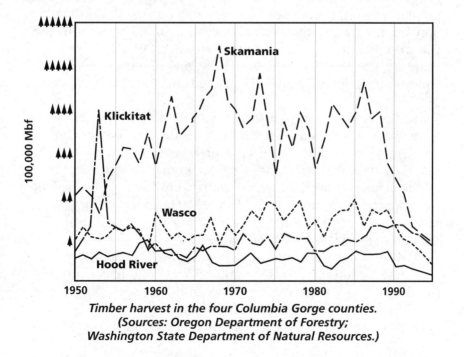

Timber harvest in the four Columbia Gorge counties.
(Sources: Oregon Department of Forestry;
Washington State Department of Natural Resources.)

51

cords of wood an hour and "their hungry boilers provided gainful employment to hundreds of woodcutters." Cordwood was also carried upstream to timber-scarce eastern locales.

The center of the American timber industry shifted at the turn of the century from the Great Lakes states to the Northwest, where the value of timber lands inflated rapidly. After cutting the most accessible stands along the lower Columbia, Puget Sound, and Pacific coast, loggers looked to mid-Columbia timber. Between 1900 and 1930, logging railroads penetrated the high plateaus between the river and the volcanic peaks of Mount Hood, Mount Adams, and Mount St. Helens. Railroads and flumes connected now-vanished lumbertowns like Palmer (in eastern Multnomah County) to riverside mills.

The postwar years brought a new cycle of prosperity to the Northwest timber industry. Except for the recession in the early 1980s, Oregon and Washington harvests were relatively steady from 1964 through 1989 despite declining land devoted to commercial production. This reflected national patterns in the National Forests, where the total cut surged steadily upward from 1940 to 1965 and then held at high levels for another quarter century. Pacific Northwest politicians maintained pressure on the Forest Service for high timber sales to support the region's logging and milling communities. Federal forest managers complied by developing unrealistically inflated assumptions about sustainable cut levels that could only be met by the aggressive harvesting of old growth. In the Gifford Pinchot National Forest in southern Washington, for example, the result was clear-cut logging of ten to twenty square miles of land annually through the 1960s, 1970s, and 1980s.

In the 1990s, however, a wide variety of new pressures have sharply reduced regional timber sales and harvest in National Forests and placed new pressures on private lands. These include the maturing of eastern pine forests, restrictions on log exports, and the intense controversy over protection of the endangered spotted owl. The 1994 statewide timber harvest in Oregon was the lowest in twenty-five years. In Washington it was the lowest since 1957.

52

Patterns in public and private ownership of timber lands in the gorge are different in Oregon and Washington. The Mount Hood National Forest in Hood River and Multnomah counties reaches nearly to the south bank of the Columbia River along a lengthy expanse of the Scenic Area. Much of this forest was protected from harvest before the Scenic Area Act. The Columbia Wilderness covers the plateau above Bonneville Dam and Cascade Locks in the heart of the gorge. The Forest Service also has a long-standing practice of not harvesting its steep lands within the gorge. In Skamania County, in contrast, almost all the timberland visible from the river is in private hands. One result is continued conflict over the visual impact of clear-cutting on the Washington slopes, since the Scenic Area legislation explicitly leaves timber harvest under existing regulatory systems.

Timber harvest has both direct and indirect effects on county governments. Income from Washington state timber harvests goes into the common school trust fund and helps pay for construction of new schools. Under federal legislation of 1908 and 1911, one quarter of the revenues from National Forests go to counties (via the states) for schools and roads. These federal forest revenues accounted for 39 percent of Skamania County's budget in 1991 and transfers from the State Forest Board provided another 14 percent. These sources of income dropped in 1992 and 1993, continuing a downward trend from 1986. Klickitat County timber receipts are on the order of $300,000 per year, only about 2 percent of the budget. Oregon counties similarly receive revenue from federal timber harvests for roads and schools. For instance, two-thirds of Wasco County's 1991-92 road budget was derived from timber revenues. Hood River County, in addition, manages substantial acreage of its own timber holdings. Finally, the National Scenic Area Act provides counties that have adopted a Scenic Area implementing ordinance with five years of additional payments in lieu of taxes for lands newly acquired by the Forest Service, to minimize the fiscal pain of decreased timber cutting.

Timber Harvests

The timber industry in the four gorge counties has mirrored the regional trend. Between 1951 and 1988, annual timber harvest for the four-county area fluctuated between 500,000 and 750,000 Mbf [thousand board feet], with a gradual upward trend within that range (see figure p. 51). Peak years were 1968 and 1986. Precipitous decline began in 1989 for reasons unrelated to the Scenic Area. Timber harvest for the four counties plummeted to far less than half the 1986 level, with only 238,000 Mbf in 1994 and a comparable level in preliminary 1995 data. Future harvests are uncertain because of the Endangered Species Act and other environmental regulations. This issue has also contributed to the delay of exchanges by the Forest Service of privately owned commercial forest land inside the Scenic Area for federal timberlands in other areas as provided for in the Scenic Area legislation.

53

Agriculture

"There was a time shortly after 1900 when, basking in the world fame of its fruits, Hood River's widespread self-publicity, abetted by the Union Pacific Railroad looking for transcontinental passengers to the valley, gave the impression that the very soil where the extra fine fruit grew had been "made" by the orchardists here."

Ruth Guppy, 1992

In Hood River County, fifteen of the twenty thousand acres of cropland in 1992 were in orchards. Fruit—first apples and now pears—has been the heart of the Hood River farm economy since the turn of the century. Hood River County actually had more agricultural workers in 1990 than in 1980. Cherries are a significant crop in northern Wasco County. Around Mosier and The Dalles there are over seven thousand acres in orchards, dating from the first decade of the century. Across the Columbia, only three thousand acres are in orchards, mainly east of the mountains in Klickitat County, where grape production is a significant industry.

Orchards east of Mosier, Oregon.
(Photo: USDA Forest Service)

The early orchard industry attracted not only experienced farmers but also a set of wealthy outsiders enticed by the amenities of the mid-Columbia valleys. In the decade before World War I, dozens of easterners and Californians established themselves as "fruit ranchers" in the Hood River area. Buffered from the uncertainties of agriculture by family fortunes, these gentlemen growers enjoyed a leisurely lifestyle that included a set of exclusive social institutions laid like a veneer over the normal patterns of small town social life. In many ways, they were a preview of the affluent outsiders who began to settle in the gorge in the 1980s, again creating sharp differences in cultural and social expectations between old-timers and newcomers.

54

The fruit industry, with its high demand for labor for pruning, tending, and harvesting, also diversified the ethnic mix of the gorge. Japanese immigrants came to the middle gorge in 1902 to work on the spur railroad up the Hood River valley and stayed to work in lumber mills, clear land for orchards, and tend new trees. As Japanese Americans worked their way into land ownership or decided not to return to the mid-Columbia region after their internment in 1942-45, orchardists increasingly turned to Mexican-American farmworkers, who formed a substantial permanent presence in the central and eastern gorge by the 1970s and 1980s. Native Americans from nearby reservations and towns have been another source of seasonal labor, as depicted in Craig Lesley's novel *River Song*. While farm owners of Japanese heritage have become important members of the small business community, they and their families number fewer than a thousand in the four counties. In contrast, the 1990 census recorded 2,752 Hispanic residents in Hood River County and nearly two thousand more in Wasco and Klickitat counties, proportions higher than in the Northwest as a whole. Hood River Valley High School graduation ceremonies in the early 1990s included speeches in Spanish as well as English.

Grain production and grazing are the heart of eastern Oregon and Washington agriculture. The farms of the dry eastern counties are large, with an average size of 2,528 acres

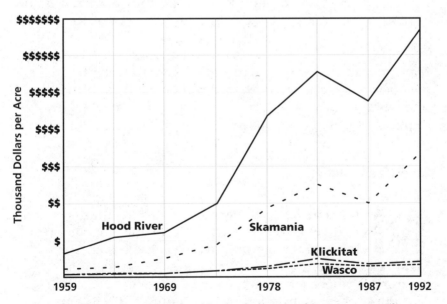

55

The average value of farmland in the four Columbia Gorge counties.
(Sources: U.S. Bureau of the Census, Census of Agriculture.)

Farmland

Wasco County farmers harvested approximately 79,000 acres of wheat and barley in 1992, mostly on dry-land farms. Another 10,500 acres produced hay. Klickitat County farmers cultivated 47,000 acres in grain and 44,000 for other crops. The grasslands of the two eastern counties supported more than fifty thousand cattle, evenly split north and south of the river.

Wasco County reported a total of 1,153,000 acres in farmland in 1992, roughly 76 percent of the total land area in the county. Klickitat County had 690,000 acres of farmland, or 58 percent of the land area. Most of this acreage is grazing land or land in rotation for dryland wheat. In contrast there are only 27,000 farm acres in Hood River (8 percent of the total land area) and fewer than 4,000 farm acres in Skamania County (under 1 percent of the land area).

in Wasco County and 1,358 acres in Klickitat County. In Skamania County, the average farm is just 67 acres. The irrigated and labor-intensive orchards of Hood River County are the smallest farm units in the region, with an average of only 48 acres. This contrast in size is inverse to the value of the farmland, with Hood River County farms valued at $6,830 per acre in 1992 and Wasco County farms at $355 per acre.

The Scenic Area Management Plan distinguishes between small-scale, part-time farms and full-time farming, whether in huge ranches or small family-run orchards. In the manner of Oregon's land use planning system, it protects agricultural land from conversion to non-resource uses and fends off incompatible uses on adjacent lands. It also exempts ongoing agricultural practices, including maintenance of existing buildings and fences, from regulation. Some landowners in the eastern portion of the gorge worry, however, that classification of their land as "pastoral" or "grassland" may lock in the status quo of 1986 despite the possibility of changing markets and technologies. Because the Management Plan requires review of new cultivation, ranchers who now run cattle worry that they may not be able to plow and plant, farmers who grow alfalfa that they may not be able to put in irrigated orchards.

Manufacturing

56

Manufacturing in the gorge has historically depended on direct access to natural resources—salmon runs, stands of timber, and hydroelectric power. These manufacturing sectors have been parts of vast regional enterprises whose fortunes they have shared.

Prior to the construction of the Columbia River dams and the advent of inexpensive electric power, manufacturing meant

The cannery at Warrendale, 1882. (Photo: Oregon Historical Society, neg. 73279)

canneries and sawmills. In the late nineteenth century, the Columbia River from Astoria to The Dalles supported thousands of fishers and cannery workers. Industrial fishing came to the gorge in the 1880s when Portland investors such as William S. Ladd financed huge fish wheels that looked like crude ferris wheels. Placed where rocks and sandbars confined migrating salmon, the wheels turned with the current and dipped fish from the river with huge baskets. After 1910, however, Columbia River fisheries declined as a result of overfishing, ocean trolling, and competition from Alaska. The last canneries at Dodson and Warrendale, Oregon, shut down in the Great Depression.

Declining timber harvests have meant a much more recent decline in wood products manufacturing. As late as 1976, twenty-five sawmills still operated in the area from Tygh Valley, Oregon, to Goldendale, Washington, west to Cascade Locks. In the 1980s and 1990s, Northwest manufacturers have closed dozens of mills as second-growth pine forests in the southern United States have matured and as new technologies have demanded investment to upgrade mills in the face of uncertain markets. The number of mills operating in the gorge counties plummeted to fifteen by 1986 and to four in 1993. The remaining mills buy many of their logs from as far away as Montana and Utah.

57

Employment in key industries in the four Columbia Gorge counties						
	1959		1990		1993	
	Total	% of All	Total	% of All	Total	% of All
Hood River County, OR	1,934	100.0	6,240	100.0	7,069	100.0
Total Manufacturing	628	32.5	1,113	17.8	1,306	18.5
Wood Product Mfg	469	24.3	487	7.8	508	7.2
Services	253	13.1	2,062	33.0	2,419	34.2
Klickitat County, WA	1,612	100.0	2,883	100.0	3,246	100.0
Total Manufacturing	869	53.9	1,343	46.5	1,446	44.5
Wood Product Mfg	837	51.9	~700	~25	~750	~23
Services	94	5.8	586	20.3	656	20.2
Skamania County, WA	801	100.0	1,011	100.0	861	100.0
Total Manufacturing	608	75.9	580	57.4	302	35.0
Wood Product Mfg	~575	~72	510	50.4	174	20.2
Services	36	4.5	171	16.9	162	18.8
Wasco County, OR	3,239	100.0	5,228	100.0	5,780	100.0
Total Manufacturing	529	16.3	978	18.7	875	15.1
Wood Product Mfg	337	10.4	~250	~5	~375	~6.5
Services	964	29.8	1,554	29.7	1,655	28.6

Source: U. S. Department of Commerce, *County Business Patterns.* Annual data by SIC code on employment covered by Federal Insurance Contributions Act (FICA). Does not include government, railroad, self-employed, agricultural, or foreign employed persons.

On the Washington side, the wood products industry as a whole—logging plus milling—remains a major although declining factor. Again as recently as the 1976, wood products accounted for a quarter of Klickitat County payroll employees, 70 percent of payroll employees in Skamania County, and virtually all of that county's manufacturing jobs. The Oregon side diversified earlier, largely due to the fruit canning and packing industry.

The problems of the forest products industry, and perhaps of the aluminum industry, can be understood as examples of a frequent pattern of economic change. Mature industries face declining profit rates and stiff competition from newer products; they respond either by modernizing operations or closing down excess capacity. The forest products industry is a classic case of a mature industry undergoing restructuring according to this model. Plant closings have been endemic in the Pacific Northwest as firms decide to shut down operations rather than reinvest in the face of uncertain markets and log availability. Several major forest products companies, such as Champion International, have sold their land holdings in the

58

Employment in key industries in the four-county gorge area compared to the states of Oregon and Washington

	1959 Total	% of All	1990 Total	% of All	1993 Total	% of All
Four County Gorge Area	7,586	100.0	15,362	100.0	16,953	100.0
Total Manufacturing	2,634	34.7	4,014	26.1	3,929	23.2
Wood Product Mfg	~2,218	~29	1,947	~13	~1,800	~10
Services	1,347	17.8	4,373	28.5	4,892	28.9
State of Oregon	359,214	100.0	1,017,239	100.0	1,074,184	100.0
Total Manufacturing	123,738	34.4	211,660	20.8	210,957	19.6
Wood Product Mfg	65,452	18.2	60,747	6.0	51,549	4.8
Services	54,190	15.1	291,218	28.6	328,043	30.5
State of Washington	594,578	100.0	1,762,046	100.0	1,859,662	100.0
Total Manufacturing	217,710	36.6	373,911	21.2	328,223	17.6
Wood Product Mfg	37,927	6.4	37,122	2.1	33,428	1.8
Services	85,572	14.4	501,383	28.5	590,736	31.8

Source: U. S. Department of Commerce, *County Business Patterns.* Annual data by SIC code on employment covered by Federal Insurance Contributions Act (FICA). Does not include government, railroad, self-employed, agricultural, or foreign employed persons.

area. SDS Lumber in Bingen is a contrasting example of a company which has shut down an old sawmill, but has opened a new computerized mill and expects to continue as one of the few viable forest products manufacturing firms in the gorge.

Portland's 1930s vision of electricity-guzzling factories at the gateways to the gorge is today's reality for another manufacturing industry. The Northwest aluminum-smelting industry dates from the completion of Grand Coulee and Bonneville dams and federally sponsored industrialization during World War II. The industry continued to grow through the 1950s and 1960s as new dams came on line and new uses for aluminum increased demand. In the early 1990s, the ten Northwest aluminum reduction plants in the Northwest accounted for 8 percent of world capacity.

The aluminum plants at The Dalles, Goldendale, and until recently at Troutdale have been the largest power users and among the largest employers in the gorge and its immediate environs. The Troutdale aluminum reduction plant, just outside the western boundary of the Scenic Area, dates to the defense mobilization of 1941. In 1992, Reynolds Metals curtailed most operations and reduced employment from eight hundred to one hundred. The aluminum plant in The Dalles

59

opened in the 1950s and now operates as Northwest Aluminum after an employee-assisted reorganization, employing 475 workers in early 1996. Just east of the National Scenic Area, a new plant opened at Goldendale in 1970/71; after several transfers of ownership and another employee-assisted buyout in 1986, it operates as Columbia Aluminum with 640 workers in early 1996. Power rates and availability continue to be the major issue for the aluminum industry. Fluctuations in power and aluminum prices have caused periodic closings and reopenings as well as transfers of ownership. Bonneville Power Administration (BPA) in 1986 negotiated a new rate structure with the aluminum plants under which the cost of power varies inversely with the market price of aluminum. Over time, the cost of power to the aluminum plants is equal to or greater than standard rates, but they pay less when profits are low, and more when profits are up. The plants, which take approximately one-third of all BPA power sales, are also subject to power cut-backs when there is a shortage. There are concerns in the industry about the long-term viability of the Pacific Northwest aluminum industry in the face of continued uncertainties in power supply and rates and stiff price competition from Russian plants.

Only in the past thirty years have more varied and smaller manufacturing industries become important employers. In 1992, Maritime Services Corp, a Hood River firm specializing in the labor-intensive work of refurnishing the interior living space of ships made a national list of the five hundred fastest-growing companies in the United States. This is one example of the kind of company that is starting to change the economic base of the gorge: specialized and small scale, with low transportation costs and/or an advantage from a gorge location. Customized sailboards, electronics, fishing lures and flies, microbreweries, and other specialized food products are produced in Hood River and to a lesser degree in The Dalles and on the north side of the Columbia. There is anecdotal evidence of substantial cottage industry throughout the gorge—whether it involves sophisticated telecommuting or piecework sail-making to supplement farm or timber income.

60

A New Wave—Boards, Tourists, and Brew

Tourism in the gorge has boomed since the 1980s. Indeed, the Scenic Area explicitly promotes sightseeing and convention business. The infusion of dollars for the northside conference center (opened 1993 in Stevenson), southside interpretive center (scheduled to open 1997 in The Dalles), and other tourism projects express one vision for creating a new economic base that is dependent on retaining the scenic character of the region. The Forest Service estimated 1.5 million visitors in 1988 and 2.1 million in 1993. Such attractions as the Mount Hood Railway excursion train, the Cascade Locks sternwheeler, and the Maryhill Museum in Washington reported banner years in the mid-1990s.

Sailboarders on the Columbia River. (Photo: USDA Forest Service)

Developing apart from these efforts, the most prominent new element in gorge recreation has been boardsailing or windsurfing. The international windsurfing community discovered Hood River in the mid-1980s in the midst of a worldwide boom in the sport. The combination of prevailing west winds and west-flowing currents in mid-gorge allows expert sailors to tack back and forth across the river. By the

61

Tourist Dollars

As tourism booms, visitors to the Scenic Area have had little choice but to spend money in Oregon rather than Washington. Oregon accounted for 90 percent of the 812 motel or bed and breakfast rooms available in 1987 and 55 percent of the campsites. The same imbalance can be found in restaurants, shops, and other services, with Oregon businesses receiving 80 percent of tourist dollars. This stronger retail and service sector reflects the larger communities that developed to serve Oregon farmers, the opportunities to supply motorists along the Columbia River Highway and later I-84, and the advantage of locating in a state without a sales tax.

The most significant change from these established patterns was the February 1993 opening of Skamania Lodge, the new convention center envisioned in the National Scenic Area legislation. Its location at Stevenson, Washington, is outside the Mt.. Hood-Mt.. Adams corridor, highly accessible to Portland and Vancouver, and extremely important to the depressed Skamania County economy. It attracted twice its projected conference business in its first year, with nearly three hundred full-time employees (in a county with roughly three thousand total jobs). Success has been helped by the architectural decision to copy Timberline Lodge, a New Deal project on the southern slope of Mount Hood that is an acknowledged masterpiece. Skamania Lodge imitates Timberline in profile, in materials, and in interior finish. Day visitors support a sprinkling of new delis, antique shops, and art galleries in Stevenson.

early 1990s, Hood River and environs were the venue for several national/international events with names like Gorge Blowout and Rushwind River Rampage.

The industry has been described as having "grown from a bunch of designers/sailors into a group of people who have matured and gotten more into the business part and less into the sailing part." Sailboarding brings practitioners and viewers and also retailers, distributors, and manufacturers, several of which are linked to Hawaiian firms. Product development, so often located in the large urban centers, is also finding a place in the gorge. Many of these firms design the sails, boards, and accessories they manufacture. Testing new equipment and developing sails and boards for the high winds of the Columbia Gorge are part of the new economy.

"Gorge Tested and Approved" is a label that goes with equipment developed under the extreme local conditions. One of the larger companies, Rushwind, mass-produces sails in Hong Kong, but custom makes its top 5 percent in Hood River. Manufacturing related to boardsailing is centered in Hood River, but is slowly inching into other counties. Skamania County has captured some business in new business incubator buildings in Stevenson. Firms have begun to consider Bingen to get away from the higher rents in Hood

White Salmon, Washington. (Photo: USDA Forest Service)

River and to obtain a more visible location on the highway between Hood River and Doug's Beach, where windsurfing "air time" is about as good as you can get.

Sailboarding has keyed a diversification of leisure-oriented businesses along a north-south axis from Mount Hood in Oregon to Mount Adams in Washington. Hood River and Mosier, Oregon, and White Salmon, Washington, in the Scenic Area, along with Trout Lake, Washington, located north of the boundary, attract recreational and retirement homes. Home owners enjoy proximity to the mountains for skiing, hiking, and hunting, quick access to the best sailing beaches, and the best balanced climate in the gorge. Communities along the axis have begun to offer an expanding range of recreational opportunities—new golf courses, an excursion railroad on an abandoned Union Pacific spur, a highly successful microbrewery. The number of vacation homes in the four counties jumped from three hundred to sixteen hundred during the 1980s.

Hood River and White Salmon are a long way from "Aspenization," but dollar signs and dread compete in local dreams. Boardsailing is a prototypical replacement industry. It provides jobs that are independent of local resource supplies but have the disadvantage of dependence on outside customers, investors, and fashions. There is a strong fear that tourism creates only low-paying jobs, requiring multiple incomes to support a family. At the same time, housing prices have risen dramatically in mid-gorge communities. View

63

houses in White Salmon and Underwood more than doubled in value between 1988 and 1992, while the average home price in the city of Hood River jumped from $51,000 to nearly $90,000. These changes are making it difficult for young families to afford to live in the gorge. Long-term residents and those who identify with primary industries are particularly negative about tourism, which they see as forcing sharply reduced lifestyles.

Is There a Boom? Four Counties, Four Economies

The economies of the four counties offer sharp contrasts, with a substantial urban sector in Oregon and a resource-dependent economy in Washington, reversing the prevalent pattern of stronger growth in Washington.

Until recently, the differences in economic activity between the four counties had been stable for several decades. With the spillover from the Portland metropolitan area and the advent of windsurfing, the balance is shifting. Hood River County has garnered the fastest-growing, highest-value components of a new wave of growth. Even more recently, Skamania County has seen the spread of expensive housing east from Clark County, small-scale sailboard manufacturing, and the Skamania Lodge resort and conference center.

64

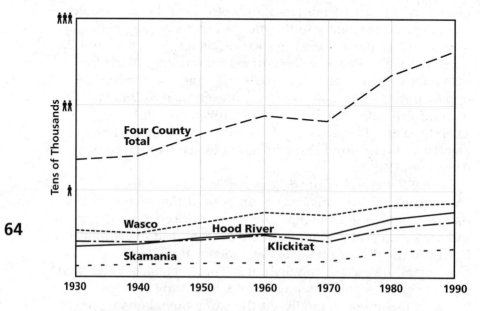

Employment in the four Columbia Gorge counties compared to total employment for the region. (Source: U.S. Census.)

Some measures of growth and income in the four Columbia Gorge counties

	Number of Housing Units		% of House- holds in different house, 1985-90	1990 Population	% Growth 1980-90	1989 per Capita Income
	1990 Total	New Housing Units 1980-90 percent increase				
Clark County	92,849	26.3	55.1	238,053	23.8	$13,993
Camas Division	8,995	19.3	46.6	23,846	15.4	$13,122
Hood River County	7,569	19.8	50.3	16,903	6.7	$11,421
Cascades Locks Division	420	10.0	59.3	948	-8.2	$10,127
Cascade Locks City	412	10.2	59.5	930	11.0	$9,974
Hood River Division	3,872	21.6	53.1	8,916	5.9	$12,212
Hood River City	2,272	20.6	64.5	4,632	7.0	$12,007
Klickitat County	7,213	20.2	52.2	16,611	5.0	$10,776
White Salmon Division	2,608	19.7	52.3	6,114	9.9	$11,070
White Salmon City	816	13.8	55.6	1,861	0.4	$11,863
Bingen	316	13.6	56.4	650	0.9	$7,354
Wahkiakus Division	1,694	18.3	48.7	3,700	9.0	$10,792
Multnomah County	255,751	9.3	53.4	583,887	3.8	$14,462
Corbett Division	1,337	15.6	41.2	3,766	1.5	$14,114
Skamania County	3,922	19.1	46.3	8,289	4.7	$11,621
Bonneville Division	1,207	25.4	43.6	2,759	21.7	$12,666
Stevenson Division	700	9.1	47.2	1,730	-13.9	$10,262
Stevenson City	457	8.1	50.0	1,147	-2.1	$9,770
Wind River Division	1,647	17.7	49.0	3,725	3.6	$11,527
Carson Valley	735	15.4	46.8	1,758	N.A.	$9,879
Wasco County	10,476	15.4	51.1	21,683	-0.2	$12,542
The Dalles Division	8,266	14.9	53.8	17,629	-0.3	$12,828
The Dalles City	4,843	8.9	54.4	11,060	2.2	$12,142
Chenowith	1,377	16.6	61.1	3,246	15.1	$11,061
Mosier	112	15.2	25.1	202	-41.2	$10,541

Source: U.S. Census

Data on housing construction from 1970 to 1990 give additional detail about pockets of growth in the gorge. New construction has pressed eastward from Vancouver across southeastern Clark County and into Skamania County. This growth, and to a lesser extent, growth in the Corbett district of northwestern Multnomah County, are extensions of the greater Portland-Vancouver metropolitan area. White Salmon and Hood River have been the biggest gainers from the

65

boardsailing boom. In the southeastern corner of Skamania County, over 32 percent of the housing stock dates from the 1970s and 25 percent from the 1980s. The city of Hood River and its immediate surrounds show similar rates of expansion from a much larger base, with 25 percent of the housing stock built in the 1970s and 20 percent in the 1980s. In distinct contrast, only 9 percent of the housing in the Stevenson area dates from the 1980s.

These differential growth patterns reflect accidents of geography and local conditions; they also influence local responses to the National Scenic Area legislation and planning process.

To some, Hood River *is* the gorge. It has the cachet of world recognition in windsurfing circles. It has a glamorous site at the base of the two valleys peaking at Mount Hood to the south and Mount Adams to the north. It has an aggressive sense of its own attractions. While the other three gorge counties have struggled to bring employment back to the levels of the early 1980s, Hood River County posted new employment highs in 1990, 1991, and 1992, keeping it far below state averages in the proportion of residents on public assistance.

Together with companies manufacturing sailboard equipment, Hood River County has wineries, microbreweries, and custom food product firms. Construction businesses (321 employees in 1990), lodging services (288 employees), and eating and drinking places (435 employees) all thrive. But the largest employment in the service sector, surprisingly, is not in tourism but in health services (610 employees). The opening of a Wal-Mart and a super Safeway on the west end of town signal competition for the regional retail business that has traditionally gone to The Dalles or Portland. Hidden in the statistics are information workers and entrepreneurs attracted by the amenities of Hood River—landscape architects, development consultants, editors. Often self-employed or small proprietors, they are further changing the character of the community.

In contrast, Wasco County has historically been the regional center for services, finance, and wholesaling businesses. Almost a third of its jobs have been in the retail sector, especially with large building material, farm equipment, and automobile dealers serving multi-county markets. Until recently it also had the largest wholesale sector, a role now relinquished to Hood River County. Wasco County is also unique in the gorge in its extremely small forest products sector, accounting for only 5 percent of jobs in the county.

66

North of the Columbia River, the resource-based economy is sputtering. Klickitat County still depends on resource production and processing, with nearly half of its employment in the manufacturing sector. It also benefitted from a relatively high level of diversification because of Columbia Aluminum, the largest employer in the county. The county budget is buffered by the presence of a regional landfill, whose long-term operating agreement gives the county a share of revenues. White Salmon is seeing a slow influx of artists, craftspersons, and small specialized manufacturers. Nevertheless, the county had the third highest proportion of food stamp and welfare clients in Washington in 1995.

Skamania County has been the most interesting case. Depending on wood products for over 50 percent of its employment as late as 1990, the county economy has changed dramatically in the last few years under the multiple strains of national recession and changed timber management and harvest schedules. With nearly four-fifths of the county in federal ownership, primarily in the Gifford Pinchot National Forest, Skamania County seemed to have few options and fewer resources. Timber industry employment since 1990 has dropped with the decreased harvest and the closing of two Stevenson Co-Ply mills in 1992, an action that idled 175 workers. As resource production has declined, Skamania County has become a bedroom community out of necessity. A county commissioner estimated that 60 percent of employed residents worked outside the county in 1992.

On the positive side, county officials in the 1990s have vigorously pursued diversification that has helped to drop unemployment from 30 percent to 10 percent and moved many families off public assistance. "From Pine Boards to Sailboards" headlined a 1992 story in *Timber Times* (a publication of the Washington Governor's Timber Team) about the use of state and federal economic development funds by the Port of Skamania County. Skamania leaders have been equally aggressive in pursuing windsurfing equipment manufacturers and tourism, despite the relatively low wage rates for most tourist industry jobs. The county rescued the Skamania Lodge project with a $5 million loan when Congress sat on the expected appropriation until 1994 and 1995. The Skamania County Historical Society raised private funds for an eclectic but well-received Columbia Gorge Interpretive Center that opened in May 1995 across the road from Skamania Lodge and adjacent to the abandoned Stevenson Co-Ply mill, once the largest employer in the county.

Responses to Change

These changes in the early 1990s—diversification of tourism, selective increases in land values and housing prices, severe decline of the timber industry—are unsettling to gorge residents. But they also continue a long-standing pattern in which successive generations have remade the Columbia Gorge economy. The Native American trading system gave way in turn to the British, Canadian, and U.S. fur business of the 1830s, the Portland-centered transportation empire of the 1860s, the fishing economy of the 1890s, the orchard and timber communities of the 1920s, the new manufacturing industries of the 1950s, and the expanding tourist economy of the 1980s. There is every reason to expect further rounds of growth and change in the next century.

In this volatile situation, each county has responded differently to Scenic Area mandates. Beyond the contingencies of individual leadership, these responses are rooted in local circumstances—industrial mix, demographic change, proportion of newcomers in positions of influence, sophistication and capacity of local governments themselves. Multnomah and Clark are metropolitan counties for which the Scenic Area is a minor consideration. Hood River has experienced the most prolonged transition from Old West to New West, while Skamania County has changed rapidly in the 1990s after lagging in the 1980s, with a consequent transformation in local government attitudes toward the Scenic Area. In contrast, old industries and attitudes are stronger than ever in Klickitat County, where established resource industries have resisted the encroachment of tourism. Wasco County, with the largest gorge city and a history as a commercial center, balances a relatively sophisticated government with a sometimes reluctant citizenry.

The Scenic Area and Economic Change

The Scenic Area thus differs from Cape Cod and Lake Tahoe, where little is left of the old fishing or logging economies and the social systems that they supported. The basic issue in both these cases was between environmental protection and recreational land development, often by relatively new owners, not between environmental protection and continuation of resource extraction.

In contrast, the New Jersey Pinelands program is similar to the Scenic Area in explicitly defining the three goals of ecological integrity, agricultural viability, and appropriate economic development. By implication, maintenance of the established economy carried a commitment to established ways of life. As a result, regional regulators in both the Pinelands and the gorge find themselves negotiating among local economic interests with sometimes conflicting goals. In New Jersey, for example, cranberry and blueberry growers in the heart of the Pine Barrens have different needs than farmers in peripheral lands. In the gorge, a comparable example is a three-way debate over the future of the Hood River waterfront among advocates of industrial development, hotels, and open space, with the latter two options meeting needs of different parts of the tourist industry.

One of the central goals of the Scenic Area is to provide tools to mediate among different industries while recognizing the power of economic modernization. Unlike New York's Adirondacks legislation, which ignored the indigenous economy, the Scenic Area Act invites all players to the table. Many who live within the gorge disagree with the tools created and with at least portions of the vision of economic change. Some residents feel caught by unfamiliar rules and frustrated by new bureaucracies. Their opposition, however, has been far less bitter and entrenched than that in far upstate New York.

The economic history of the Columbia River gorge makes it clear that continuing change is far more likely than economic and social continuity. In this context of uncertainty, mechanisms for thinking about and shaping the future can be among the most valuable community resources. Within the Columbia Gorge, there is no effective alternative to the Scenic Area program for attempting to manage transitions that are already underway.

CHAPTER 3

Choosing Sides

"If you don't solve the problem, it will be solved for you."
    Charles Cushman, 1981

"Local officials are the problem not the solution in the gorge."
    Chuck Williams, testimony to Congress, 1983

When Colonel George A. Rizor, Jr., U.S. Army (Retired) sought in 1980 to divide property he had owned for nearly twenty years, Skamania County did not have a zoning ordinance. The county had a comprehensive land use plan, and it also had adopted a shoreline management plan in response to a Washington state mandate. But the county commissioners had not yet seen the need for zoning. Land use control in Skamania was primarily informal, as it is in many other rural places, its dynamics shaped by the social structure of the community. Rizor wanted to build homes and recreation facilities on his waterfront property directly across from Multnomah Falls, one of Oregon's premier tourist attractions, located in the heart of the Columbia Gorge.

Rizor's actions deeply disturbed Yvonne Montchalin, a thirty-year resident of Skamania County who owned land adjoining Rizor's property on the east and another tract one ownership removed on the west. Montchalin wasn't a member of any environmental organization, but she believed that Rizor's proposal would damage the scenic splendor of the gorge. She was also troubled by what she thought were procedural violations. Montchalin claimed that Rizor had deeded parcels to members of his immediate family to deliberately avoid Washington state and Skamania County laws regarding the creation of subdivisions, including environmental review and public hearing requirements.

Telling her story to a U.S. Senate committee, Montchalin later noted that Washington's Columbia Gorge Commission, the advisory body created by the state in the 1950s, and Multnomah County officials requested Skamania County to comply with the subdivision laws, but the county would not do so. The commission requested an opinion from the state attorney general in January 1981, but never got a response. The issue came up in the local press and in informal public meetings. County officials said repeatedly that development was unlikely because permits for septic tanks probably would not be granted. But Montchalin later learned that, while county officials were downplaying the proposal in public, they were quietly granting Rizor two extensions of his deadline to complete application procedures. In mid-September 1981, Montchalin and other neighbors heard and saw road construction on the Rizor property. They discovered that the commissioners had, indeed, granted approval for twenty-four septic tanks. In October, Montchalin reluctantly became the lead plaintiff in a lawsuit filed in Skamania County Superior Court, with Rizor, members of Rizor's family, and the county as defendants. The plaintiffs sought to enjoin further development. Before they were due in court, the county commissioners formally approved Rizor's project. The court subsequently granted a temporary injunction.

Joining Yvonne Montchalin in opposition was John Yeon, the owner of the property adjoining Rizor's on the west. A well-known architect and conservationist, Yeon as a young man had chaired the Columbia Gorge Committee of the Northwest Regional Planning Commission, which in 1937 issued a report calling for gorge protection (see page 35). He now wrote a scathing critique of Rizor's proposal, expressing several deeply felt concerns, including his doubt of the capacity of local governments in the gorge to manage, in an environmentally sensitive manner, the residential development that he saw looming ahead.

Montchalin and Yeon believed that Skamania County's informal approach to land use control had broken down when faced with Rizor's challenge to environmental resources and rational planning practices. Montchalin felt that, "Had the plaintiffs not had the courage to file the suit, post the very substantial bond and bear the attendant risks and verbal abuse, the subterfuge resorted to by the individual defendants, aided and condoned by Skamania County officials, would have resulted in a poorly planned development becoming established." Yeon was even more alarmist, warning that "Skamania County approval of . . . Rizor . . . shines a revealing light on the standards considered acceptable by the county planning staff, planning commission, and county government. It is a chilling preview of the calibre of planning and land usage which will be allowed in this section of the gorge."

71

The controversy encapsulated a basic difference in attitudes that would continue to structure debates about the future of the gorge. Advocates of scenic and environmental protection turned increasingly to formal rules as a way to override what they saw as entrenched local growth coalitions. Many gorge residents, in contrast, would view the growing emphasis on rule making as devaluing local social networks; such systems might be necessary in complex metropolitan regions, they believed, but not in communities structured by local knowledge.

Introducing the Park Service

Supporting the neighbors in opposition to Rizor was Chuck Williams, a former national parks expert for Friends of the Earth, a national organization that spoke for strong environmental protection. In the short term, Williams's contribution to the emerging political debate was to help organize and lead the Columbia Gorge Coalition, formed in 1979, before Rizor's plans brought the question of development in the gorge to a head. About four hundred households were dues-paying members of the Coalition; most of them, including all of the organization's directors, lived in the gorge. Using Williams's contacts, the Coalition was instrumental in getting the National Park Service to initiate a study of the gorge in 1979, building on a Park Service study of urban recreation issues in the Portland area conducted in 1976.

The project took local government officials by surprise. Many of them and their constituents became distressed after seeing copies of letters that Williams had written to the Park Service director and to the secretary of the interior outlining a strategy to incorporate the gorge as a Park Service unit. A journalist noted that, "There is a local belief that the National Park Service study is part of an environmentalist conspiracy." A draft of the study released in November 1979 triggered conflicts that would reverberate in the gorge for years to come and shape the political evolution of National Scenic Area legislation.

72

The draft identified several threats to resource values, primarily industrialization, resulting from continuing efforts by port districts and other local agencies to recruit new firms, and residential and commercial development pressures, especially in eastern Clark and western Skamania counties. Interestingly, the Park Service noted: "Both Clark County, which has indicated a political domination by development interests, and Skamania County, which has yet to adopt a zoning ordinance, appear to be subject to major land use changes and significant population increases." Surface mining was another problem, for certain counties had ignored recommendations by the state Columbia River Gorge Commissions to deny new extraction permits. The draft argued that clear-cutting of forest land in large areas of the gorge was responsible for the degradation of water quality. Moreover, charged the draft, "little if any land use laws exist to protect threatened farmlands."

The Park Service also worried that more than fifty governmental agencies were involved in gorge management, without an authoritative entity that could protect environmental resources. They noted that the state gorge commissions had adopted a Resource Management Plan in 1976 that included guidelines for compatible forest management, surface mining, recreation, housing, and commercial and industrial development. Moreover, both state governments had directed local governments to take these guidelines into account when making land use decisions. But the state commissions did not have the financial means to manage implementation, especially to acquire lands that their 1976 plan identified for purchase. In addition, their plan did not specify what changes were needed in existing county zoning ordinances; it simply identified areas of concern. Without a legal mandate—and substantial sums of money—implementation of the plan was uncertain.

Chuck Williams

Chuck Williams was tied to the gorge by Native American ancestors on one side of his family and by nineteenth-century pioneers on the other. Although he grew up in California, the gorge remained "the mystic center" of his childhood memories from visits to the family home ground in Skamania County. After working as an engineer and a VISTA volunteer, he went to work for Friends of the Earth in 1975 and soon began preparing an eloquent and beautiful book on the gorge that appeared in 1980. Moved by a vision of the gorge as a special place and instrumental in generating local support for systematic protection, Williams remained deeply involved in gorge politics through the 1980s but became increasingly angry about the compromises of the political process. (Photo: Hood River News)

73

State regulations were mixed on both sides of the river. Oregon's forest practice law, which regulated the use of privately owned forest land, did not take scenic resources into account, though the U.S. Forest Service was already applying a visual management system in much of its extensive Oregon holdings. In addition, Oregon had a statewide land use planning program with statewide land use goals with which city and county plans and ordinances had to be consistent.

The quality of state regulation was even more important in Washington, where most of the gorge land was privately owned. The Washington forest practice law was no better than Oregon's with regard to scenery. Washington did require the preparation of shoreline management plans, and an environmental impact review process when either public or private actions were deemed to have potentially significant environmental consequences. But the lack of statewide goals and reliance on local initiative to regulate led to implementation inconsistencies.

The Park Service draft report considered four alternatives to the status quo: strengthening the existing commissions; creating a multigovernmental commission; establishing central federal management; and forming a bistate compact. The analysis generated intense controversy.

The gorge commissions split along characteristic political fault lines. A majority of the Oregon commission favored federal intervention to protect the gorge. The Washington commission disagreed. Environmental activists on both sides of the river disparaged the advisory status of the commissions; they were especially critical of Washington efforts. John Yeon continued to feel about gorge preservation in 1980 as he had in 1967, when he wrote to former Oregon governor Tom McCall: "The Washington side of the Gorge is an orphan which Washington has abandoned and Oregon cannot adopt." Yeon believed that the existence of the commissions had lulled area residents into complacency.

Oregon governor Victor Atiyeh broke with his gorge commission to join Washington governor Dixie Lee Ray in writing to the secretary of the interior opposing any change in the governance structure or federal intervention, although he did acknowledge that the commissions might need some money to acquire land.

74

Alternatives for the Gorge: The Park Service Report

The intensity of the reactions to its draft report took the Park Service by surprise. Efforts to be responsive are evident in revisions to the draft and an unusual public review period was initiated. As a result of this public input, the Park Service strengthened the alternative which expanded the role of the existing commissions. Since the governance structures designed by the Park Service reappeared in a variety of legislative proposals leading up to the 1986 National Scenic Area Act, a brief discussion provides context for the political dynamics analyzed in the next chapter.

Strengthening the Commissions

As the Park Service envisioned it, expansion of the role of the existing gorge commissions depended upon the states finding funds to match a special congressional appropriation to implement the commissions' 1976 Resource Management Plan. Such money could be used to acquire land, monitor implementation, revise and update the plan, and provide technical assistance to local governments. The Park Service would participate as an ex officio member of the commissions, advising them and administering the federal funds. The gorge commissions would develop use classifications and adopt performance standards for lands within their existing jurisdictions and attempt to persuade city and county governments to incorporate these into local plans and ordinances. Implementation would be more consistent, the Park Service added, if the states would mandate that local government land use regulations comply with the Resource Management Plan. This idea was put forward as a suggestion, however, in the context of a governance structure designed to leave existing federal-state-local relations as undisturbed as possible. The Park Service would watchdog other federal agencies to monitor consistency with gorge plans, and the states would be expected to do the same at their level.

The theory underlying this governance alternative is that the problem of protection is basically one of adequate financial resources and technical capacity. Federal funds would leverage state contributions to buy land and regulate land use to preserve the gorge environment. Following the arguments in the governors' letter, this scenario assumed that local and

75

state leaders and citizens on both sides of the river were generally supportive. The analytical parts of the Park Service report, of course, cast doubt on that assumption. But throughout the lengthy course of legislative debate, local gorge officials, especially on the Washington side, would insist that their planning bodies were both willing and able to do what was necessary. They would argue they didn't need federal technical help. Federal money, though, would introduce complications for both friends and foes of a federal role in the gorge. Indeed, the Park Service clearly recognized that land acquisition was a very sensitive issue. All of the alternatives stressed that government should acquire something less than full ownership of land, such as a scenic easement, whenever possible, and that condemnation should be held to a minimum.

A Multigovernmental Commission

Establishing a multigovernmental commission, the second alternative to the status quo, would mean replacing the existing commissions with a congressionally legislated planning and monitoring agency to which federal, state, and local governments would appoint representatives. The Park Service might have a representative, but would not play a central management role. The Park Service would, though, be charged with identifying and recommending the acquisition of sensitive lands.

The federal government would give the new commission money to hire a staff, prepare and adopt a comprehensive plan, give planning grants to local governments, monitor plan implementation, and establish a revolving fund to buy sensitive lands that could be resold with restrictions. Commission staff would persuade local governments to make their own plans and ordinances consistent with the comprehensive plan and make recommendations regarding timber harvesting practices.

The commission's relationship to the locals would still be, as in the previous alternative, advisory—but with a new twist: incentives. Local compliance would open the way for federal funds for new recreational facilities and other purposes. Jurisdictions losing tax revenues due to acquisition would get compensation. The Park Service also suggested that the commission adopt the Oregon land management strategy of

76

Lands in the west end of the gorge vulnerable to development. (Photo: USDA Forest Service)

encouraging future commercial, industrial, and residential development to locate within the growth boundaries of established urban areas. And the report recommended legislation mandating consistency between the actions of other federal and state agencies and the commission's plan.

Money and technical capacity were the key elements in the first alternate governance structure. While these were also important in this second alternative, the multigovernmental commission is based on the potential of participation to change hearts and minds, along with material incentives to stay on board. The theory is that if the various jurisdictions, particularly local governments, could participate in shaping the commission's planning processes and outcomes, then they would be disposed to implement the plan. A broadly representative participatory process would engender mutual trust and cooperative behavior. Local interests could be defended honorably, balanced by equally honorable regional concerns.

77

This alternative, like the first, assumes the validity of a journalist's observation of the politics surrounding the draft: "Everyone agrees that the gorge is beautiful and worth protecting. No one seems to agree on how to do it." A multigovernmental commission was intended to facilitate the emergence of an agreement. Incentives were intended to lubricate the process and motivate local governments to address threats identified by the Park Service.

While local officials argued throughout the legislative process for maintaining the status quo, the governors picked up the idea of a multigovernmental commission as one that suggested a way of responding to environmentalist advocacy while preserving a large role for state and local officials. The Park Service was deliberately vague, however, regarding the composition of the commission. How much weight would local, state, and federal representatives each carry? Answering this question—deciding whether locals or outsiders, Old Westerners or New Westerners would control it—was just as complicated and divisive as spending money to acquire land.

Federal Management

The third Park Service alternative started from the assumption that local governments lacked the desire or capacity to address environmental threats, and suggested a federally managed National Recreation Area in the western portion of the gorge. The concept of a National *Recreation* Area did not really fit the situation in the gorge for three reasons: (1) there was far more population and economic activity in the gorge than was typical; (2) passive recreation would predominate; and (3) the cost of buying the necessary private land would be prohibitive. However, the idea did resonate with the underlying concept of the 1976 Park Service study of the gorge as a recreational zone for the Portland metropolitan area. Moreover, the most environmentally sensitive lands are in the western part of the gorge. The eastern part could be protected either by the status quo commission arrangement, or through the first or second alternatives.

To create a National Recreation Area, Congress would designate a lead federal agency to prepare a comprehensive plan, identify compatible land uses outside incorporated areas, and acquire sensitive lands when appropriate. The agency would work with local officials to define growth boundaries for incorporated areas consistent with protection goals and would then manage federally owned and controlled lands. An advisory committee—perhaps the same entity that would be in

78

charge of the eastern gorge—would consult with the federal agency regarding planning and implementation.

The Park Service noted that the primary strategies to preserve gorge values in this alternative—public ownership and restricted use of private lands—"would be relatively inflexible compared to the other alternatives and would be applied forcefully." The political and financial cost to the federal government to buy full ownership of certain lands and easements or other sorts of partial ownership elsewhere would be large. The theory in this case is that relatively inflexible means—and a leading role for a federal agency—are necessary to transcend the limits of local government land use control. Even when spirits are willing and plans and ordinances are in place, local government officials have a very hard time restraining themselves in the face of specific development proposals.

According to the analysis of land use politics in Clark and Skamania counties mentioned in both draft and final reports, the level of local government commitment to protection might vary dramatically by place and over time. Skamania County commissioner Ed Callahan—a former Washington Gorge Commission vice-chair—worried that zoning would depress property values in his jurisdiction. In Wasco County, orchardist Barbara Bailey successfully led a grassroots citizen movement to drive away a proposed zirconium plant that local officials had been assiduously courting. But she worried about the capacity of citizens to prevail in the face of a continuing stream of such proposed pollution-generating industrial projects. Central federal management was the governance structure preferred by environmentalists, who despaired of local government's capacity to effectively implement protection plans.

A Bistate Compact

The Park Service originally intended to analyze a fourth alternative to the status quo—a bistate compact between Oregon and Washington creating a joint commission

empowered, among other things, to override local land use controls. "However," wrote the Park Service, "as the provisions and scope of this alternative were studied, it became clear that it would have been extremely complex to implement and that certain ramifications would have made it infeasible." Basically, the Park Service believed that Oregon and Washington, given their differing philosophies regarding land use, would never agree on such a compact, and that state legislators, even in Oregon, would not support overriding local decision makers. Moreover, a bistate compact would lack authority over federal lands and agencies. Ironically, however, the National Scenic Area Act eventually did incorporate the notion of a bistate compact, mandating that Oregon and Washington create a commission empowered to do just what the Park Service believed, left to their own devices, the states would resist. The Columbia River Gorge Commission would not, however, be an agent of the federal government. As the Park Service said, this alternative is extremely complex.

The Park Service report discussed crucial issues that would remain at the center of debate throughout the legislative period. Suggestions regarding governance structures, land acquisition, land use controls, and incentives would be mixed and matched by participants in forthcoming congressional battles. And though it tried to emphasize the purely conceptual nature of its report—and to respond to local government worries—the Park Service would itself become embroiled in controversy about the future of gorge protection.

Troutdate, Oregon, at the entrance to the Scenic Area. (Photo: authors)

From Proposal to Politics

While controversy simmered around the Rizor proposal and the idea of federal protection, Skamania County invited Charles Cushman to the area. A fiercely competitive man who started his business career as a soft drink and peanut vendor at Dodger Stadium, Cushman had taken on the National Park Service in the 1970s on behalf of himself and other owners of private cabins within Yosemite National Park. His National Inholders Association was an early player in the growing "wise use" or "property rights" movement, bringing him in the 1990s to the leadership of several property rights lobbying organizations.

Coming to Skamania County at local invitation in 1981, Cushman told angry stories of the Park Service forcing people out of their homes and off their lands. He warned that the Columbia Gorge could see a replay of what had happened in Cuyahoga National Recreation Area in Ohio, where the Park Service had displaced rural residents and created a *cause celebre* of heartless federal disruption of a local community. More than seventy-nine thousand families across the country had lost their homes to the Park Service, Cushman charged. He set out before worried Skamanians the future of the gorge as he saw it, assuring them that they did have the political clout to combat pressure for federal management if they would support local county executives. Cushman observed that a major obstacle to organizing effective opposition to federal intervention in threatened areas like the gorge was the isolationist mentality of residents. Local property owners vehemently resisted anyone who might impose any limits on them. But he pleaded with his audience, "You don't want to be simply anti-managerial . . . you want to be pro local government, or they will take it [the gorge] away from you."

Col. Rizor—who told a U.S. Senate committee that God's plan "specified private individual ownership of land, with minimal local level supervision, and no national land use control, except for boundary defense"—was willing to allow a minimal amount of local government intervention, indicating that even Skamania County isolationists took Cushman's advice to heart. Cushman had made a significant impact on the local political culture and opponents of federal gorge protection would lean heavily on his advice to stress local government capacity to manage natural and scenic resources. They also regularly attacked the logic of federal protection. The

81

newly formed Committee to Preserve Property Rights in the Columbia River Gorge argued that ponderous federal agencies with rigid rules and nationalized agendas were as likely to harm the gorge as to help. Articulating views that would echo repeatedly in criticisms of the Scenic Area Act, the Committee argued that "the Gorge's well-preserved state to date, despite its proximity to a major metropolitan area, and without—in fact, often in spite of—federal actions, seems to be attributable primarily to the concerted efforts of an environmentally aware and conservation-minded local citizenry and local government . . . One must question whether transferring the authority and responsibility for the future of the Columbia River Gorge to the Federal Government—whose primary contribution to preservation of this 'scenic treasure' has been three hydroelectric dams, a four-lane freeway, and miles of transmission lines strung across the face of our cliffs—is at all a good idea."

A Coalition for Protection

The Committee saw political pressure building in the urban areas for federal intervention. Many supporters of protection did dwell in the metropolitan areas of Oregon and Washington, and they were sounding alarms, as had John Yeon and the Gorge Coalition. Yeon had learned of Nancy Russell, a Portland Garden Club member whose slide shows of gorge wildflowers were attracting interest. He had approached her in August 1979 to encourage her to work for gorge protection. Not long after, Russell also attracted the attention of Multnomah County executive Don Clark. At the suggestion of U.S. senator Mark Hatfield (R-OR), Clark had initiated a broad-based, bipartisan coalition-building effort for gorge protection legislation. Clark asked Russell to take a leadership role in this effort, and Russell emerged as a founding member of Friends of the Columbia Gorge. The Friends were largely a metropolitan-based organization, although there were members who resided in the gorge. Catalyzed into being in early 1981 by the Rizor proposal, the Friends actively participated in the lawsuit against it, and began to work closely with members of the Oregon and Washington congressional delegations on federal legislation.

82

Friends of the Columbia Gorge argued that rapid population growth in the metropolitan area, the absence of

Nancy Russell

Nancy Russell would soon cast a long shadow over gorge politics. She was quiet, determined, and often caustic about aesthetic values that did not match her own. Beginning in the early 1980s, Russell became a skilled champion of gorge protection. She worked through the Friends of the Columbia Gorge and used her deep commitment, impressive energy, and blossoming political skills to turn gorge preservation into a prominent Portland issue. In the process she displaced other Portlanders who also shared an interest in gorge conservation but who were more willing to consider compromise with local interests. By the 1990s she was a hero in many eyes and a conspirator in others—but always deeply committed to her vision of the gorge, working through the Trust for Public Lands and buying select properties with her personal funds.

controls on land development, and the existence of more than fifty governmental agencies with authority in the gorge necessitated federal intervention. The recent opening of a north-south interstate freeway near the western end of the gorge (I-205) appeared to present a clear and present danger. Painting an ominous portrait of impending medium-density rural residential development, a study of land use trends in western Skamania County by the existing state commissions added fuel to the fire. The Friends saw that a new urban West was supplanting the old gorge resource economy, and believed that the region should be managed in accord with new realities.

This local political support for protection paralleled the origins of other similar efforts. Metropolitan residents within range for weekend use were central in identifying these comparable areas as sensitive regions and creating the political constituency for public action. Regulation of the Adirondacks has involved state-level decisions driven by downstate legislators. Federal legislation for Cape Cod, Lake Tahoe, and the Pinelands came in response to local requests filtered through state congressional delegations, and the minimal federal action was to authorize, facilitate, and prod state legislative action.

83

The Columbia Gorge Coalition—led by Chuck Williams—supported National Park Service management of the western part of the gorge, though the Park Service had not specifically put itself forward as the lead agency in its report. The area should be managed, the Coalition believed, along the lines of Santa Monica Mountains National Recreation Area near Los Angeles and Golden Gate National Recreation Area north of San Francisco. The Coalition acknowledged that the usual National Recreation approach wouldn't fit in the gorge. It favored a National *Scenic* Area as a compromise, albeit one entailing more risk to environmental protection than a Recreation Area.

The Battle LInes Are Drawn

The Committee to Preserve Property Rights scoffed at concerns about development, claiming that population in the gorge had been decreasing for years (in fact population in the four counties had decreased in the 1960s, but increased in the 1970s). Extensive land use laws in Oregon and Washington, they argued further, prevented uncontrolled development. Nor, they claimed, would federal legislation limit the capacity of national government agencies—a majority of the fifty-plus agencies in the gorge—to act autonomously. They believed that the *real* problem in the gorge was a chronically high level of unemployment and a population that had been falling for years—scarcely signs that the booming New West was replacing the Old West. They feared that a protectionist policy would exacerbate this economic decline. The Friends and the Gorge Coalition countered with support for recreation and tourism development, and a strategy to concentrate future commercial and industrial activities in the gorge's small urban and rural centers. While the gorge counties appreciated whatever investments were associated with recreation and tourism, they heaped scorn on this notion as a serious alternative to their traditional sectors of employment.

84

In April 1982, the superior court ruled for the plaintiffs in the Rizor case. Rizor then submitted a slightly scaled-down version of his proposal, still located directly across from Multnomah Falls. The Skamania County commissioners, once again, unanimously approved it. The Trust for Public Land stepped in at this point to purchase the Rizor property. The

Residents by Choice

Significant voices in support of the Scenic Area and the region's economic transformation are residents who have chosen the gorge over large cities. Portlanders Kate and Jack Mills, who retired to the upper Hood River Valley in the early 1970s, actively supported environmental protection, joined the Friends, and invested in new enterprises that diversify the gorge economy. They supported the Scenic Area because it puts "development where development already is," in Kate's words. Ten years later they continue to regard it as pioneering legislation whose benefits far outweigh its problems. (Photo: Hood River News)

Another example is Will Macht, who stumbled on Hood River in the early 1970s while looking for an alternative to the pressure-cooker of Washington, D.C., where he had worked for Robert Kennedy. Will and his wife Mimi were on a town-hunting swing through the West when they took a side trip to Hood River; despite the fall drizzle, they decided instantly that it was the right place. In the ensuing decades, Will has worked as a real estate developer and consultant in Portland-Vancouver, taught at Portland State University, and fought for creative approaches to the economic development component of the Scenic Area.

Friends were also appealing Skamania County approval of another, much larger, riverfront project to the Washington State Shorelines Hearings Board. Klickitat County had a gorge scenic protection overlay zone in place, but Gorge Coalition members were suing that county, charging its officials with violating their own law.

When Skamania County commissioners announced early in 1983 that they were developing a zoning ordinance, reluctantly taking up Cushman's advice, Chuck Williams didn't attach much importance to this apparent change of heart: "Zoning protection is temporary at best, and it seems reasonable to assume that the Skamania commissioners, with their philosophic opposition to land use planning, will give out

85

variances upon request." Moreover, the commissioners balked at participating with Clark and Klickitat counties in a serious effort to establish a regional commission to coordinate planning and zoning on the Washington side of the gorge. This refusal confirmed environmentalists' fears about local government's lack of commitment to protection. Environmental activists therefore sought federal government intervention to protect natural and scenic resources in the gorge.

Underlying the battle between the two sides were issues that would continue to be debated in legislation and plan making but would never be fully resolved.

One was a basic disagreement about the long-term future of the gorge. Was the Old West resource economy viable? Could a New West economy emphasizing service industries replace logging and resource processing? The middle ground eventually embodied in federal legislation was to protect the resource economy but to encourage a shift to tourism—but whether as a supplement or a replacement was left undetermined.

The second disagreement revolved around the proper level of control. The governance structure for gorge management—a topic introduced by the Park Service report—remained central to congressional deliberations. Environmental organizations did not believe that county governments could protect natural and scenic resources. They saw two, three, many Rizor cases ahead. The existence of a comprehensive land use plan and a shoreline management plan didn't offer much comfort.

Finally, the question of *level* of control intersected with disagreement about the proper *style* of management. County-level management was associated with case-by-case decisions. It would be sensitive to nuances of local values and knowledge, said advocates of localism, subject to manipulation and growth coalition pressures, said opponents. Bistate or federal management meant more systematic rules and regulations—the essential tools of the modern state more familiar to city-based environmentalists than to farm and forest workers.

86

CHAPTER 4

The Politics of Protection

"Great visions must always accommodate practical reality."
　　Oregon governor Victor Atiyeh, 1983

Because of their distrust of the structure and dynamics of local land use politics, environmental activists looked to federal government intervention to protect the natural and scenic resources of the gorge. Increasingly their efforts were led by Portland residents, stereotyped as "Volvo and brie liberals" by their opponents, and gorge residents were squeezed toward the margins of the lobbying effort. Their options were complex, but the basic goal was simple—a set of rules applied systematically to the entire Columbia Gorge.

At every step, the politics of protection revolved around the tension between bureaucratization and trust. Advocates of scenic protection tended to favor management by an externally accountable bureaucracy that would reflect the interests of a service-economy nation—ideally a federal resource agency. Advocates of local prerogatives argued that the gorge was already well managed by residents who valued it as a home, and that local governments deserved to be trusted with continued management. The more the negotiation process built in local representation in decision making, the more environmental advocates pressed for specific guidelines rather than vague goals.

In brief outline, the legislative process evolved as follows:

(1) Working closely with the Friends, U.S. Senator Robert Packwood (R-OR) emerged as the first congressional champion of protection. However, the lead federal agency approach embodied in legislation sponsored by him in 1982 and 1983 failed to overcome fierce local resistance, especially on the Washington side of the gorge.

(2) Oregon governor Vic Atiyeh and Washington governor John Spellman then suggested dramatic modifications in Packwood's proposed governance structures. However, the governors' ideas created much consternation in the environmentalist camp; they, too, failed to produce agreement.

(3) U.S. Senator Dan Evans (R-WA) then assumed the lead in bringing the senators together to work toward an acceptable

87

compromise. This resulted in a new piece of legislation introduced in 1986.

(4) U.S. Senator Mark Hatfield (R-OR) played the lead role in guiding an amended version of the bill through congressional and executive branch minefields. A last-minute plea by Hatfield to President Reagan to sign it even if he had to hold his nose while doing so put the bill over the top.

The Packwood Bill: The Forest Service in the Lead, 1982-83

Senator Packwood's Columbia River Gorge Act of 1983, S. 627, focused on governance issues, expressing environmentalist concerns about local government capacity and about the consequences of the multiplicity of jurisdictions involved in the gorge. Packwood believed a lead federal agency was necessary to resolve existing and potential differences between jurisdictions. He thought that federal agencies had demonstrated the capacity to manage effectively in partnership with local governments and private land owners, in mixed ownership situations such as that in the gorge, pointing to the accomplishments of the Cape Cod National Seashore and the Sawtooth and Santa Monica Mountains National Recreation Areas.

The bill proposed a Scenic Area as part of the National Forest system. By doing it this way, Packwood and the Friends of the Columbia Gorge hoped to enable the U.S. Forest Service to apply to private forest land the visual management guidelines used to protect aesthetic values in the Mount Hood National Forest. "State forest practices laws . . . ignore the scenic values of the forests," Packwood noted.

The bill designated certain areas as critical, while exempting nine towns and their urban growth boundaries. This followed the Oregon approach to planning. Oregon land use goals aimed at containing population and urban economic activity within designated growth boundaries, and preserving farms, forests, and open spaces beyond these lines. The exempted Oregon towns had established such growth boundaries, but their Washington counterparts had not.

88

The Scenic Area was to be administered by the secretary of agriculture acting through the U.S. Forest Service. A regional commission, composed of local, state, and federal appointees, would advise and assist the Forest Service in preparing a Management Plan, approve the plan before its adoption by the secretary of agriculture, and monitor its implementation.

Packwood's choice of the Forest Service was controversial. The Columbia Gorge Coalition had suggested the National Park Service, as had an early paper drafted by the Friends of the Columbia Gorge board of directors. However, the Friends, wishing to be responsive to local concerns, shifted their support to the Forest Service after hearing that many gorge residents would feel more comfortable with that agency. A visit to Sawtooth National Recreation Area, administered by the Forest Service, also helped persuade the Friends to switch. The Sawtooth area, like the gorge, had private property within its boundary, and the Friends felt that the Forest Service was doing a good job. The Gorge Coalition believed that reliance on the Forest Service would further weaken an already compromised proposal for a Scenic, rather than a Recreation, Area, but was willing to accept it, though within a few years the Coalition and other environmental organizations came to oppose a Forest Service role.

The Forest Service chief would have two years to prepare a plan and submit it to the regional commission for approval. If a majority of commission members voted to approve, the secretary of agriculture would adopt the plan. If not, the plan would go to the secretary with the commission's objections specified. The secretary would then revise, if deemed appropriate, and resubmit the plan to the commission and might, without the commission's approval, adopt the plan as resubmitted, or after dropping any part not approved by the commission.

Local Involvement

The Friends and Senator Packwood clearly meant to emphasize the role of the Forest Service and downplay the regional commission. The fact that the measure did not prohibit locally elected officials from serving on the regional commission indicated that the advocates of protection believed the Forest Service would be willing and able to withstand any challenges from local interests. The experience of regional planning at Lake Tahoe exemplified the dangers: activists believed that the Tahoe environment had deteriorated badly following passage of protective legislation because locally elected officials were eligible to serve on the regional planning board. They claimed that the Tahoe planning agency had approved 96 percent of proposed developments between 1971

89

and 1977. The bill also contemplated a limited staff capability for the regional commission. In addition, the secretary would be able to adopt the plan prepared by the Forest Service even over commission objections. Finally, and most significantly, S. 627 did not mandate substantive standards for plan content. The bill's silence with regard to detailed, specific environmental requirements eloquently testified to the faith in federal intervention and the insulation from local pressure that the sponsors felt were embodied in the proposed act.

The Packwood bill gave local governments in the gorge the option to implement and enforce the Management Plan.

Blanche Barnes of Home Valley, Washington, protests Scenic Area hearings, 1983. (Photo: Hood River News)

However, it included stringent tests if they wished to take up this challenge, clearly revealing the sponsors' concern with governmental capacity. Those local governments wishing to assume responsibilities "shall submit . . . a land use plan which demonstrates that such local government entity intends to and is capable of carrying out the provisions of the Act." This meant adoption of a zoning ordinance consistent with the plan, including sanctions for violations. Nor were local land use plans to be approved unless the local government demonstrated that it had adequately skilled and funded planning staff. To build administrative capacity, the bill authorized the secretary to make annual technical assistance grants to local governments. If the local governments did not submit plans, or if local plans were disapproved, the secretary would take charge of implementation and enforcement.

90

Other Sensitive Issues

L and acquisition was a highly controversial issue, of course, and Packwood attempted to allay fears of a federal juggernaut. His bill restricted the use of eminent domain to those areas designated as critical, and no more than ten percent of the entire Scenic Area was to be acquired by condemnation. Condemning land was to be used only as a last resort, with regional commission review, and land exchanges were authorized.

In order to increase local comfort with acquisition authority, S. 627 said specifically that "no such lands or interests which, on July 1, 1981, were primarily used for single family residential purposes, farming, or grazing may be acquired without consent of the owner as long as the existing character of that use is not substantially changed." To sweeten the bill, the secretary was authorized to make payments to local governments when acquisition would significantly increase taxes on remaining private property. This provision responded specially to Skamania County, where only 8 percent of land was currently taxed at full valuation due to extensive federal, state, and private timber company holdings.

Because environmentalists were sensitive to the issue of protection during the interim between passage of the law and the adoption of a Management Plan and implementation ordinances, the Packwood bill included a moratorium on new building. The secretary was directed to promulgate Interim Guidelines within six months of passage of the act, which would be used to administer the Scenic Area until plans and ordinances were adopted.

Provisions addressing the management of an industrial transition, beyond those concerning land acquisition, payments to local governments, and the designation of lands for recreation and interpretive facilities, were conspicuous by their absence. There were no economic development incentives to respond to concerns about the impact of protection on the gorge economy. Timber companies, in particular, worried about harvesting trees on private lands if aesthetic criteria were in effect. These issues became increasingly important as Scenic Area legislation evolved.

91

The Governors Step In, 1983-84

Packwood's Gorge Act stimulated a bustle of political activity on both sides of the river and on both sides of the issue. The most significant immediate development, however, was a joint statement by the governors of Oregon and Washington at a hearing chaired by Senator Hatfield shortly after Packwood had introduced his bill in March 1983. Speaking on behalf of himself and Washington governor John Spellman, Oregon governor Vic Atiyeh told the Senate committee that they had signed an "unprecedented agreement, setting forth principles and key elements that we believe must be reflected in Federal legislation. . . . [A]greement between two sitting Governors is historic." The two governors endorsed a congressionally created joint state-federal management agency to develop a binding Management Plan. This regional commission would be composed primarily of representatives appointed by the governors, with some federal representation, and would certify local land use plans and implementation ordinances. Their objective was to transform the governance structure proposed by Packwood into one more palatable to opponents of a top-down approach.

Atiyeh explained the political logic of the proposal. "You will agree," he told Hatfield and the others in attendance, "that a Federal lead agency concept, whatever its merits, simply will not be acceptable to citizens and officials on the Washington side of the river. They want assurances of greater state and local control, and for the first time are prepared to accept binding regional management with Federal participation if they feel their voices can be adequately heard." Atiyeh then added a reminder, based on the elementary dynamics of congressional politics. "Great visions must always accommodate practical reality. None of us is blind to the plain fact that no proposal, no legislation before the Congress, that seeks to protect the Columbia Gorge will move forward without the support of both States."

Ironically, shortly after the agreement between the two governors was reached, Booth Gardner replaced Spellman as Washington governor. He assumed office advocating a primary role for the federal government in gorge protection, and a moratorium on development in the interim. Gardner later changed his stance, but in 1984 his representative was hooted and booed after outlining the governor-elect's position at a Skamania County hearing.

92

Reactions, Alliances, Controversies

This dramatic intervention fundamentally altered the course of legislative evolution. Representatives from the Oregon and Washington congressional delegation incorporated the governors' ideas in a new bill. While these particular proposals did not survive, Northwest senators and the Friends no longer thought Packwood's approach politically viable. The governors' proposal presented a fundamental challenge to the Coalition-Friends alliance, and to the other environmental organizations involved—the Wilderness Society, Sierra Club, and Oregon Natural Resources Council. The Wilderness Society feared that management by a state/local commission would be ineffective without detailed guidelines for gorge protection, yet also believed that, "It is highly unlikely that Congress would spell out the kind of detail necessary in legislation directing action by state and local agencies."

These organizations felt a deeply rooted suspicion of the exercise of discretion by state and local governments. The Washington state Audubon Society warned that "the State Forest Practices Act will not protect the Gorge." As the possibility of a lead federal agency receded, environmentalists intensified efforts to incorporate detailed, specific standards and requirements into any Scenic Area legislation.

The timber companies had had a great deal of difficulty with the way that the Packwood bill proposed to manage the transition from resource extraction-based industry to recreation and tourism. They were particularly concerned about the application of visual management guidelines to private forest lands. However, many timber firms believed that some sort of legislation was inevitable and sought a voice in the legislative process in order to protect their interests.

Large timber firms supported the governors. The Washington Forest Protection Association explained why the industry was so concerned about federal regulation:

> The current Forest Service "visual" management guidelines in effect on the Mount Hood National Forest in the Oregon portion of the Gorge, are an economic anathema to any private landowner. . . . A series of mandated aesthetic requirements means shut-down.

93

The issue of land acquisition created strange allies. Crown Zellerbach called on Congress to appropriate sufficient funds to acquire land when scenic preservation must take precedence on private property. The Gorge Coalition's Chuck Williams made a similar argument. He believed that without land acquisition as an alternative to zoning, "large landowners in the gorge will be treated unfairly . . . because the people who had protected their land . . . would then be penalized by not being able to develop their land and not having the option of either selling a scenic easement or the land to the Government. . . . It just rewards the developers, the people that are already dividing it." Williams was concerned that legislators would move quickly to accommodate the timber industry, but that other private landowners outside the designated critical areas—including Williams himself—might not fare so well. As he prophesied, a reluctance to acquire land necessitated a strict regulatory approach to resource protection, generating profound feelings of inequitable treatment.

The question of development was controversial as well. Columbia Gorge United, an umbrella opposition organization, argued that the Packwood bill exempted too few towns and that the absence of urban growth boundaries around Washington communities would unfairly constrain their growth. Economic development activists in the gorge suggested that federal legislation should incorporate development initiatives aimed at facilitating industrial transition. William Macht, a commissioner at the Port of Hood River, proposed creating a Columbia Gorge development bank to facilitate preparation of tourism plans and to provide loans and guarantees to compatible development projects. Senator Dan Evans (R-WA) was clearly attracted to the development bank idea, and also to an argument made by North Bonneville's planner that any legislation must stress development as much as landscape preservation in order to address high unemployment. Balancing resource protection and economic development, like dramatically limiting federal agency control and maintaining state-approved timber industry practices, would be key elements in future legislative proposals.

94

Senatorial Compromises, 1985-86

As Packwood's original bill languished in committee and died in the crossfire of interest group and gubernatorial criticism, Senator Evans began a search for a balanced approach by bringing together members of his and Senator Packwood's staffs in early 1985 to inventory gorge land and define critical areas. He apparently hoped that such an exercise in rational planning would enable the parties to transcend the conflicts that had stalemated earlier legislative efforts. He also articulated his favored approach: a two-tier system with Forest Service administration of federally owned lands and state-local administration of the rest of the gorge. When the land studies were nearly complete, Evans, Packwood, Hatfield, and Senator Slade Gorton (R-WA) announced a workshop to discuss their findings. In an invitation to state and local officials they indicated their unified interest and their conclusion that coordinated planning and regulatory activities in the gorge were needed. Packwood and his staff believed, however, that disagreements about governance structures remained the key issue. Meanwhile, environmental organizations, including the Gorge Coalition and the Friends, announced their support of the federal agency approach to gorge protection with the National Park Service as the lead agency.

Evans nonetheless persevered in his efforts to bring the parties together. Orchestrated by governors Atiyeh and Gardner, key congressional staffers and staff from the governors' offices came together at a retreat in August 1985. They reached agreement on several crucial points, including a two-tier governance structure, designated critical areas, and a development corporation authorized to give grants and loans. Disagreement remained regarding which federal agency ought to be involved, although it appeared that only Packwood was committed to the Park Service, supporting the position of environmental activists who had returned to a pro-Park Service position. The meeting produced compromises on planning and implementation relationships in the context of a two-tier system: maintaining a right for the federal government to reject regional agency plans and strengthening private property rights in areas subject to stringent federal protection.

These agreements threatened to unravel, however, because of a dispute over the extent to which detailed, specific standards ought to be written into the law. Staff members on

95

the Washington side continued to press for more autonomy for the regional commission. In a major concession, their Oregon counterparts were willing to permit the regional commission to override—with a two-thirds vote—a veto by the federal government of plans developed by the commission, if the law contained detailed, specific standards and enforcement mandates. When the Oregonians submitted a list of such requirements, however, the Washingtonians refused to include most of them in the last draft of the legislation. The sense among the staff was that they had gone as far as they could; a resolution of the remaining issues by the principals was necessary in order to break the stalemate.

Several environmental organizations openly criticized the Washington senators for resisting the inclusion of strict standards and enforcement mandates. Senator Hatfield, worried that the impasse would delay passage of any gorge legislation for a year or more, began further negotiations with his Washington colleagues, hoping for consensus, and all four senators sponsored the introduction of S. 2055, the Columbia Gorge National Scenic Area Act, in early February 1986. However, at a June hearing both Evans and Packwood said they viewed this joint bill as a starting point for congressional consideration, rather than as a finished legislative product.

S. 2055

The jointly sponsored Scenic Area Act carved out four Special Management Areas (SMAs) from a larger Scenic Area; these SMAs, rather than the entire Scenic Area as in the Packwood bill, were established as a unit of the National Forest system. Twelve Urban Areas were designated exempt from the act, an increase of three over Packwood's bill, all in Washington.

The designation of new Urban Areas generated controversy. The existing gorge commissions questioned the principle of exempting Urban Areas from all regulation, including F. Stuart Chapin, who was a member of the Washington commission, one of the nation's leading authorities on land use planning, with forty-five years of academic and practical experience, and a Klickitat County resident. Because some critical Scenic Areas were within the cities, he believed that some regulation ought to be imposed there. The exemption idea, however, was solidly in place.

The Bingen-Hood River area, with its complex mix of industrial, commercial, agricultural, and residential uses, epitomized the problem of protecting scenic resources in a working landscape. (Photo: U.S.D.A. Forest Service)

Both environmentalists and local opponents thought that Senate staff members had been arbitrary and capricious in delineating Urban Area boundaries. A Skamania County commissioner fumed at the exclusion of the community of Home Valley from the exempt list, since the county's recently revised comprehensive land use plan clearly contemplated substantial growth there. The gorge commissions, the Friends, and the Coalition all felt that more land had been placed within the boundaries of some Washington Urban Areas than could reasonably be justified. These groups also believed that Skamania County's recent plan changes regarding Home Valley were an outrageous effort to circumvent anticipated legislation.

97

In larger perspective, the exempt Urban Areas were safety valves. To the extent that economic survival requires new development, management systems must make some division between buildable land and areas that are off limits. Similarly, the Adirondacks plan exempted existing "hamlets" from its regulations. New Jersey omitted the Atlantic City area, largely left villages to develop as they had been, and planned to allocate growth within the Pinelands to selected areas.

The 1986 bill outlined a Columbia Gorge Commission, to be established by action of the states. If the states failed to act, the secretary of agriculture would establish the commission as a federal agency. This regional commission would have twelve voting members, including one resident from each gorge county, appointed by the county, three residents of each state, appointed by their governors, and one Forest Service employee, ex officio, appointed by the secretary. Neither elected nor appointed officials were permitted to serve.

The commission was mandated to prepare a Management Plan within two years of legislative enactment, including land use designations based on a resource inventory that was to be cooperatively developed by the commission and the Forest Service within one year. The plan was required to incorporate, without change, land use designations for the SMAs to be developed by the Forest Service. The commission would then develop guidelines for the adoption of zoning ordinances to regulate non-federal lands. These guidelines would also have to incorporate, without change, the guidelines developed by the Forest Service for the SMAs. A majority of members within each state voting to approve would be necessary to adopt the plan, which would then be reviewed by the secretary. If the secretary disapproved, the commission would either revise and resubmit or, by a two-thirds vote, override the secretary.

Senator Packwood, governments in the metropolitan area, the Friends, and other environmental organizations were deeply disturbed by the provision for a two-thirds vote to override. Because this was the same number of affirmative votes—eight—that it would take for the commission to adopt a Management Plan, and because at least half its members would be gorge county representatives, protectionists felt it would be too easy for the commission to stick to its plan despite Forest Service objections. They thought that it ought to take at least nine votes to override the secretary.

Within one year after getting guidelines from the Forest Service for the SMAs and from the commission for the

98

remainder of the gorge, the counties were mandated to develop zoning ordinances. If a county failed to do so, or if a proposed ordinance was disapproved either by the secretary or by the commission, the commission would adopt regulations for that county; SMA regulations would be subject to the secretary's approval. Once implementation ordinances were in place, the commission would "monitor activities of counties . . . and may take such action as necessary to ensure compliance." The use of the word "may" regarding enforcement troubled Senator Packwood and the environmentalists, who insisted that the regional commission be mandated to enforce adopted plans and implementing ordinances.

Differences Between S.2055 and Packwood's Bill

Responding to the political turmoil that had surrounded Packwood's 1983 bill, the 1986 measure approached gorge protection in a dramatically different way. Under its proposed two-tier system, the regional commission would have a much more prominent planning and administrative role than in Packwood's bill. In order to balance this prominence, elected and appointed officials were barred from service, an effort to allay fears of reproducing the Tahoe experience. In addition, carving out the SMAs, designating the Forest Service to plan and write guidelines for those sensitive lands, and requiring the commission to incorporate these without change were clearly intended to insulate the most critical parts of the gorge from local pressure.

These provisions reflected the strength of Lake Tahoe as a negative reference. Tahoe was personally known to many Portlanders and familiar to the Forest Service, while parallel cases in the northeastern states were not. The result was that most attention went to a program that was constitutionally similar but substantively dissimilar. The Tahoe area faces environmental and development pressures very different from those in the gorge. What attracted the attention of Portland activists, however, were the problems of bistate coordination: the difficulty of coordinating California and Nevada policies that reflected the very different political cultures of the two states.

Even more importantly, the 1986 bill contained planning standards, which had been completely lacking in the 1983 bill. The inclusion of these standards reflected the opinion of

99

Oregonians and environmentalists that if the Forest Service, rather than the Park Service, was going to be involved, and if a regional commission, rather than the federal government, was going to play the lead role, then the law had better be specific. The new bill was—to a certain extent. It defined major development actions as (1) land division proposals and (2) permits outside Urban Areas for multifamily residential, commercial, or industrial facilities, and prohibited them in the SMAs. Outside SMAs, they would be allowed only if the commission determined that they would not "substantially impair or detract from" gorge resources.

Some of the content of the Management Plan was also detailed. The commission was mandated to designate lands suitable for the production of agricultural and forest products, and to protect and enhance those lands. A similar stipulation was set forward for open spaces. The process of concentrating future development in already existing Urban Areas, and designating, protecting, and enhancing agricultural and forestry lands reflected the Oregon approach to land use planning. Statewide goals 3 and 4 sought to protect resource lands from residential or other uses that would undermine their productive integrity.

In addition, the Management Plan was to require industrial development to occur in Urban Areas and to encourage commercial development in such areas. Outside the designated cities, standards for residential and commercial development were to "minimize impacts" on resources. Finally, the plan was to encourage, but not require, that surface mining take place outside SMAs.

From the environmental point of view, these content specifications were a mixed bag. The location of various activities was "encouraged" but not "required." Words such as "minimize," "substantially," and "detract," used to characterize potential impacts, also appeared to expand the local exercise of discretion beyond the environmentalists' very small comfort zone.

The 1983 bill had called for a moratorium on development during the period between legislative enactment and the
100 preparation of Interim Guidelines by the Forest Service six months later. The 1986 bill gave the Forest Service six months to prepare Interim Guidelines for the SMAs, and the authority to review all proposals for new residential development in SMAs prior to plan adoption. The commission was given one year to prepare Interim Guidelines for land outside the SMAs,

and the authority to review all major development actions in the remainder of the gorge prior to adopting its plan. However, the moratorium was dropped, another concession to private property rights and local control.

Whereas the Packwood bill had made local implementation optional, S. 2055 mandated county preparation of zoning ordinances. The secretary was ordered to provide technical assistance and grants to counties for the development of implementation measures, covering up to 75 percent of costs. However, if a county failed to obtain approval of its ordinance within three years, the secretary was authorized to seek reimbursement. As had been the case in 1983, liberal standing to sue was incorporated in order to keep the various officials honest.

The Columbia Gorge Coalition had criticized Packwood's bill for failing to attend to the issue of hydroelectric dam construction in the region, and to the status of rivers tributary to the Columbia. They argued that dams threatened the rivers and the wildlife dependent on them from both environmental and recreational points of view, but they were also concerned that protecting the Columbia would have the unfortunate consequence of shifting development to lands surrounding the tributary streams. The Coalition and other groups called, therefore, for including six tributaries in the National Wild and Scenic River System, or at least studying them for possible inclusion. In response, S. 2055 mandated that the secretary and the commission determine that dams proposed within their respective domains would not substantially impair or detract from gorge resources. It designated one tributary for a Wild and Scenic River System study and protected another by including its canyon in a Special Management Area. From the environmentalist perspective, once again, the 1986 bill was somewhat, but not very, responsive.

The new jointly sponsored measure, unlike Packwood's earlier bill, had a number of suggestions for facilitating the transformation of the gorge economy. The timber companies got what they wanted to ease the transition. The bill said that state forest practices acts would supersede the federal act except within the SMAs; the remainder of the Scenic Area would not be considered a part of the National Forest system.

The timber companies wanted the federal government to either buy their land when it was deemed necessary for scenic protection (a demand also voiced by Chuck Williams on behalf of all landowners, including George Rizor, Jr.) or do an

101

exchange. The bill authorized the appropriation of $35 million for land acquisition in the SMAs, and authorized land exchanges as well.

The sponsors of the bill, hoping to convey the seriousness they attached to the land acquisition program and their responsiveness to private property owners, noted that Congress intended that exchanges be completed within three years. The bill gave teeth to the deadline by saying that adopted regulations would no longer apply to parcels in SMAs three years after the date a landowner had offered to sell at fair market value to the Forest Service. (The gorge commissions, however, thought the deadline for exchanges should be five years instead of three, to permit the Forest Service to make more judicious choices.) The measure included authorization for the secretary to make grants to Oregon and Washington to buy land and proposed that acquired land would become part of the National Forest system for purposes of calculating timber receipts due the counties from the federal treasury, an additional carrot not found in the 1983 bill. Moreover, the counties would be permitted to use these receipts for a broader array of public purposes than generally allowed. Acquisition by the Forest Service outside the SMAs was not contemplated, much to the dismay of Chuck Williams and the existing gorge commissions.

Unlike the earlier bill, the 1986 bill mandated the secretary to prepare a plan for acquiring lands within SMAs, in consultation with the regional commission. When the plan was adopted, any further acquisitions were to be consistent with it. The gorge commissions wanted to delay acquisitions until the plan was completed, or at least until an interim plan was developed; they also thought that the three-year deadline to complete willing-seller transactions ought not to kick in until the plan was in place. They were concerned that the time constraint would push the Forest Service to acquire lands that were not critical, regardless of plan priorities.

Finally, S. 2055 included a constraint on condemnation similar to that in the Packwood bill, although without a numerical limit on the amount of property that could be so acquired. Land used for educational, religious, charitable, single-family residential, farming, or grazing purposes, so long as the existing character of the use was not substantially changed, could not be condemned.

In order to more directly facilitate an industrial transition, the bill authorized the commission and the Forest Service to

102

cooperatively develop and implement a recreation plan. In addition, the secretary was authorized to make loans to a Columbia Gorge development corporation—if the states would create it—to provide low-interest loans in counties that had adopted implementation measures. The bill authorized the appropriation of $15 million for the corporation and required it to loan all the money loaned to it by the secretary within five years. Finally, the secretary was directed to prepare a plan, in cooperation with relevant others, to preserve and restore the Old Columbia River Highway as a National Historic Road; $600,000 was authorized to begin the work. Wasco County pressed for an additional item: funds for a major interpretive center in the gorge.

The Forest Service Role

Senator Packwood had argued for a lead federal agency approach based on the Forest Service's experience in dealing with private landowners, and its success in managing similar areas elsewhere. Advocates of gorge protection signaled their trust in the Forest Service by insisting on a major role for it either as lead agency or—especially—as a partner with a regional commission. The irony is that the Forest Service was very reluctant to accept this responsibility. The Forest Service was satisfied to continue managing the lands it owned in the gorge primarily for scenic and recreational purposes, as it had been doing since 1915, when it had set up the Columbia Gorge Park Division of the Mount Hood National Forest. However, during the Reagan era the agency believed that "the regulation of the use of privately owned lands is and should remain the prerogative and the responsibility of State and local governments. . . . The federal government should not: approve or disapprove plans for controlling private land use . . . [or] enforce regulations applicable to the use of private lands."

Advocates of federal legislation and a strong federal agency role had sought to nationalize the gorge protection issue. Unable to overcome deeply rooted resistance to strict regulation at the state and local levels, and profoundly distrustful of the local capacity to regulate effectively even when the spirit was willing, environmentalists wanted to base a governance structure on a federal champion armed with detailed, specific standards. The Forest Service, though, had

103

the following worst-case scenario in mind. If the states failed to create the regional commission, then the 1986 bill said the Forest Service should create such an entity as a federal agency. "This Commission would have the responsibility to plan and develop zoning regulations for private lands if counties fail to comply with the planning and zoning responsibilities outlined in the Bill. This would amount to federal zoning of private lands. This is clearly not an appropriate federal role. We strongly oppose, on the basis of principle, the concept of the Federal government developing zoning for non-federal lands." The Forest Service was especially worried about the prospect of imposing the mandated fines for violations of implementing ordinances. Moreover, the Service was extremely worried about takings-related lawsuits, which stringent regulation might well produce. "In light of the uncertainty in this area of the law, we cannot suport legislation which would expose the Federal government to liability."

The Forest Service also thought that its relationship to the Gorge Development Corporation was unclear, and questioned the mandate for a land acquisition plan. It had prepared this sort of plan in Lake Tahoe, but had actually pursued acquisition in a reactive way, responding to willing sellers as they presented themselves, rather than seeking to purchase according to a priority order. Given the very high level of political opposition to federal intervention in the gorge, proactive acquisition policies would likely generate much resistance. Finally, the Forest Service, speaking now as an executive branch agency, was concerned that the total cost of implementation could not be estimated. In an era of budget restraint, this open-endedness was, in its view, a fatal flaw.

S. 2055 Becomes Law

The four Oregon and Washington senators introduced the Scenic Area Act (S. 2055) in the face of strong local opposition. The Skamania County commissioners voted **104** to evict the Columbia Gorge commissions from their meeting place in the county building. Nancy Russell left the June hearing held in Stevenson, Skamania County, to find the tires on her car slashed.

In this context of intense controversy, regional activists and legislators concerned with national implications worked over the bill. The opposition of the Forest Service was a profound challenge; responding to its concerns caused significant changes to both governance structures and the management of industrial transition.

The provision requiring the Forest Service to establish the regional commission as a federal agency if the states failed to act was dropped and replaced by a number of sticks and carrots to ensure that the states took the necessary actions. The mandated land acquisition plan disappeared. The only remaining guideline was that the Forest Service could spend no more than one-fourth of the money authorized for acquisition during the interim management period. The timeline for land exchanges was increased from three to five years, as recommended by the gorge commissions. Gorge protectionists lost on the issue of the votes necessary to override the secretary regarding plan approval. Indeed, the concept of "approval" disappeared; the secretary would either concur with the regional commission's plan, or deny concurrence. Eight votes—at least four from each state—would be sufficient to override the secretary on both the Management Plan and county-developed ordinances to implement the plan in SMAs. If the secretary failed to concur regarding an ordinance, however, various economic development funds would not be available to that county.

In general, the prominence of the Forest Service in gorge management was reduced in favor of the regional commission and counties. This change, in turn, generated efforts by protectionists to shore up other aspects of the legislation. In early August 1986, the four senators announced a sweeping set of amendments to the bill, including agreements by the Washington senators to strengthen the standards incorporated in it. Without a federal champion to stand up to local growth pressures, the Oregon senators and their allies demanded tighter, more explicit standards to defend gorge scenic and natural resources. Commercial and residential development outside Urban Areas and mineral extraction activities would have to take place "without adversely affecting" gorge resources (replacing language about not "substantially impairing" or "detracting from"). The definition of major development actions—actions prohibited in SMAs—was expanded to include the siting or construction of any residence or related major building on any parcel of land of fewer than forty acres.

105

Advocates of greater state/regional/local autonomy generally gained on issues of governance and industrial transition. Home Valley in Skamania County was added to the list of exempt Urban Areas, but there was still grumbling on both sides of the river about worthy places left off the list. A new rule would increase local influence: at least one of the members appointed to the regional commission by the governors would have to be a gorge resident. Of the twelve members of the commission, then, at least eight would be gorge residents.

But environmentalists also gained. The Gorge Coalition and their allies secured the designation of parts of two of the tributaries for which they had sought protection as Wild and Scenic Rivers, and studies for designation of other parts of the same streams. The changes also added a measure of protection for several other tributaries in the face of dam proposals. Indian treaty and other rights were protected.

The bill picked up several more incentives intended to induce state and local actors to participate in a managed industrial transition. In addition to a recreation plan, the regional commission would also prepare an economic opportunity study. Wasco County's idea of an interpretive center in the gorge was taken up and a conference center was added. The interpretive center would go to the Oregon side and the conference center to Washington. The Gorge Development Corporation was replaced by a mandate that each state produce an economic development plan based on the commission's opportunity study. The secretary would directly disburse up to $5 million to each state upon receipt of its plan, after the commission certified that proposed economic development projects were consistent with the Management Plan and implementing ordinances. The role of the Forest Service in economic development, outside of building and maintaining recreation facilities, diminished.

Funding for development-related activities increased as well. Money available for land acquisition grew from $35 to $40 million. The interpretive and conference centers would receive $10 million and recreation facilities were budgeted at another $10 million. Funds for the restoration of the Old Columbia River Scenic Highway grew from $600,000 to $2.8 million. Also included was a $2 million set-aside for payments to local governments to make up for losses of taxable property. The secretary's concurrence regarding plans and ordinances would be required for the allocation of all of these funds to counties, with the exception of money for land acquisition.

The timber companies got even more than they had asked for, but with a twist. The Forest Service would be able to cross state lines to work out land exchanges, and the legislation explicitly set out a pool of federal lands eligible for exchange. Exchanges would not be subject to environmental review. Moreover, the SMAs as a whole were no longer designated part of the National Forest system; only those lands within SMAs acquired by the Forest Service would be. In response to the Forest Service's complaint that it did not want responsibility for regulating private property, its jurisdiction was limited to lands owned by the federal government. Though the Forest Service would develop guidelines for timber activities mandating no adverse impact on non-federal lands within SMAs, it would not itself regulate forest practices on private property. But the amended bill was not quite clear regarding who would—the states, the commission and/or the counties.

Senator Packwood, the Friends, and other environmental organizations all had argued for mandatory enforcement by the commission to ensure that the counties complied with the plan and implementing ordinances. They disliked and distrusted the phrase, "may take such action as necessary to ensure compliance," which permitted, in their eyes, too much discretion, especially by a commission composed primarily of gorge residents. Senator Evans and Richard Benner, representing 1000 Friends of Oregon, the land use watchdog organization upon which the Friends of the Columbia Gorge had been modeled, discussed a number of alternatives, but the final language was not greatly changed: "The Commission shall monitor activities of counties . . . and shall take such actions as it determines are necessary to ensure compliance." "May" was now "shall," but "as it determines" still implied a good deal of discretion.

Final Maneuvering

The last stage of the legislative process was enormously complicated. Shortly after the four senators reached their compromise agreements in August, the Senate Energy and Natural Resources Committee unanimously approved the amended bill. However, when they sought to bring it to the Senate floor, opposition surfaced. Republican senators James McClure of Idaho and Malcolm Wallop of Wyoming opposed federal regulation of private land within

SMAs, as had the Forest Service. The bill remained in committee. Meanwhile, three Democratic Northwest representatives, Jim Weaver and Les AuCoin of Oregon and Don Bonker of Washington, introduced an essentially similar bill in the House. The Interior and Agriculture committees both had jurisdiction over it. A solid wall of Republican opposition greeted the bill in both committees, led by Bob Smith and Denny Smith, both Oregon Republicans representing heavily rural constituencies. Indeed, it is a telling point about patterns of support that AuCoin represented affluent Portland suburbs while Bob Smith's district included Wasco and Hood River counties. A congressional urge to adjourn greatly heightened the level of anxiety.

The compromise that removed Forest Service jurisdiction over private lands in SMAs satisfied McClure and Wallop. The Senate passed the bill without opposition in early October, but House dynamics remained complex. Since the bill was bottled up in the authorizing committees, advocates sought to persuade the House Rules Committee to suspend the rules, permitting the full House to consider the bill. The sponsors worried, though, that if any amendments were attached in order to secure agreement, the measure would have to go back to the Senate, where renewed opposition from McClure and Wallop potentially loomed. As Congress rushed to adjourn, House majority whip Thomas Foley (a Democrat from eastern Washington) convinced the Rules Committee to forward the bill to the floor. Unanimous support among Washington legislators facilitated Foley's action. Bob Smith, however, attached an amendment that required one of the gubernatorial appointments to be a gorge resident. The legislation passed by a vote of 290 to 91, although Oregonians Bob Smith and Denny Smith remained opposed.

The bill then went back to the Senate, where McClure and Wallop did have objections. But Senators Hatfield, Evans, and Gorton provided the assurances that McClure and Wallop sought regarding the role of fedral agencies in the gorge. The Senate then approved the bill on a voice vote.

President Reagan very reluctantly signed the Columbia River Gorge National Scenic Area Act in November 1986. "While I am strongly opposed to the federal regulation of private land use planning," Reagan said, "I am signing this bill because of the far-reaching support of both states for solution to the long-standing problems related to the management of the Columbia River Gorge."

What Congress Wrought: Retrospect and Prospect

How effective are the major provisions of the Act? We can evaluate them using the six conditions of effective implementation identified in the influential theoretical work of Daniel Mazmanian and Paul Sabatier.

Clear and consistent policy objectives that at least provide substantive criteria for resolving conflicts. Whereas S. 627 and S. 2055 had listed a great many findings and purposes, the final Scenic Area Act contains just two: (1) protect and enhance gorge scenic, cultural, recreational, and natural resources; and (2) protect and support the economy of the gorge "by encouraging growth to occur in existing Urban Areas and by allowing future economic development in a manner that is consistent with protecting the resources mentioned in (1)." These goals are clearly stated, and growth and development are subordinate to the primary goal of protection, but there are still multiple, vague, and potentially conflicting objectives, a bane of effective implementation.

Enhancing recreational resources, a priority objective, may conflict with protecting scenic or cultural resources. The spectacular growth of windsurfing in the gorge, for example, would present a conflict-resolution challenge. The notion of development "consistent with" protection is clearly vague and prone to problems. And encouraging growth in existing Urban Areas is problematic as well, since the Act sets out conditions under which Urban Area boundaries might be changed by a two-thirds vote of the commission.

A valid theory that links the problems identified and the solutions contained in the statute. The provisions of the Scenic Area Act reflect a multitude of theories. First, if regional commission and Forest Service planners do a scientific inventory within the framework of the standards set out in the law, they will be able to produce technically adequate and politically stable solutions to existing and potential land management conflicts. These solutions, in turn, will be translated into technically adequate, politically stable regulations by county governments, as well as acquisitions and exchanges by the Forest Service. Second, if planners prepare development plans based on scientific economic and recreational studies, then various implementing agencies will be able to invest in recreation, tourism, and other projects that will facilitate an industrial transition in a politically acceptable

109

The Columbia River Gorge National Scenic Area Act mandated the following steps:

The Columbia Gorge Commission will do a resource inventory, an economic opportunity study, and a recreation assessment. The inventory will be used to develop land use designations. These designations, in turn, will form the basis for a land use Management Plan, which will include guidelines for the adoption of county implementation ordinances. Land use designations and guidelines developed by the Forest Service for a set of Special Management Areas are to be incorporated in the Management Plan without change. The plan is required to incorporate a set of detailed, specific environmental protection standards that were written into law. The commission is mandated to adopt this Management Plan within three years of its establishment.

manner. Concentrating such investments in already existing Urban Areas, an additional theory borrowed from the Oregon planning system, will enhance the technical and political effectiveness of these plans.

Ironies abound. Despite Chuck Williams's plea, the Act restricted land acquisition to SMAs. Unable to buy land in order to protect resources, planners would have to lean heavily on a regulatory approach to implementation in the remaining General Management Areas (GMAs), especially the open space designation. Profound challenges to the technical and political validity of the planning theories embodied in the Act would be in store. On the technical side, questions would be raised about the decisions made by a centralized planning agency for a highly diverse region—a clash of rule making with the very different imperatives of small-scale place making. On the political side, deploying the open space designation would greatly exacerbate the level of private and public anxiety. The Forest Service had resisted responsibility for regulating private property in part because of a fear of takings-related litigation. Now this responsibility had fallen on the shoulders of the counties, the unit of government least able, politically, technically, and financially, to bear it. A county could refuse to play along, but at the cost of access to economic development benefits, nearly guaranteeing political conflict. The rationality of the link between land use plans and Forest Service acquisition practices would be problematic as well.

110   A host of uncertainties attached to the Act's theory of managing an industrial transition. Whether or not the projects and programs set out in the Act would be able effectively to shape market forces in a politically acceptable time frame was an open question, as was the idea of concentrating economic and population growth in already existing urban areas.

A probability that agencies, organizations, and individuals involved will perform as desired. The Scenic Area Act created a complex governance structure; it was frequently described as a "partnership" between the federal government, the states, and local governments. Although the federal partner would set up a new office that initially was quite enthusiastic about its mission, the headquarters of the Forest Service was very hesitant about the entire venture. The sympathies of the new bistate commission would depend both on the points of view of the people appointed and on their experiences in office.

The local partners were similarly mixed in their feelings about planning and implementation. The Oregon counties had a good deal of experience with statewide land use goals, comprehensive plans and zoning ordinances; there was less experience on the Washington side. Most of the privately owned land in the gorge, though, was in Washington. The more urbanized counties, Multnomah and Clark, had been strongly supportive of gorge protection, while the rural counties were mixed in their views. Ironically, Skamania County, center of opposition during the legislative struggle and, at the outset, the county least committed to regulating land use, would respond constructively to the economic development incentives. Klickitat County, on the other hand, had instituted regulations in advance of Skamania, and was forthcoming during the legislative process; after 1986, however, the county would refuse to take part in plan implementation.

Leaders of implementing agencies who possess managerial and political skills and are committed to statutory goals. Key issues in this case would be the choice of executive director for the bistate commission and Scenic Area manager for the Forest Service. The Act required the states to fund the regional commission; its staff capacity would thus be subject to state and local political currents, as would be the capacity of the counties to prepare and implement ordinances.

Active support by constituency groups and by key legislators throughout the implementation process, with the courts supportive or neutral. While many national and statewide environmental organizations actively participated in the lengthy legislative struggle, and would participate once again during plan preparation, Friends of the Columbia Gorge was pretty much on its own at the end of the congressional session and would continue to be after plan approval and

111

concurrence. The national and state groups moved on to other battles. The Columbia Gorge Coalition had become disenchanted with the Friends and with the law that seemed to be emerging, but muted its concern in order to maintain a united front and secure a bill it thought better than nothing. Once the Act passed, the Coalition would bitterly critique the concessions to local governments and the timber companies, and protection opportunities foregone. Except for a few dramatic confrontations, it would remain distant from day-to-day implementation dynamics. The Friends, on the other hand, had the technical, legal, and financial resources to continue to play an extremely active role in monitoring planning and plan implementation. Their capacity to do so would be enhanced by the Act, which authorized citizen suits to compel compliance.

Hatfield, Packwood, and other members of the Northwest congressional delegation indicated their willingness to ward off threats to the Act and work to ensure the smooth flow of implementation actions. Ron Wyden (D-OR), for example, would successfully parry an effort in the House to slap a capital gains tax on land exchanges. Hatfield would remain a supporter of the Scenic Area through the 1990s.

Another critical area would be the willingness of the Congress to actually appropriate the funds authorized for the economic development projects included in the law, and for land acquisition. The commission and the counties would turn to the congressional delegation with other requests as well. The continuing capacity of the delegation to protect and advance the interests of the Scenic Area in the face of shifting state and national political dynamics would be uncertain.

Goals of the legislation should not be undermined by the adoption of conflicting public policies or by changes in socioeconomic conditions that weaken its political support or validity. It is still too early in the implementation process to say much about this. Thus far, continuing decline in the traditional gorge economy and rapid population growth in the metropolitan areas have highlighted the strains of industrial transition, and the pressures on recreational resources. An increasingly fierce attack on Oregon's land use regulatory apparatus is taking place, while Washington has recently adopted a growth management law. Land use governance issues, within and without the gorge, remain extremely controversial, not least the question of how much discretion ought to be exercised at the local level.

112

Lessons Learned

In retrospect, several points stand out about the legislative process. One is the ability of metropolitan interests to override rural interests. The Friends supplanted the Gorge Coalition. The senators who drove the process knew how to count—and found more votes in middle-class Portland and Vancouver neighborhoods than in the gorge counties. In a political sense, the Scenic Area is one more step in the incorporation of the gorge into Portland's sphere of influence. To the extent that the New West is an urbanized West, the Scenic Area is part of the transition from Old to New.

The tension between old and new appeared as well in debates over the scale of intervention. New Westerners as we have defined them are more comfortable than Old Westerners with wide-ranging bureaucracies and complex regulations. These approaches emphasize portable technical expertise rather than carefully cultivated local knowledge. They are more compatible with mobility rather than rootedness. The irony that pervades the Scenic Area study is that these abstract tools seemed to many to be the only available means to protect the very specific landscape of the Columbia River gorge.

chapter 5

Making a Management Plan

*"There isn't anyone who is against protection, it's just how you
go about it."*
      Joyce Reinig, Columbia River Gorge commissioner, 1996

*"The twenty-five year mark will be a good time to assess
whether it worked."*
      Art Carroll, Forest Service manager, Columbia Gorge, 1996

Passage of the Columbia Gorge National Scenic Area Act
—creating the nation's first such area—galvanized many
parties into action. The Forest Service began to write
Interim Guidelines and review land use proposals until the
new bistate commission was ready to take over with its own
Management Plan. The Forest Service and the Gorge
Commission would have to deal both with environmental
activists who strongly supported protection, and with local
governments and property owners who bitterly resented the
distrust and criticism implied by federal intervention. The
Forest Service and commission would plan, but county
governments would implement. Clearly, every aspect of Forest
Service and commission activity would be thoroughly
politicized.

    Many skirmishes occurred during the interim period, while
the Forest Service and the commission were developing their
plans. Given the climate of hostility, the planners
understandably sought to use the incentives for industrial
transition included in the Act to overcome fear and establish
cooperative relations. They also tried to manage the gorge
during the interim with an eye toward future cooperation,
although this proved tricky, since environmentalists were ever
on the alert for signs of agency appeasement of the interests
who were supposedly being regulated.

    Two issues stood out during plan preparation: the takings
issue; and the balance between protection and development.
The first was especially significant. Since Congress did not
permit land acquisition outside the Special Management
Areas, a regulatory approach largely based on zoning land as
open space necessarily figured prominently elsewhere. Given
the federal government's reluctance to acquire land except

from a willing seller, the Forest Service would likely hesitate to use the open space designation in the SMAs as well. The fear of takings-related litigation profoundly influenced plan making, as well as the politics of plan adoption and implementation.

The balance between protection and development, of course, was the same issue that been prominent in five years of legislative maneuvering. It now dominated substantive discussion during another five years of plan writing. In the process, it continued to pit a vision of a prosperous and *stable* gorge that depended, as it traditionally had, on resource production and transportation against a vision of a prosperous and *changing* gorge—the visions of the Old West and the New West.

Another central issue during plan preparation, as it had been throughout the legislative phase, was that of flexibility versus specificity, case-by-case negotiation, trust versus control, with actors and interests lining up on the same sides as during the legislative hearings. Regulators in the various agencies in the Scenic Area and similar programs around the country have had to move quickly to establish their legal validity and have had to make sure that interim review actions do not undermine forthcoming Management Plans. They have therefore been inclined toward strict interpretation of the law. The Tahoe Regional Planning Agency developed its initial Management Plan in 1970-71 by strictly applying technical environmental assessment criteria. Without adequate local participation, the plan was dead on arrival. The Adirondack Planning Agency offended local residents by treating public hearings as formal evidentiary proceedings without the give and take of open discussion. The Pinelands Commission was more forthcoming in style, but still emphasized legal precedent over education and outreach in its first years.

Residents in such situations are likely to be offended by what they see as rigidity and hyper-legalism. Exacerbating these tensions has been the problem of deadlines. Cape Cod planners had less than a year to develop a Management Plan; Pinelands planners had under two years. Managers of the Scenic Area were required to prepare land use designations within two years and to adopt a Management Plan within three years. There may also be a cultural clash between local people who are accustomed to talking problems through and regulators who are comfortable in a world of memos and rules.

115

Residents may argue that local circumstances often require reasonable flexibility. But officials may reasonably fear that initial flexibility might destroy their legal ability to tighten standards later and might simply encourage demands for more and more exceptions. Can regulators afford to trust the good will of local governments whose poor track record is presumably the reason for the additional regulation? This is, again, the tension between rule making and place making.

The Forest Service Starts to Plan

Immediately following President Reagan's reluctant signing of the Scenic Area Act, the Forest Service announced the appointment of twenty-five-year veteran Art DuFault as Scenic Area manager. The new manager and his staff decided to locate in the gorge, and to establish their personal households there as well, to integrate themselves into the community. They began working with timber companies on possible exchanges of commercial timber land. They also started work on a set of Interim Guidelines, which had to be completed within 180 days.

The twelve-member Interim Guidelines team included Forest Service planners assigned to the gorge and from similar areas elsewhere in the country, including Sawtooth National Recreation Area and Mono Basin National Scenic Area. The planning directors of Multnomah and Klickitat counties were also invited to serve on the team to increase the technical and political credibility of the guidelines, since they had the necessary expertise and experience in dealing with private land development projects. The lead Forest Service planner—Katherine Jesch—wanted another woman on the guidelines team. Lorna Stickel, the planning director of Multnomah County, welcomed the opportunity to articulate strongly a local government point of view.

Planners and implementors generally try to develop guidelines, rules, and regulations that are (1) consistent with legal mandates, (2) appropriate given professional and bureaucratic values, and (3) politcally feasible, given the distribution of power among relevant interest groups. Forest Service and local government members of the Interim Guidelines team brought different approaches to the process. The local planners were accustomed to more specificity than were their federal counterparts and argued that specificity was necessary to give structure to case-by-case decision making. They worried that the absence of specific guidelines would necessitate elaborate case-by-case justifications for decisions, increasing the possibility of inconsistent policy. This line of thought was similar to that voiced by environmentalists during the legislative campaign, and became the basis for incorporating detailed, specific standards in the law.

Forest Service professionals, on the other hand, historically had enjoyed a great deal of discretion in managing resource allocation. They viewed wide-ranging discretion as necessary for balancing multiple uses in the public interest. However, since they were acutely aware both that the law was full of specifics and that they had limited experience regulating private land, they were disposed to adopt the local government professionals' point of view. The Interim Guidelines that were submitted to the national Forest Service headquarters contained a substantial number of detailed, specific requirements, though not quite so many as a traditional zoning ordinance.

Scenic Area planners were shocked to learn that top Forest Service officials opposed the guidelines. Two main sources of opposition surfaced. One was a general reluctance to have the federal government engaged in controlling local land use in such a detailed way, even during an interim period. The other was headquarters' fear that detailed, highly specific guidelines would produce a host of presently nonconforming uses and future disapprovals of development that would, in turn, generate pressure to condemn land. Given the Reagan administration's ideological hostility to the condemnation of private land, top Forest Service officials rejected the Scenic Area planners' work and demanded that all specificity be eliminated from the Interim Guidelines.

Art DuFault. (Photo: USDA Forest Service)

The gorge planners now faced a profound dilemma. They believed that what headquarters had ordered would neither be appropriate from a professional/technical standpoint, nor be acceptable to important local, state, and congressional political actors. However, they saw the culture of the Forest Service as discouraging challenges to top authority, and reluctantly decided to follow headquarters' direction. As a result, Scenic Area professionals went to local public hearings with guidelines essentially lacking in substance. While they

117

were careful not explicitly to encourage critical responses to the guidelines, they did not advocate on behalf of their regulations either, tacitly expressing their dissatisfaction.

The Interim Guidelines were criticized in the hearings, in written comments, and in the metropolitan press for their lack of specificity. Local government planners and Friends of the Columbia Gorge led the critique. The Friends' executive director wrote to the Forest Service chief:

> The draft guidelines are extremely general and lacking in critical detail. This flaw makes it highly unlikely that counties will incorporate the guidelines into their zoning ordinances, or that the Gorge's resources will be adequately protected during the interim period.

In the context of these conflicting pressures, Forest Service planners turned to performance standards as an approach that would meet the tests of legal consistency, professional appropriateness, and political feasibility. Interestingly, they did not consciously set out to do so but, as they designed a revised set of guidelines, they gradually became aware that performance standards were emerging. Environmental activists, the metropolitan press, and Forest Service headquarters generally supported the revised approach. The staff convinced top officials that performance standards would permit planners to be flexible in dealing with gorge property owners, thus reducing pressures to condemn land.

Environmentalists and Planners

The critical comments by local planners and environmentalists regarding the initial set of guidelines were extremely important in securing headquarters' approval of the revised standards. Scenic Area planners were able to document how the standards reflected input received during public review. The supportive relationship between the Friends and planners carried over into the early implementation period. An activist sat in the Scenic Area office on a weekly basis to monitor case processing; the staff welcomed and facilitated such monitoring.

About a year after the passage of the Scenic Area Act, the bistate Columbia Gorge Commission was ready to assume responsibility from the Forest Service for carrying out the Interim Guidelines. During the last several months before the

118

transition took place, the relationship between the Forest Service planners and environmental activists deteriorated. The Friends worried that Forest Service planners were reproducing the failure of the Tahoe planning agency by approving the vast majority of development applications.

The organization's executive director charged that implementation of the Interim Guidelines was doing little to stop damaging development patterns. "If development continues at the rate of the past 11 months the impact on the gorge would be devastating. At the very least key areas of the gorge will have been lost forever before the management plan and implementing ordinances are even adopted."

The Scenic Area manager responded that staff planners considered a proposal approved by a gorge county prior to passage of the Act as "vested." Because most of the proposals approved were of this type, the early wave of approvals was not a valid indicator of future Forest Service actions. Friends of the Columbia Gorge remained unconvinced.

The political dilemma for the Scenic Area staff was clear. Vesting projects previously approved by county planners was a way of showing cooperative behavior and they in turn would need the cooperation of the counties in the future. The Forest Service was also trying to neutralize potential political opposition. But this high approval rate reinforced the fears of environmentalists.

The Friends' critique of the Forest Service came as no surprise to members of the Columbia Gorge Coalition, who had felt marginalized by the Friends during the later stages of the legislative process. Although full of dark foreboding about the future of the gorge, the Coalition had closed its office "since both the organization and . . . key activists were financially in ruins." Various timber company actions during 1987 and 1988 greatly disturbed Coalition activists, who were outraged by what they thought were Forest Service failures to protect the gorge.

The Coalition had been successful in establishing Wild and Scenic River status and studies for segments of two gorge streams, but boundaries and regulations were left to the Forest Service. The Act did not provide interim protection for

> **Forest Service Land Acquisition Policy**
>
> *During the interim period the Forest Service only bought land from willing sellers. Hardship cases (where the legislation had affected the ability of the owner to sell or use land) got top priority. This aspect of Forest Service practice was consistent with past agency behavior and the cooperation theme, though it raised again the concern about the amount of development.*

119

these segments, nor did it authorize acquisition funds. The Coalition, the Friends, and another local conservation organization, Friends of the White Salmon, vehemently disagreed with the study boundaries proposed by the Forest Service. So did a prominent timber company whose land would be affected. While the parties contended, the timber company began logging in contested areas. Conservationists responded with pressure on the Forest Service and a lawsuit. The company pulled back from logging in one area, but began cutting elsewhere within the proposed boundaries.

During the conflict Chuck Williams of the Coalition chained himself to the door of the Forest Service office in Hood River and to the door of a downtown Portland hotel owned by the same family that controlled the timber company. Following his two arrests, the Forest Service decided to purchase the lands in question. The Coalition looked forward to at least a temporary reprieve. It also lamented that, "If our proposal had been enacted [to place the National Park Service in charge], we'd now be planning trails. Instead . . . we're having to put our bodies on the line to stop the continuing destruction."

The Columbia River Gorge Commission Gets Organized

While the Forest Service wrestled with its interim management responsibilities, the Oregon and Washington legislatures set up the Columbia River Gorge Commission as specified in the Scenic Area Act. The gubernatorial appointments were people strongly committed to planning and to environmental protection.

Oregon governor Neil Goldschmidt appointed Barbara Bailey, Don Clark, and Stafford Hansell. All three were members of Friends of the Columbia Gorge. Bailey, an orchardist in Wasco County, was a Friends board member and former member of the county planning commission. Clark, former Multnomah County sheriff and commissioner, had helped give birth to the organization. Hansell, in addition to his membership in the Friends, was an eastern Oregon farmer who had served in leadership positions in the state legislature. He would be chosen the Gorge Commission's first chair, in recognition of his experience in land use matters and his stature as a moderate Republican.

Washington governor Booth Gardner appointed Dave Cannard, Stuart Chapin, and Gail Rothrock. Cannard was a

Vancouver, Washington, insurance executive and civic activist and a founder and board member of the Friends. Chapin had belonged to the Friends until his appointment to the Washington Gorge Commission. A resident of Klickitat County, he was retired from a faculty position at the University of North Carolina. He was widely recognized as one of the country's leading authorities in the field of urban land use planning, and was coauthor of a highly respected textbook. Chapin would be an invaluable resource to both staff and fellow commission members during his term in office. Rothrock, a management and public affairs consultant from Vancouver, was a former member of the Washington State Shorelines Hearing Board and the state Pollution Control Hearings Board.

The county appointments were mixed. Hood River County appointed Joyce Reinig, a former member of the county planning commission, a nurse, and a small business owner. Wasco County appointed Ray Matthew, a former city council member and county commissioner, and also a small business owner. Multnomah County chose attorney Kristine Olson Rogers, a specialist in cultural resource law and Native American affairs.

The absence of Nancy Russell's name from the list of finalists made Multnomah County's choice controversial. The chair of the county commission had encouraged Russell to put her name forward, and strongly supported her candidacy. The associate editor of *The Oregonian* wrote that "Russell is acknowledged as one of the persons—if not the person—most knowledgeable about the natural and cultural resources of the . . . Gorge. She has more gorge information at her fingertips than most other gorge panel members are likely to acquire in a

> ## Columbia River Gorge Commission Vision Statement
>
> *The Columbia River Gorge is an area of worldwide importance,*
>
> *Where scenic qualities and diverse landscapes, together with their natural and cultural components, are paramount,*
>
> *Where development and recreation are carefully placed in a manner that protects resources,*
>
> *Where the human presence is lightly demonstrated, and where lessons from the past are a constant guide and inspiration for the future.*
>
> *To achieve this vision, the Columbia River Gorge Commission will provide:*
>
> *Stewardship of this legacy and trust,*
>
> *Leadership for implementation of the National Scenic Area Act and the Management Plan,*
>
> *Partnership with communities, tribal governments, and agencies, and*
>
> *A vision of the Gorge as a region and the river as a bond.*
>
> **Columbia River Gorge Commission, 1988**

121

year." However, the commissioners received a letter signed by 250 people who lived within the Scenic Area boundary opposing Russell because of fears that she would give little consideration to the economic health of their communities. Taking note of this opposition, the commissioner whose district included the petitioners refused to support Russell, citing reservations about her ability to work with gorge residents. This was sufficient to block her appointment by the county.

Clark County appointed Bob Thompson, who worked for the county public utility district. Skamania County designated Nancy Sourek, a former Forest Service employee who was the director of the county's Department of Emergency Management. Klickitat County chose Pat Bleakney, a cattle rancher and former county commissioner and county planning commission director, who had actively opposed the Scenic Area Act during the legislative phase.

Five of these six—Bleakney, Matthew, Reinig, Sourek, and Thompson—were expected to articulate the local government, prodevelopment perspective that had worried environmentalists, although Reinig was experienced in Oregon-style land use planning. Rogers, representing the metropolitan county that had strongly supported the Scenic Area Act, was expected to favor protection.

Hansell quickly became the dominant figure on the Gorge Commission. His background as a hog farmer from Umatilla County in eastern Oregon freed him of the taint of Portland, but thirty years of experience in the Oregon legislature and several executive departments had convinced him of the need for systematic management of Oregon resources. That service had also given him impressive political skills and a deep reservoir of respect as a person who operated on principle and who was motivated by "a love affair with Oregon." As a managerial Republican, he had served both Democratic and Republican governors, most recently as chair of the Oregon Land Conservation and Development Commission—a position that made him favorably inclined to extending the Oregon planning approach throughout the Columbia Gorge.

122   A condition of effective implementation is assignment to a sympathetic agency. Gubernatorial appointments of Friends activists to the Gorge Commission reflected an effort to create a supportive context for resource protection. The Act also sought to encourage economic activity consistent with protection goals. Most of the county appointments supported this second objective. As members of a new entity, commissioners sought to create a shared identity. Acutely aware of the controversies surrounding the creation of the commission, and of the need for local cooperation in order to survive and prosper, commissioners and their staff sought to respond to the concerns of important local stakeholders. Industrial transition would be one arena within which they could show sensitivity to local needs.

Stafford Hansell, a hog farmer from Umatilla County, shared the award for Oregon Conservation Farmer of the Year in 1977.
(Photo: Oregon Historical Society)

Members of the Friends became the commission chair and vice-chair. The chair appointed a three-person committee to search for an executive director; two of these three were Friends. However, when Friends on the commission sat as judges deciding contested land use cases that also involved the Friends organization playing its watchdog role, controversy erupted. In the latter part of 1988, an attorney from Hood River County argued that former Friends members—the four had recently resigned from the organization—should disqualify themselves from deciding cases in which Friends was a participant. An assistant Washington attorney general, citing the state's "appearance of fairness doctrine," supported the challenge. The commission's executive director asked the Friends to stop intervening while the issue was resolved.

The newly appointed commissioners set about hiring an executive director. The short list of finalists included the planning director of Multnomah County, who had worked closely with the Forest Service on Interim Guidelines development; an extension agent at Washington State University; and Richard Benner, senior attorney with 1000 Friends of Oregon, and strong advocate before Congress of a detailed, specific Scenic Area law. The commission chose Benner to take advantage of his very highly regarded legal skills, deep knowledge of land use and environmental matters, and political experience gained on Oregon land use planning

123

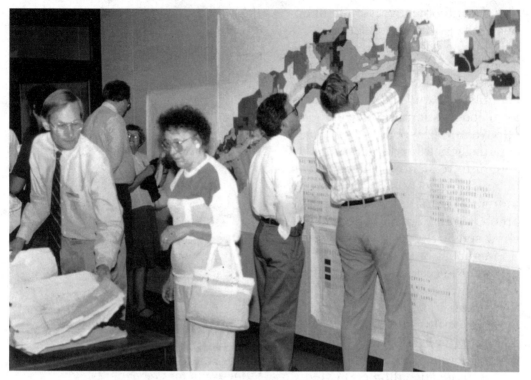

Forest Service planner Jurgen Hess (left) and citizens discuss the plan.
(Photo: USDA Forest Service)

issues. Given the commission's profound concern with producing a plan that could survive takings-related scrutiny, Benner seemed especially well qualified.

Benner was thoroughly grounded in the Oregon system, and identified as the Friends' choice by already suspicious Washington gorge residents. He hired a land use planner with a great deal of experience dealing with gorge agricultural and forest issues who was respected on both sides of the river. The other planners hired to work on cultural and natural resource issues, and on recreation and scenic resources, were from outside the area.

124

The Columbia River Gorge Commission Starts to Work

B enner and his staff were ready to take over development review from the Forest Service Scenic Area office in early 1988, just after the Friends had blasted Forest Service implementation of the Interim Guidelines. The commission adopted the existing Interim Guidelines as its own, with two amendments that defined agricultural and forest lands in much greater detail. The changes reflected the influence on Benner and the commission's land use planner of Oregon's statewide land use Goals 3 and 4, regarding agricultural and forest lands. Benner and his staff were strongly committed as well to Oregon's Goal 14, which aims at concentrating development within urban growth boundaries.

The commission also jumped right into managing an industrial transition, beginning an economic opportunity study and working with the Forest Service on a recreation assessment. The commission also designated two "Rural Centers," one in each state, while rejecting several other candidates. Rural Centers were clusters of development that did not merit inclusion on list of exempt Urban Areas. The designation was intended to encourage the location of certain kinds of economic activity in these places, expanding the possibilities for growth in depressed parts of the gorge.

Struggle for the Interpretive and Meeting Centers

A mong the economic incentives in the Scenic Area Act were an interpretive center on the Oregon side and a meeting center in Washington. These highly desirable prizes generated a great deal of competition and selecting their location was a major political challenge for the commission. The commissioners first addressed the interpretive center. Although building a center in each of the three Oregon gorge counties—a politically expedient approach—was initially considered, the commissioners decided to support just one. Thirty-nine proposals flooded in. Finalists were all from Wasco and Hood River counties. The commission settled on a Wasco County location, just west of The Dalles; delays in federal and private funding set back ground breaking until May 1996.

The commission wanted a public-private partnership for the meeting center, which was a much more elaborate undertaking than the interpretive center. If the competition in

Senator Mark Hatfield at the ground breaking for the interpretive visitor center, May 1996. (Photo: USDA Forest Service)

Oregon was intense, there was an air of desperation on the other side of the river. Five proposals came in, at least one from each of the three Washington gorge counties. The commission narrowed the choice to one each in Skamania and Klickitat counties, both of which were experiencing high levels of unemployment. Advocates attached great importance to the potential economic benefits associated with their projects. Skamania County proposed a partnership with developer John Gray to build a $20-million facility on county-owned land. The county would contribute $5 million, the developer $10 million, and the $5 million federal contribution would round out the package. Klickitat County entered a $28-million hotel/ conference center, trade center, and condominium package in partnership with a Seattle-based firm. In addition to the federal government's $5 million, the private partners would come up with $19 million, and the Port of Klickitat, which owned most of the land, would put up $4 million.

Both counties worked very hard to line up commission support. The commissioners developed a set of criteria, then asked a group of private consultants to evaluate the two proposals. This task force rated the entries about equal for

126

design quality, access, and natural amenities, but gave an edge to the Skamania County project on finance because of the private partner's superior track record. Then the commissioners split 6-6 on an east end/west end basis. Benner persuaded them to impanel another task force, composed of people suggested by the private developers, but unfamiliar with either of them, to recommend a top choice.

While the second panel was gearing up to visit the gorge, the Klickitat County package threatened to unravel when the private owners of a piece of land in the center of the project area said they were taking their land off the market.

The panel favored the Skamania County proposal. The commission initially voted 9-3 in its favor, then made it unanimous. Chair Hansell referred to the Klickitat project as a "pig in a poke," due to the financing and land acquisition uncertainties. The commissioners were troubled by the turmoil in Klickitat County, which highlighted a problem in managing an industrial transition. Ironically, just a few days later, a lumber mill in the town of Klickitat shut down, leaving only one mill still operating in the county.

Skamania County had flown the flag at half mast when the National Scenic Area Act passed. It now stood in line to get $5 million in federal aid, *if* it adopted a plan implementation ordinance acceptable to the commission and the secretary of agriculture. Klickitat County had given the conference center competition their best shot. Having lost, lacking the financial incentive, and internally divided, Klickitat County would refuse to participate in plan implementation.

Other Commission Decisions

Meanwhile, other manifestations of industrial transition gave the Gorge Commission chances to show its responsiveness to economic development concerns. During 1989 the Broughton Lumber Company proposed a mini-destination windsurfing resort on the site of a closed sawmill in Skamania County. Since it would be a large commercial project outside existing Urban Areas, the Friends opposed the resort. Worried about interference with tribal fishing rights, the Yakama Indian Nation opposed it as well. After Broughton scaled down its proposal, Richard Benner, supported by the commission, reversed his initial disapproval, over the continuing objections of the Friends. (The project

127

Skamania Lodge. (Photo: USDA Forest Service)

remains unbuilt in 1996.) Despite the concerns of both staff
and the Friends, the Commission also decided to amend the
Interim Guidelines to facilitate efforts to replace mobile homes
with modular or site-built houses.

Generally speaking, the commission's land use decisions
during the interim period were much less controversial than
the Forest Service's. During the four years leading up to plan
adoption in October 1991, when it was responsible for
development reviews, the commission dealt with about 950
applications. Skamania and Wasco counties accounted for
about 60 percent of the cases, 38 percent in Skamania County
alone, reflecting the large amount of private land in the county
inside Scenic Area boundaries. Just 5 percent of the cases
were from Clark County, while those from Multnomah,
Klickitat, and Hood River counties ranged around 10 percent
of the total. About three-quarters of the applications involved
residential land uses, mostly single-family homes. Sixteen
percent involved land divisions, and the remainder included
small percentages of commercial, industrial, and other uses.

Overall the commission approved (with conditions) 82
percent of the applications. Single-family home applications
met a 91 percent approval rate, commercial applications 61

128

percent, and land divisions 40 percent. These percentages are slightly lower than those reported for Tahoe when the Scenic Area legislation was under discussion. During the three years from 1988 through 1990, gorge applicants appealed 40 percent of the denials (about seventy cases). The commission sustained the executive director in about 80 percent of these appeals. Very likely the existence of the guidelines deterred the submission of some proposals that were unlikely to gain approval. The specifics in the Act, and the performance standards approach of the Interim Guidelines, appeared to permit the commission to maintain a politically acceptable balance between flexible responsiveness and resource protection.

As the Forest Service and especially the commission moved from the Interim Guidelines to the Management Plan, however, that acceptable balance of local discretion and specific protection would become harder and harder to find. The commissioners found themselves damned from both sides as they sought a middle course that acknowledged property rights and economic interests but also prevented alteration of scenic values.

The Draft Management Plan and Its Critics

In October 1990, the Forest Service released its draft plan for the Special Management Areas, comprising about 40 percent of the National Scenic Area. Gorge commissioners released their draft for the General Management Areas, comprising about 50 percent of the total, in December. (The exempt Urban Areas accounted for the remaining 10 percent.) Embodying three and a half years of work, these plans were complex documents that wove together the findings of many consultants, the comments of citizen participants, and staff judgments. The plans brought to a boil several controversial issues that had simmered since passage of the Act. Significant changes to preliminary drafts occurred on the way to adoption of a final Management Plan by the Gorge Commission in October 1991. As had been the case during the legislative struggles, the nature and extent of discretion available to the counties to implement the proposed plan was a major source of conflict.

129

Consultants did most of the analytical work for the gorge plans. Much of the inventory work was, in fact, coproduced by

Hearing the Public

All told, from the beginning of the planning process through plan adoption, the Gorge Commission conducted thirty meetings with county boards and twelve meetings with tribal governments. There were 62 "key contact" meetings with persons thought to be informed and influential, twenty open houses with several hundred participants, and four public hearings at which 340 people testified. In addition, the Forest Service received 286 written responses to the draft plan for the SMAs and the commission received 1,038 written comments regarding its draft and final planning documents.

environmental organizations such as the Native Plant Society of Oregon and the Nature Conservancy in cooperation with the Oregon and Washington Natural Heritage Programs. But tribal governments did not coproduce the cultural resources inventory; the commission deferred to the Forest Service, which contracted with a professional archaeological firm to survey already published information about gorge cultural resources. Since very little of the gorge had been physically studied, the inventory was seriously incomplete.

Based on the inventories and other studies, the Forest Service and the commission developed land use designations and guidelines, recreation intensity classes, and recreation development plans. While these were under development, and after the release of the preliminary drafts, the commission and the Forest Service sponsored an extensive public involvement program. Yet many opinion leaders felt that, while the planning process had been open in a formal sense, the planners really had not listened to what local people told them.

The plans were daunting documents. Many people found them excessively bureaucratic, legalistic, and hard to understand. They were so long and complex that they were difficult going for the counties, let alone individual citizens. Clearly, neither the planning process nor the plans themselves resolved long-standing conflicts. Instead, contending parties found many of the same sorts of problems they had seen in the legislation.

Some county officials felt that the tribal governments were accorded more respect by the commission than they were. The commissioners responded that county officials had designated **130** representatives on the governing body; the tribes did not have such direct representation. The tribes did have a champion on the commission throughout the planning process in the person of Multnomah County appointee Kristine Rogers. Respect for the principles of tribal sovereignty and government-to-government relationships was critically important for her. Staff recommendations for the protection of cultural resources in the preliminary draft plan built on an existing federal government process for assessing the significance of sites, supplemented by an advisory committee—including tribal representatives—that would monitor and review commission and county actions regarding cultural resources. Rogers believed that this process failed to reflect either a Native American worldview or the tribal participation called for by the Scenic Area Act. She argued that the recommendations were entirely inadequate. She persuaded the commission, in the face of opposition from the Forest Service, county governments, and the state historical preservation offices, to adopt language allowing the tribal governments in the gorge to identify cultural resources needing protection.

Environmentalists Respond

Environmental organizations—including the Native Plant Society of Oregon, the Nature Conservancy, the Friends, the National Wildlife Federation, the Wilderness Society, and the Gorge Audubon Society—had a few major concerns with the Forest Service's preliminary draft for the SMAs, but except for the Columbia Gorge Coalition, they generally liked what they saw. Their primary concern was that the Forest Service overemphasized recreational development.

Squally Point, in Wasco County, crystallized this issue. The Forest Service proposed to classify Squally Point in the most intense recreational development category, allowing a parking lot for up to two hundred cars and campground with up to one hundred and fifty sites. The Columbia Gorge Boardsailors' Association strongly supported this recreational development, as did Wasco County officials. The Boardsailors pointed out that at a workshop sponsored by the Forest Service and the commission, Squally Point had emerged as the highest-rated potential recreation site in the gorge. They and county officials stressed the economic development benefits likely to be associated with intense recreation there. Moreover, the Boardsailors had sought out opponents of development to ascertain their objections and consider mitigation measures. The Boardsailors believed that environmental and Indian fishing rights issues could be resolved. But environmental activists thought Squally Point a much too fragile sand dune and valuable wildlife habitat area to accommodate intense

131

recreation. They insisted that this classification and those of several other areas be changed to a much lower intensity category.

Environmental organizations also questioned some of the Forest Service's proposed forest land designations and guidelines. The groups felt that the SMA plan should have designated several key forested areas as open space rather than forest land. Moreover, while the Forest Service clearly stated that clear-cutting would be prohibited on federally owned forest lands in the SMAs, there was no such stated restriction on non-federal lands. Environmentalists felt that clear-cutting should be banned throughout the Scenic Area and uneven-aged timber management practices mandated on both private and public lands in the SMAs. The Columbia Gorge Coalition in particular was deeply disturbed that the extensive use of the forest land designation would allow logging to continue in the SMAs.

The Friends criticized several proposed Forest Service guidelines for failing to give explicit directions to local governments, fearing that, without specific standards, loose implementing ordinances would let residential construction diminish scenic resources. They saluted the Forest Service, however, for its prohibition on the alteration or destruction of wetlands.

Environmentalists also greeted the Gorge Commission's preliminary draft plan for the GMAs with a general chorus of approval. They did see some problems, including the treatment of wetlands and riparian areas in the commission's plan for the GMAs. Grazing and other agricultural activities on and around these sensitive lands were of particular concern. Environmentalists worried that the commission's more flexible approach to regulation would provide substantially less protection than would the Forest Service proposal for the SMAs. The Friends and others argued that the commission's policy of calling for no net loss of wetlands, while appealing in theory, would not work in practice. Environmentalists also worried that the ways the commission proposed to categorize agricultural and forest lands would lead to the conversion of some small-scale farms and woodlots to housing.

132

The commission approached the challenge of designating open spaces very gingerly, and their trepidation is understandable. In comments on the introductory chapter in the preliminary draft, Friends noted a significant silence: "The Plan lists the types of land use designations the Act directs the

Commission to make. The list mirrors Section 6(b) of the Act, with one exception; Section 6(b)4 which refers to open spaces, is omitted. This implies that the Commission is not directed to make open space designations. We assume this is an oversight." In fact, the commission designated the Columbia River and another one thousand acres as open space and about ten thousand acres (9 percent of the GMA not counting the Columbia River) as "candidate open space." The commission meant by this that another use designation (forest, agriculture, etc.) might also apply to the lands in question. The commissioners had not yet decided. Environmentalists, of course, wanted all the candidate lands to retain the open space label.

The commission suggested two options that alarmed the Friends and other environmental organizations. One was to limit the open space designation to public lands; the other was that improved lands should not be designated as open space. An improvement was defined as something subject to a county property tax, or land that had seen agricultural, forestry, or mineral resource activity within the previous five years. The environmentalists strongly protested both these options. The Friends enthusiastically did support, though, a policy of working to establish a vehicle, such as a land trust or a conservancy, to acquire lands and easements in the GMAs.

Environmental organizations generally offered congratulations, advice—and warnings. The Northwest office of the Sierra Club thanked the commission for "hard work and outstanding effort. The draft Plan goes far in establishing standards that can help assure that this marvelous treasure will exist for the benefit and enjoyment of all Americans." But the club's Columbia Group (Portland) noted that "the state of Washington has criticized this Plan and called it 'unworkable,'" and urged the commission to "look to the broader constituency in rejecting the state of Washington's call for weakening the Plan. This is a National Scenic Area and the approach to this Plan must be from a National perspective." The Friends advised the commission "to stick to its guns and follow through with the open space designations." The Natural Resources Council reminded the commission that "Land use **133** policies in the state of Washington were the impetus for the legislation. Congress determined that existing plans and procedures in Washington were not adequate to protect the sensitive resources of the Gorge. Do not heed the urgings of the state of Washington to ignore statutory direction."

Opposition to the Plan

The preliminary plan did run into substantial opposition. Officials from five of the six gorge counties—Multnomah County was the sole exception—were sharply critical. They attacked what they felt was the lack of flexibility in the proposed guidelines, the absence of attention to existing local plans and policies, and the exposure to massive takings liability they were certain would result from aggressive use of the open space designation on private land. They were particularly incensed over a perceived overemphasis on resource protection at the expense of economic development.

Washington Department of Community Development officials agreed with this critique. The assistant director charged that the plan was "extreme, unreasonable and unworkable . . . a recipe for confusion and conflict . . . We don't believe the plan will have the willing compliance of the people who are the most affected. . . . That means endless litigation." Washington governor Gardner was also critical; Gorge commissioners heard his letter read in "stonyfaced silence." Gardner agreed that the commissioners had failed to form a true partnership with gorge jurisdictions. He counseled building in much more flexibility to encourage creative implementation at the local level, and planning in a manner consistent with existing state laws, including Washington's environmental policy act.

The withering critique by local opponents did not surprise the commission. Washington state's opposition was more troubling, especially the charge that the commissioners had failed to take local concerns seriously. Many points in the plan had been clearly intended to assuage local worries. The commissioners and staff had taken great pains to use the open space designation conservatively, and to maintain some economic use of land even in the most restrictive categories. The commissioners wanted to respond to the critical comments and scheduled several intensive all-day workshops in April 1991.

134 Cultural resource issues were especially controversial during the workshops, pitting the staff against Commissioner Rogers and her supporters. Staff proposals to revise the preliminary plan, Rogers felt, went much too far toward accommodating those who opposed a strong tribal role in resource identification and protection. A divided commission voted to maintain the policy of "allowing tribal governments to identify sensitive resources and allowing the Cultural Resources Advisory Committee (with tribal representation) to intervene in a disputed development review."

Shortly before they were to release the final draft for public comment, the Gorge Commission and the Forest Service were hit with a lawsuit seeking to block further work on the plan. Klickitat County and the city of Washougal, located at the gorge end of Clark County, joined SDS Lumber Company, the Klickitat County Livestock Growers Association, and three gorge businesses to claim that the commission and the Forest Service were required by federal and Washington state environmental laws to prepare impact statements assessing the proposed plans' environmental, economic, and social consequences. The suit asked that all work on the plans be halted until such impact analyses were completed. An attorney for the U. S. Department of Agriculture countered that the Scenic Area Act exempted the commission and the Forest Service from an impact statement requirement. The commission's attorney argued that the Oregon and Washington statutes creating the Gorge Commission did not require impact statements, and that the commission, as a bistate entity, was not bound by Washington state law.

In early May a U.S. district court judge in Yakima, Washington, granted a temporary injunction, ordering the commission and the Forest Service to halt work on the plan until he could decide whether or not the document must incorporate an impact analysis. In mid-June the judge denied the plaintiffs' request for a permanent injunction and threw out the suit.

The draft Management Plan was an effort to create a unified approach to allocating gorge land resources. Explicitness is the most important characteristic of such a comprehensive plan. The plan makes visible the implications of changes it proposes. The preliminary gorge plans weren't quite as explicit as environmental activists wished. But they were sufficiently explicit for many gorge property owners and local and state officials, especially on the Washington side, to see threats to traditional political processes and to dislike the contents of the proposed package deal.

The Management Plan

The *Final Draft Management Plan for General and Special Management Areas*, released in July 1991, contained many changes that the commission and the Forest Service thought were responsive to concerns about the preliminary drafts. The commissioners, in particular, believed they had tried hard to accommodate Washington state, local official, and gorge property owner interests. But these efforts did not elicit much support, or even mute the opposition from former critics, while they incurred the wrath of the Friends and other environmental organizations.

The final draft plan was an inch-thick document, including four maps. It was, like the preliminary drafts, a great deal to digest. The new document reflected the commission's tight schedule and limited budget. A specific problem was the commission's decision to leave for the adopted plan any discussion of "the overall intended effect of the plan—the vision for the future of the Gorge." The plan started off with land use designations, and goals, policies, and guidelines for each category. Then came scenic, cultural, natural, and recreation resource protection and enhancement goals, policies and guidelines; action programs; and a final section on future roles for the commission, the Forest Service, and Indian tribes.

Evident throughout is the planners' desire to stay close to the data developed in the land use and resource inventories. Land suitability, key viewing areas, scenic travel corridors, landscape settings, and recreation intensity classes were tools created by the planners to transform these data into place-specific policy arguments to protect and enhance resources. Awareness of implementation politics is also evident in the choices of designations, boundaries and regulatory approaches. The commission believed that the final draft had

- reduced demands on and costs to property owners;
- reduced implementation demands on the counties and the states;
- eliminated some specificity in guidelines to give the counties more flexibility;
- dropped some regulations where existing state and federal regulations offered the same level of protection;
- and clarified confusing policies and guidelines.

136

Economic Development

To address the local concern that economic development had been neglected in the preliminary draft, the commission pulled all the relevant material into a new 13-page section. The commission argued that protections for land designated for agriculture and forestry would stabilize and enhance those economic sectors. New commercial activity would be funneled into the exempt Urban Areas, the two designated Rural Centers, and five areas along important travel corridors. Small-scale commercial uses, such as bed-and-breakfast inns, cottage industries, and home occupations would be permitted uses in many land designations. The plan stressed recreation development and other projects to be financed with federal funds. The counties and local property owners, however, saw the new section as totally inadequate. The Friends, on the other hand, thought that a lot of cottage industry and home occupation activity outside Urban Areas and Rural Centers would conflict with resource uses.

Recreation

Recreation had generated more comments than any other aspect of the preliminary plans. The Forest Service reduced intensity classifications in several places, including at Squally Point, where it was concerned about the impact of intense recreational use on environmental values and Native American fishing rights (see page 131). The Gorge Boardsailors' Association was outraged. This clash recapitulated the conflict between active and passive recreation that had simmered since the 1950s and fights about the aerial tramway.

The commission, on the other hand, also angered the Friends by stating that its goal was to "increase recreational access to the Columbia River and its tributaries as much as possible." The Friends had also complained about the possibility that counties might be given discretion to increase the number of parking spaces and campsites in the most intense recreation classification. In the final draft the commission itself set out increases in several classifications in the GMAs. The commission declared, though, that exceeding the new guidelines would require a plan amendment.

The commission had heard local concerns that visibility from Key Viewing Areas would lead to denials of proposed development. Commissioners responded with a policy clarification: "Except for production and/or development of mineral resources, nothing in the Key Viewing Areas or Landscape Setting sections shall be used as grounds to deny proposed development otherwise consistent with other provisions of this Plan." The commission also relaxed its guidelines to permit new and expanded quarrying and mining under certain circumstances, even if visible from key viewing areas. The Friends believed that both these final draft changes would fail to protect scenic values. The commission was very sensitive to quarry-related concerns, because Hood River County owned one that was visually troubling but economically very important. Hood Rver County's representative made the commission acutely aware of the significance of the quarry to the local political economy. The commission ws clearly trying to be responsive on this issue.

Environmentalists had loudly criticized the commission's reluctance to follow the Forest Service regarding stringent wetlands protection. In the final draft the commission not only stuck to its policy mandating only no net loss, which the Friends and others found inadequate, but actually reduced regulations in wetlands and riparian areas. The commission was persuaded that existing state and federal laws permitted the removal of wetland regulations from the main stem of the Columbia River. It also dropped regulation of livestock grazing and other agricultural practices in wetland and riparian areas and buffer zones. Many environmental groups bitterly protested, pointing out that many Oregon and Washington resource agencies had urged that agricultural practices in these areas be strictly regulated. Environmentalists also thought that final draft regulations would exacerbate the likelihood that owners would convert small agricultural and forest parcels to residential uses.

Environmentalists had strongly urged the Forest Service to extend the ban on clear-cutting to non-federal lands within SMAs. The commission had been urged to ban clearcutting as well, because of the destructive impact on scenic and natural resources. The Forest Service declined to do so in the final draft. The commission could not, of course, under the terms of the Act. Just to be clear, it added a policy in the scenic resource protection and enhancement section declaring that, "The goals, objectives, policies and guidelines in this chapter shall not affect agriculture or forest practices." Seeing this

138

together with the policy statement about Key Viewing Areas and Landscape Settings, the Friends feared that scenic protection regulation in the GMAs had effectively been gutted.

The Forest Service designated about 62 percent of the SMAs as open space in the final draft. The attorney who had represented the plaintiffs in the lawsuit to block release of the final draft plan called attention to looming problems regarding the implementation of the open space designation. One of the conditions of effective implementation is that conflicting public policies not undermine the possibility of achieving goals. The attorney noted that a very large proportion of the stock of forest land that the Forest Service had hoped to use for exchange had been designated critical habitat for the endangered spotted owl. By the beginning of 1991, the Forest Service had spent $19 million of the $40 million authorized to acquire lands. The attorney claimed that the remainder of the money would be grossly inadequate to acquire the remaining forest lands placed in restrictive land use categories.

The commission made changes in the parts of the plan dealing with open space. The open space designation for the Columbia River disappeared because port districts in the gorge had worried that the designation would disrupt river-based economic activities. The commission also cut the amount of land that had been designated candidate open space to 5 percent of the GMAs (not including the river), dropping the total from the 11,649 acres initially proposed to 5,710 acres. It declared a policy to use the open space designation as a scenic protection device to compensate for the commission's inability to regulate forest practices in GMAs, except if there was an improvement on the land. The commission clearly sought to limit, to the greatest possible extent, the use of the open space designation on private property. Environmentalists took the cut as a profoundly troubling political statement.

Most of the official commentary on the Final Draft Management Plan came from environmental groups and people living outside the gorge, who attacked the document for its perceived weakness. The Friends wrote to Richard Benner expressing feelings of abandonment by a commission it believed was trying too hard to make peace with its local opponents:

> As you know, we supported and defended the Preliminary Draft Plan. However, the Final Draft is a blueprint for disaster and we cannot support and defend it. If weakened further or left unchanged, the magnificent

landscape of the Columbia River Gorge will be forever destroyed. The publication of the Final Draft reveals that the Commission has lost the vision which drove the preparation of the Preliminary Draft. When controversy arose, instead of standing fast and recognizing that protection and enhancement of Gorge resources are the primary purposes of the Act, the Commission gave in to the loudest voices. The result is a Plan that is clearly contrary to the intent of Congress. Where the Preliminary Draft struck an excellent balance between protecting resources and providing for reasonable growth, the Final Draft is shifted entirely too much in favor of economic development.

Anticipating a future filled with intense watchdogging and legal activity, the Friends wanted the commission to change the appeals procedure. The final draft said that only those parties who had participated at the county level would be eligible to take part in the appeal proceedings. The Friends saw a threat to their watchdog capacity in this requirement to keep an eye on six counties. The commission declined to change the process.

Chuck Williams summed up the environmentalist dismay in characteristically blunt language: "We understand fully the dilemma you commissioners are in. Thanks to Congress' awful legislation . . . you are forced to choose between protecting important lands and treating landowners fairly. Thus, we are very upset that you gutted the plan. . . . Folks, it's all over in the Gorge—and we lost."

Yet Washington state and local gorge officials didn't feel that they had won. Quite the contrary. Klickitat County thought that the final draft was still far too rigid. Words such as "shall" and "must" angered county officials, who wanted the discretion to shape implementation to fit local circumstances. If the document was not changed, the county said, Klickitat County would simply refuse to adopt it. Hood River County took a similar stand. Skamania County likewise found the final draft unacceptable. County leaders were deeply disturbed at the prospect of being held liable for takings-related claims. They demanded that counties be held harmless for any liability resulting from the implementation of Gorge Commission guidelines. And after all the commission's efforts to respond to economic concerns, Skamania County still found "that the management plan is generally hostile to Gorge residents and to economic development. . . . There is no

140

balance between environmental protection of Gorge resources and the economic well-being of Gorge people."

Most troubling to the commission was Washington governor Gardner's continuing dissatisfaction. The governor wrote a lengthy letter to the commission that began with unequivocal support for the Act and resource protection. However, he felt that the plan did not distinguish between the Special and General Management Areas in its stringency, adding that "The plan's guidelines are still much too specific." Gardner went on to tell the commission what it ought to do: "The simplest way to accomplish our objectives," Gardner wrote, "would be to redefine plan policies as 'guidelines' and refer to existing guidelines as 'examples' . . . Use of numerical standards and the word 'shall' are appropriate for implementation ordinances, but should be avoided in the management plan. Guideline language should clearly express a policy objective or performance expectation." He also believed that the plan should offer generalized rather than specific descriptions of uses within land designations, while counties should identify specific permitted and review uses; the open space designation on private property within GMAs ought to be eliminated to reduce the possibilities of legal challenge; and nonregulatory strategies, including technical assistance and public education, ought to be employed to a much greater extent.

The commissioners struggled with Gardner's proposals. The ideas clearly resonated with the three Washington county appointees—Sourek, Bleakney, and Thompson—and Gardner appointee Rothrock. The Oregonians, plus Cannard and Chapin, saw too many risks. Variable designations and procedures might diminish protection, they feared. Reinig felt that plans need specifics. "The two states have different philosophies . . . and it comes down to a difference of opinion by those who have worked with and have experience with land use planning," she argued. "Broader definitions will depend on appointees and the political atmosphere. . . . The plan would be open to a subjective viewpoint and development would not be controlled." Clark's instinct was "not to give any more. . . . We have given a lot; in fact, I think we have given too much." Hansell summed up the feeling of the majority of his colleagues when he said that he could not see a way "to accept the Governor's proposal without lessening the standards of the plan."

141

This stance over specific standards, performance zoning, and trust of local governments contrasts with New Jersey, where the Pinelands Commission was very flexible in its approach to the process by which it approved local plans for meeting regional goals. The commission negotiated individually with townships and counties to achieve its broad objectives while meeting many local concerns. The Pinelands flexibility was possible, however, because of the power of the Pinelands Commission to override local decisions. Lacking any such power, the Gorge Commission has tried to make sure that county ordinances are adequately specific and stringent to stand on their own.

Amendments and Adoption

The commission was not yet done with changes, though. Before voting on adoption of the Management Plan, it incorporated several amendments. These included a few more deletions of open space, more flexibility for the counties regarding recreation development, and a pledge by the commission to extend appropriate assistance to any county defending against a takings claim. Benner wrote to the commissioners that these and other changes aimed at greater flexibility for the six gorge counties and reduction of their implementation costs. In response to the Friends' concerns, the commission eliminated the phrase "as much as possible" regarding increasing recreational access to the Columbia River and its tributaries, and clarified the status of Key Viewing Area and Landscape Setting guidelines. They still could not be used as grounds to deny proposals that were otherwise authorized, but compliance was mandatory.

Staff also proposed to diminish the substantial tribal government role in cultural resource protection that a commission majority had written into the draft plan. These recommendations surprised the commissioners. According to Rogers, "No one had imagined that the Commission would be fighting its own staff, in addition to the Governor of Washington, five counties [Multnomah was the exception], and officials within the Department of Agriculture." The commission voted unanimously to maintain their policy.

The commission finally took up the question of approving the Management Plan at an emotional meeting on October 15, 1991. Skamania County appointee Nancy Sourek, with the

142

Acreage of land use designations		
	GMA	**SMA**
Agriculture	**68,114**	**7,449**
Large-scale agriculture	58,673	
Small-scale agriculture	6,766	
Agriculture—special	2,675	
Agriculture		7,449
Forest	**30,209**	**33,820**
Commercial forest land	21,322	
Large woodland	2,885	
Small woodland	6,002	
Non-federal forest		25,947
Federal forest		7,873
Open space	**5,523**	**71,859**
Recreation	**1,036**	**1,438**
Public recreation	895	1,438
Commercial recreation	141	
Residential	**7,327**	**60**
1-acre minimum lot size	244	
2-acre minimum lot size	1,146	
5-acre minimum lot size	2,732	
10-acre minimum lot size	3,205	
Residential		60
Commercial	**195**	**0**
Rural center	171	
Commercial	24	
Water	**33,643**	**0**
Columbia River	32,907	
Major lakes	736	
Indian trust land (exempt)	**2,957**	**474**
Total	**149,004**	**115,100**
Urban Areas (exempt)	**28,511**	
Total Scenic Area	**292,615**	

Source: *Management Plan for the Columbia River Gorge National Scenic Area* (1992), page 20.

support of Klickitat County appointee Bleakney, proposed that the plan be amended to permit counties "to adopt ordinances with provisions that are equal to or provide greater protection than the provisions in the plan." She stressed that such flexibility would facilitate the partnership that had thus far been lacking in the gorge planning process. She and Bleakney saw little risk to the commission in giving the counties a chance to take ownership of the plan and act responsibly and creatively. Clark County's Thompson and Rothrock also liked the idea, but the motion lost 8-4.

Clark then pointed out that the commission was now at a historic moment. Each commissioner, even those who were greatly troubled by the plan, expressed admiration for the staff and great respect for colleagues. Rogers pointed out that they had all been together for four and a half years; she gave credit to chair Hansell for setting a high standard that discouraged parochial bickering.

Chapin moved adoption of the Management Plan as amended. Bailey seconded the motion. The vote was 9-3 in favor. Bleakney, Reinig, and Sourek voted no.

The Last Act

The commission faced one more controversy before it sent the plan to the secretary of agriculture for concurrence. The three commissioners who had voted against approval wanted to append a minority report explaining their views. They wanted the secretary, current and future commissioners, and the public to know that they supported greater flexibility for counties to propose their own implementation approaches if they were equal to or more protective than those in the gorge plan. The majority refused to permit a minority report to be attached. That did not prevent critics from otherwise communicating their opinions, of course.

The Skamania County commissioners, for example, wrote to the regional forester, whom they felt would represent the secretary in reviewing the plan, enclosing copies of their own statement of opposition and the minority report. They claimed that "the Skamania County that objected to the passage of the National Scenic Area Act is not the same Skamania County that is writing to you today." The new, improved county had adopted zoning, and was proud of its ordinance. But the Gorge

144

Commission had ignored it—and the other counties as well. Why? Why did the commission also ignore legitimate economic development needs? Skamania County officials believed the process had been biased from the start against economic considerations by an imbalanced commission and its handpicked executive. Skamania County wanted the regional forester to send the plan back to the commission for revision, "to make the plan the precedent setting and outstanding document it was originally envisioned to be; not the heavy-handed prescriptive zoning ordinance the Commission adopted."

Both governors also went to see the regional forester. Oregon governor Barbara Roberts strongly supported the plan, while Washington's Gardner explained his concerns and set out his recommendations. There were similarities between the dynamics of developing Interim Guidelines back in 1987 and the 1991 plan. The Forest Service Scenic Area office had originally proposed a prescriptive set of Interim Guidelines. Top agency officials had balked at the specificity, so gorge planners came up with an approach based on performance standards that was politically and technically viable. The Gorge Commission had now sent to the secretary a plan that resembled in its specificity the initially proposed Interim Guidelines. Gardner and the commission minority were suggesting the same performance standards approach that had evolved earlier. If such an approach had been viable in 1987, would it be viable now?

Edward Madigan, secretary of agriculture, tried hard to make it so. In February 1992, he wrote that he believed the plan was consistent with the Scenic Area law, and had to be given a chance to work. However, he conditioned his concurrence. Madigan wanted the commission clearly to express an intent to use its discretion to maximize the protection of private property. He also wanted a paragraph added to the plan that permitted the counties the flexibility to adopt ordinances that provided protection equal to or greater than plan provisions. The secretary's thoroughly ambiguous response threw the commission into turmoil. The Act had not contemplated concurrence with conditions. According to the Act, the secretary would either concur, fail to respond—which amounted to concurrence—or deny concurrence and state reasons. If concurrence was denied, the commission would either revise and resubmit, or vote to override. Had the secretary concurred or not? What was the status of the conditions he had stipulated?

145

The Friends and the Sierra Club put the commissioners on notice: if they decided against interpreting the secretary's letter as concurrence, then a lawsuit awaited them. Columbia Gorge United, bitter opponents of federal intervention, threatened a lawsuit if they did.

The New Commissioners and Executive Director

Clark and Cannard, original Friends and supporters of a unified, detailed approach to land management, had been replaced. Oregon governor Roberts appointed Louie Pitt, Jr., who worked for the Confederated Tribes of the Warm Springs Reservation of Oregon, to replace Clark. Gardner appointed Vancouver businessman Vaughn Lein to replace Cannard. Richard Benner had resigned as executive director to accept the directorship of the Oregon Department of Land Conservation and Development. Commissioner Gail Rothrock was appointed interim executive director. In her place, Gardner appointed commissioner Nancy Sourek. Skamania County designated Kathleen Butcher as its representative. While Pitt would support the plan, Lein and Butcher supported Gardner's approach.

When the commission met in March to wrestle with the secretary's response, several new commissioners were in place, as was a new executive director. All the old feelings about governance, including trust and partnership, came pouring forth. After a great deal of debate, including three tie votes, a commission majority decided that the secretary's letter was a significant change that justified consideration of a plan amendment. Commissioners then voted 9-3 to consider the secretary's two conditions when a plan amendment process was in place. Bleakney, Butcher, and Reinig, from Klickitat, Skamania, and Hood River counties, voted no. The plan would now go to the counties, which would have to declare whether or not they would produce implementation ordinances.

Why weren't performance standards a viable approach to plan implementation, as they had been for Interim Guidelines? In the eyes of the Friends, it was far more feasible to monitor the case processing activities of one implementing agency (first the Forest Service, then the Gorge Commission) than those of six counties. The Friends had supported a lead role for the Forest Service; they were prepared to trust it. The counties, of course, were a different story. Moreover, the theory of planning espoused by the Friends, as well as by commissioners Chapin, Rogers, and, interestingly, Matthew of Wasco County, placed overriding emphasis on coherence at the regional level. Performance standards applied by six counties threatened, in their view, to undermine a coherent approach to gorge management. Top Forest Service officials

146

and the secretary clearly wanted to permit local discretion in order to minimize political and legal problems, as they had during the interim. However, given continuing support from the Northwest congressional delegation, from the Oregon governor, and from environmental groups and local jurisdictions for the SMA portion of the plan, denying concurrence outright probably seemed unacceptable. Hence, the secretary's ambiguous effort to appear responsive to all interests.

The final result was a management system in dynamic tension. As the Columbia River Gorge Commission took political heat from both sides, the Forest Service quietly dropped into the background. The intense debates over flexibility, property rights, and proper attention to economic growth expressed serious differences. So did the stylistic divide between Portland and gorge leaders. Nevertheless, the adversarial tone of the debates concealed some important commonalities—most basically an affection for the gorge itself. The challenge in implementation has been to find that common ground.

chapter 6

Testing the Waters: From Plan to Action

*"The Columbia Gorge is for everyone to enjoy. To tarnish its
beauty by destructive development would be the shame of all of
us who call this place our home."*
      Tom Koenninger, 1993

The great beauty of the Columbia River Gorge should be
protected. No one disputes this basic premise, no matter
what their opinion of the National Scenic Area. Some
speak eloquently about the spiritual values of the gorge, its
capacity to renew and restore people worn down by urban life.
Others whose families have been there for a century or longer
use traditional names for places they know well, remember
where and why wells were dug, understand how the parts of
the landscape work together. Both visitors and members of
multi-generational gorge families have their favorite trails and
wildflower meadows.

The dispute over management of the gorge has remained
intense after completion of the Management Plan and its
acceptance by the secretary of agriculture in March 1992. A
number of influential leaders in the gorge claim to favor the
basic purpose of the Act; many quickly qualify that support
with complaints about implementation. The most common
criticism says the planning process was a sham that ignored
local voices. A contrasting minority believe that the Gorge
Commission has failed to move strongly enough to protect the
gorge. Virtually everyone is ready to suggest major or minor
adjustments to the Act.

The split between outsiders and residents remains as
strong in the mid-1990s as it was during the congressional
hearings a decade earlier. People who live in metropolitan
Portland-Vancouver or have strong metropolitan ties are
positive about the Act and see different strengths and
weaknesses than do gorge residents. The general unpopularity
of the Act and of Congress itself make it harder to find open
supporters within the gorge. However, there is a clear
generational split here. Younger leaders with local
backgrounds and residents by choice mix words of praise with
their criticisms and look for ways to accomplish local goals
within the framework of the Scenic Area. Older leaders are

How different groups evaluate the Scenic Area Act			
	Portland/ Vancouver	Residents by Choice	Local New Generation	Local Old Generation
Strengths of Act	**14**	**17**	**11**	**10**
Protects from development	4	5	4	5
Protects beauty	2	4	1	2
Focus on need for change	3	2	3	0
Emphasis on economy	2	3	1	0
Limits federal impact	0	0	1	1
Recognition of Tribes	3	3	1	2
Weaknesses of Act/CGC Plan	**3**	**17**	**18**	**26**
Economic hardship	0	4	5	6
Lack of flexibility	0	3	5	5
GMA/SMA designations	2	5	5	9
Forest practices	1	2	1	3
Weak environmental protection	0	3	2	3
Number of people interviewed	4	9	7	11

Source: see Sources for chapter 6

eager to talk about the weaknesses of the Act and reluctant to find any strengths. They may see the Gorge Commission as unwilling to recognize local expertise; attack the hearings process in the development of the Management Plan; lament that the Friends of the Columbia Gorge, through their influence on the Gorge Commission, seem to have achieved in the planning process what they could not achieve in Congress; or see a continuing conspiracy of Portland elitists subverting the Act's intended partnership approach.

Continued debates over the merits and effects of the Scenic Area center on two issues of balance. Arguments about how best to accommodate economic change within a preservation process are no surprise, for the legislation's two goals built such tensions into the Scenic Area. Less expected are the equally strong arguments about the proper mix of top-down decision making based on credentialed expertise and bottom-up decision making that draws on local knowledge, with county governments presenting themselves as the true voice of the people. Buried in the debate is a fundamental argument over the character of the gorge as a place. Advocates of

149

areawide planning tend to believe that Portland and the gorge are complementary parts of a single region. Defenders of localism find such arguments both unconvincing and disingenuous, for *they* see multiple microregions, with sharp contrasts within the gorge itself and a wide chasm between the gorge and the urban Northwest.

Protection Politics: New Players, New Scripts

The work of implementing the Management Plan has reshuffled the political environment of the gorge as politicians and players position themselves within the new system of land use regulation and economic development incentives.

The locally based environmentalists of the Columbia Gorge Coalition have complained repeatedly that the Interim Guidelines were weakly enforced, with development approvals for hundreds of new rural homes in the first five years. In August 1993, Coalition founder Chuck Williams angrily accused the Gorge Commission of deliberately ignoring the public input that would allow it to be an informed and vigorous defender of the gorge. More broadly, such critics accuse the Gorge Commission of bogging down in regulatory minutiae and losing any comprehensive vision of the region's future.

More commonly, residents in the heart of the gorge think that the commission has been excessively rigid. Some original members of the Gorge Commission see early inflexibility as "a necessary evil." Opponents frequently accuse the commission of insensitivity to individual hardship and disdain of local knowledge. Thoughtful opponents recognize that the tight time schedule set by Congress, a steep learning curve, and the heavy workload all pushed the early commission to be systematic or, as some see it, arbitrary. Yet even these constraints are seen by some as part of the intent to ignore local opinion through congressional mandate.

Particularly resented was control of residents' decorative choices under the Interim Guidelines. Word-of-mouth stories are often more powerful than official statistics in fixing local understanding of complex regulations. Nearly everyone in the gorge has heard about the homeowners who were forced to change the color of their drapes in a picture window prominently visible atop a bluff. A sailboard enthusiast and

150

Richard Benner

Richard Benner, the first Executive Director (1987-92), was a focus for dissatisfaction. Previously an attorney with 1000 Friends of Oregon—a land use lobbying organization that carefully monitors Oregon's cities and counties for compliance with state planning goals and mounts legal challenges when it thinks localities fall short—he advocated strict enforcement of detailed regulations. His approach may have been necessary to get the plan prepared and adopted, but many in the gorge found him abrasive and dictatorial. Benner, rather than the commission, became the lightning rod for complaints about the new regulations; local officials viewed him as the wrong person to build the strong local cooperation needed for effective plan implementation. Some early members of the Gorge Commission saw initial stringency as necessary caution. (Photo: Hood River News)

developer thinks it stupid to have allowed green houses in the east end of the gorge, where the predominant land tone is brown, but not blue on a house framed against the sky. The regulation of exterior paint colors was similarly contentious in the Adirondacks. Skamania County commissioner Melissa Carlson-Price argued the need for standards based on objective impacts such as glare rather than the plan's "subjective preference" standards.

Gravel pits, identified as an eyesore as early as the 1980 Park Service report, have been another point of contention. Proponents of the Act would like to see the elimination of the several quarries that take bites out of the riverside cliffs. Residents who have grown up with the quarries as parts of the local landscape and economy see shutdown orders as arbitrary departures from common sense. Their closure hurts owners and employees and adds to the costs of construction and road maintenance. Pit owners and county commissioners also contend that shutdowns will also increase air pollution from long-haul truck traffic.

Levels of sophistication about institutional processes clearly affect reactions to Scenic Area regulations. A local resident with limited resources and experience in dealing with

151

planning bureaucracies who is seeking five acres in a rural setting to locate a double-wide manufactured house is likely to respond differently than a moneyed and savvy outsider who wants a protected site for an expensive dream home. Members of the local real estate industry see the management process as fair but complicated and foreign to the informality of rural communities. On the other hand, it is argued that the commission's strong stance during the peak of the windsurfing boom discouraged big California developers from even attempting to build in the gorge.

From Tough Cop to Consensus Builder

Time can mellow the bureaucratic process. Once past their first deadlines and precedent-setting decisions, several of the regional management agencies to which we compare the Gorge Commission adopted more conciliatory styles. If the initial regulatory leadership has to be mindful of setting precedents, then their successors may be able to allow flexibility within rules that have become well established.

As the first round of appointees cycled off the Gorge Commission in 1992-93 and new members took their place, gorge residents similarly began to perceive a more open and compatible commission. New appointees, especially to the Washington slots, have been more local in orientation and less concerned with vigilant regulatory protection. An example is 1993 appointee Tim Southworth, a small-business owner with experience with land trusts and an interest in finding "ways to encourage people to have a more stewardship attitude toward the resources here without imposing more regulation." A Gorge Commission that is closer to the area's political center reduces the pressure on future governors to appoint active anti-regulators who might decisively shift it away from a protectionist orientation.

Similarly, local officials and economic development staff saw Benner's successor—Jonathan Doherty, a former National Park Service planner from the east coast—as an improvement. Doherty appeared more open to dialogue with gorge residents and less devoted to a preset agenda. He describes his goal as facilitating a process that includes all interested groups and individuals. He believes in alternatives to a strictly regulatory regime and in devising cooperative approaches to enhancing gorge natural and scenic values. One Hood River resident

152

	Portland/ Vancouver	Residents by Choice	Local New Generation	Local Old Generation
How different groups evaluate the management of the National Scenic Area				
Elitist/Portland control	0	3	5	6
Locals can manage	0	2	6	2
Oregon planning system imposed	0	1	2	2
Other OR/WA dichotomies	2	2	2	5
Destructive to economy	0	2	4	3
In favor of act	4	5	3	2
Benefits economy	4	5	0	2
Need for mgmt./OR system good	3	2	0	0
National benefits	4	2	2	2
Act good, implementation flawed	0	4	3	1
Number of people interviewed	4	9	7	11

Source: see Sources for chapter 6

noted "a new commitment to working with the counties and communities." Gorge commissioner Ray Matthew agreed that Doherty "has more of a tendency to help people as long as it's within the rules and within the law. He's been responsible for many changes in people's attitudes."

The Gorge Commission thus seems to be evolving from tough cop to consensus builder. Completion of the Management Plan has allowed the commission to assume a lower profile as a responsive rather than proactive agency. The move to the center has been hampered by the legacy of resentment over the legislation, Interim Guidelines, and planning process, but ironically helped by criticisms of its actions by the Friends. Members of the commission in the mid-1990s cite the bureaucrat's comfort that they must be doing something right if everyone is upset.

Role of the Friends

Many residents in the gorge remain angry at the Friends of the Columbia Gorge and their perceived control of the legislation and the planning process. Other outsider environmental groups earn testy comments, but the focus of the distaste is the Friends. Letter-to-the-editor sections of gorge newspapers testify that residents continue to believe that the Friends conspired to ram the Scenic Area through Congress and then received control of the Gorge Commission and the executive director's position to complete their agenda. The Friends, one Hood Riverite wrote, "are not friends of the gorge, but friends of some metropolitan people who would force their rule on the people of the gorge."

The changing role and composition of the Gorge Commission has recently begun to isolate the Friends as a political player. Increasingly, the Friends find themselves on the outside of commission decisions, monitoring the commission and Forest Service to make sure that they remain faithful to the intent of the Act. Their role is much like that of 1000 Friends of Oregon in relation to Oregon's land use program. The Friends have several times taken the commission to court, sometimes to seek clarification of responsibilities and sometimes to challenge decisions. Said the organization's executive director explaining a lawsuit in March 1993: "At some point the spirit of cooperation runs out."

Portland activists who helped to create the Scenic Area also have a new way to influence land use in the gorge. In 1989, the San Francisco-based Trust for Public Land established a Portland office. The Trust for Public Land is an implementing rather than lobbying organization, purchasing private lands in the Special Management Area of the gorge and (it hopes) reselling them to the Forest Service or other land management agencies.

In the mid-1990s, the Trust for Public Lands and the Friends of the Gorge are the only strong environmental organizations that are paying close attention to the gorge. Chuck Williams and the Gorge Coalition have limited resources and have stopped actively pressing a more radical approach. Other local environmental groups focus on very specific issues or subareas such as the protection of Columbia River tributaries. The result is to institutionalize the Friends of the Columbia Gorge as a continuing and long-term player and an outsider to the management process.

Flexibility and Local Control

The issue of "ownership" of the gorge and the role of local knowledge are still important foundations for political differences. Over the last decade, many individuals and groups have claimed that they best understand the gorge and its problems, continuing the debate triggered by Portland's earlier efforts to determine the future of the gorge. Much of the talk and the anger within the gorge is about who can best protect its values as a place.

Residents often take the Scenic Area Act itself as a slap in the face. They resent the implied message that they are unable to manage their own communities and protect what they also see as a valuable resource. The antipathy broadens. Some point fingers at outsiders: inept federal agencies unable to manage their own lands; throngs of tourists; pushy Portlanders looking for trophy homes. The future of the gorge, residents complain, is in the hands of "gorp for lunch people" and the "champagne and brie crowd." This anger unites people like Chuck Williams, one of the major supporters of gorge protection, and Joe Wrabek, a proponent of the free market and local control, both of whom blame the arrogant Portland elite.

Within the gorge, the ideal of local responsibility speaks to heritage, community, and stewardship. Both large and small landowners are often proud of their care for their own land. They engage in ecological restoration, reduce erosion by planting hedgerows, and leave properties open for hiking and horseback riding.

Such local knowledge and stewardship can be especially valuable because of the diversity of the Columbia Gorge. Vegetation ranges from sagebrush slopes to oak-dotted hills to dense forest. Growth has impacted each county differently, and each has its own political style. A number of local residents argue that a Management Plan that does not recognize these differences cannot work.

In part because of this intraregional diversity, the most common theme in local complaints is the lack of flexibility to recognize community differences. In other words, the Scenic Area Management Plan is said to ignore variations in landscape, existing county plans, Oregon and Washington planning and environmental laws, local expertise, and local goals for development. Opinion leaders in Skamania, Wasco, and Klickitat counties are especially concerned about the need

155

for more flexibility in gorge management. The same issue motivated the three gorge commissioners who voted against plan adoption.

Many in Washington resent the imposition of an Oregon process. The legislation itself looked to the Oregon land use system as a model, and Richard Benner brought close familiarity with that process to the planning process. Critics claim that other tools of planning that are part of the Washington system, particularly the environmental impact review process, are unfairly ignored.

Residents also object that the Gorge Commission and the planning process disdained good planning done prior to the Act. County officials were disappointed that the Gorge Commission did not start with existing county plans and adapt them to the needs of the Scenic Area in partnership with local governments. Wasco County Judge John Mabrey and Hood River County Commissioner Jerry Routson think that Oregon counties fared no better in the process than Washington. Instead, elected officials on both sides of the river believe that they have been saddled with inflexible regulations that are too specific and in some ways inconsistent with the intent of the Act.

The first direct conflict between counties and the Gorge Commission came over the takings issue and the consequent reluctance of county commissions to adopt implementing ordinances. Opponents of the Scenic Area repeatedly claim that Management Plan regulations on open space and density constitute uncompensated takings of private property. Commission and Forest Service staff counter that they carefully crafted the Management Plan to leave property owners with viable economic uses, thereby protecting local governments from lawsuits. Nevertheless, the counties continue to fear that they will get stuck with the bills for defending such suits and may find themselves faced with enormous compensation awards.

County Ordinances

156

With the takings question as background, the ongoing debates over county implementing ordinances are one more window into the differences of political culture and concern from county to county. They also continue the ongoing argument about the extent of discretion available to counties in implementation.

Chenowith Table, controversially designated as open space. (Photo: authors)

Multnomah County, with a very small amount of private land in open space designations and a large urban population, was not seriously bothered by the takings issue. Responding to Portland preservationists, it was the first county to submit an implementing ordinance and the first to receive approval in June 1993.

Skamania County, which worked hard both to meet local political concerns and also to meet the requirements of the Management Plan, was next to adopt an ordinance. The county was anxious to gain access to the economic development opportunities of the Act to counter crashing timber employment. The county planner described the effort as a "leap of faith" by a reluctant community, while several gorge commissioners praised the working relationship of "trust and goodwill." To meet local concerns, however, the ordinance contained a sunset clause that would rescind the law in January 1995 if several conditions had not been met: (1) receipt of federal economic development and conference center funds; (2) adoption of hold-harmless provisions to protect the county from takings litigation; and (3) amendment of the Management Plan to allow a locally controlled variance process for Scenic Area land uses.

Controversy over the sunset clause demonstrated the level of distrust between preservationists and local politicians. Then-gorge commissioner Kristine Olson Rogers, a Portland

157

attorney, argued that the variance idea had already been rejected during plan formulation. She also feared that the county could receive federal funds on the basis of its approved ordinance and then opt out through the sunset clause. In the end, the Gorge Commission accepted the Skamania County ordinance by a 10-1 vote in September 1993, prompting the Friends of the Columbia Gorge to sue the commission to force rejection of the ordinance as inconsistent with the Act and Management Plan (the suit failed in state courts and was dismissed on a technicality in federal court). In the end, Skamania County extended the sunset clause for one year but then tentatively repealed it in January 1996, pending satisfaction of several conditions.

The four other counties failed to submit ordinances by the January 15, 1993 deadline, causing the Gorge Commission to adopt ordinances for each county as provided by the Act. The commission's regulations went into effect July 1, 1993, making the commission the local planning board for General Management Area lands.

Wasco County then followed the lead of Skamania County and submitted an ordinance with a sunset clause to be triggered by (1) failure to receive interpretive center funds; (2) inadequate protection of the county from takings litigation; or (3) failure to secure changes in the treatment of open space in the GMA, particularly 740 acres of private land on the Chenowith Table west of The Dalles. The commission ruled the ordinance inconsistent in September 1993 but offered to cooperate in working toward a compromise. On June 3, 1994, it accepted a rewritten Wasco County ordinance with a "quasi-sunset" clause stating that the county would reconsider in January 1996. The clause was intended to protect the county from possible takings litigation if landowner concerns about the Open Space designation of Chenowith Table were not resolved. As of November 1996, one major landowner had reached accommodation, the second was pursuing administrative solutions, and the county had neither invoked nor revoked the clause.

158 **Clark County**, on the north side of the river, was too busy with meeting requirements of the Washington Growth Management Act to take quick action about its small piece of the Scenic Area. Adoped in 1990 and 1991, the Growth Management Act required large and fast-growing counties, such as Clark, to develop plans to meet state land use and environmental goals and to develop growth boundaries around urban areas. The county put a Scenic Area implementing ordinance approved by the planning commission on hold in 1995 because of uncertainties created by the passage of Washington Initiative 164, which proposed compensating property owners if their land was rendered less valuable by actions taken by governments. In May 1996, however, the ordinance was accepted by the Gorge Commission. Approval by the secretary of agriculture in June made Clark County the fourth gorge county with authority to review and approve land development applications within its section of the Scenic Area.

Hood River County completed an ordinance in April 1995 that contradicted the Management Plan on two key issues. One was the county's refusal to apply open space designations to private land. The other was the desire to continue to operate the county gravel pit located along the old Scenic Highway east of town or to receive compensation for loss of the gravel supply. The Forest Service had found the pit inconsistent with the Scenic Area under the Interim Management Plan. When the Gorge Commission returned the ordinance, as expected, opinion within the county was mixed. Officials stressed that they were simply trying to add economic balance and common sense to the regulations. With 74 percent of the county in public ownership, they were unwilling to place further restrictions on the land base. "We really do appreciate the beauty of the gorge," said the county planning commission chair, "but we also believe private landowners need to be protected." In contrast, the politically conservative *Hood River News*, perhaps aware of the importance of the tourist industry, had already criticized the county for grandstanding:"Telling Congress to go fly a kite doesn't strike us as a good way to get something approved by the federal government." The gravel pit remained active until the county, Forest Service, and state in 1996 worked out a three-way land swap that traded the quarry for timber lands of comparable value and guaranteed a supply of gravel for road work. In January 1997, the county commissioners approved an ordinance that was expected to be acceptable to the Gorge Commission, although the county included a provision calling for repeal within one year unless it sees favorable outcomes for readjustment of Scenic Area boundaries around the cities of Cascade Locks and Hood River and support for additional administrative costs.

Klickitat County refused on principle to prepare an ordinance, arguing that Washington planning and environmental regulations already provide superior protection without extra bureaucracy. The county had been relatively active in land use planning in the early 1980s. By the 1990s, however, internal political conflicts and changes on the county commission had turned it into an official opponent of the Scenic Area. Of all the gorge counties, it appeared most committed to its Old West economy. While its politicians fought the Scenic Area regulations, timber industry interests undermined an effort to compete for the federally assisted conference center.

Overlaid on the political differences between Oregon and Washington are differences among the pairs of counties that cover the western, eastern, and central gorge. In the metropolitan counties of Multnomah and Clark, the Scenic Area has strong public support from city residents and relatively little impact on private land. Reproducing a tension that antedates the Scenic Area, residents in the eastern counties of Klickitat and Wasco have the strongest antipathy for city-style regulation. There is a strong sense that the Management Plan regulations, especially for open space, are inappropriate for arid grazing lands. The central counties of Hood River and Skamania split the difference politically as well as geographically, with substantial numbers of newer residents who span the gap between Portland environmentalists and the old guard. Political leaders see great economic development benefits from the Scenic Area and tend to argue about specific concerns rather than clashing cultural values. They have been essentially cooperative, although moving at different paces.

Behind all the problems of balance among the different interests and cultures within the gorge—Washington and Oregon, east end and west end, old timers and interlopers, residents and temporary users—are questions of consideration and courtesy. Many gorge residents feel disrespected by a Portland elite. Skamania County's Ed McLarney summed up the felt need to balance decision processes as well as planning goals when talking to a reporter in 1991: "What we need is a blending of mutual respect for the people of the area and their rights, along with respect for environmental and scenic concepts."

Lyle, a designated Urban Area on the Washington side of the Columbia River. Inset: sign advertises Waterfront Property for development—14 lots available with completed streets and utilities.
(Photo of Lyle: USDA Forest Service. Photo of sign: authors)

Boundaries

In 1986, Congress split the gorge into distinct subregions—Urban Areas, General Management Areas, and Special Management Areas—ostensibly as a way to differentiate more and less sensitive lands. In the decade since, the multiple treatment of gorge lands has emerged as a serious and frequently cited problem.

Some environmentalists worry that the Urban Areas were drawn too generously, making large tracts of land available for development with only local planning and permitting controls. In particular, they point to Washington, where Congressman Sid Morrison worked with the drafters of the legislation to secure 17,990 acres of Urban Areas. The Oregon side, despite having two-thirds of the gorge's urban population, has only 10,520 Urban Area acres. With some justification, critics fear small-scale versions of suburban sprawl, with forests of backlit gasoline and fast food signs contrasting with green hills.

161

More immediately troublesome is the uneven geographical distribution and different treatment of land in the two types of management areas. During the legislative process, the Friends and other Portland-based advocates focused their attention on the heavily forested and precipitous landscapes between Portland and Hood River, making sure that the bulk of these lands were classified as Special Management Areas. They were less concerned with the dryer, more open lands in the eastern third of the gorge, leaving local environmental groups to fight for protection of sensitive areas such as Washington's Major Creek and Catherine Creek. The legislation placed 86 percent of SMA lands in the four western counties and 56 percent of the less protected GMA lands in the two eastern counties (which have 86,100 GMA acres and only 16,610 SMA acres).

Corbett, Oregon, was not designated as an Urban Area, though it is a developed community. Shown here is the old Corbett School; a large new facility sits across the road. (Photo: authors)

The Forest Service is unable under Scenic Area authority to purchase or exchange land in these GMAs. The situation is ironic: Chuck Williams pushed very hard for the inclusion of purchasing authority for such lands, but Congress denied it in order to appease opposition in Washington. The decision was a strategic mistake, for it prevents the land adjustment program from relieving economic impacts on small owners. Another quirk of the separate designations is the different parcel sizes required for a new house in forest or open space zones: 40 acres in the SMA but 100 acres in the GMA. What has become a stock story tells of individuals who were able to clear-cut their property but were not allowed to build a home.

The commission also faces the problem that congressional staff made hurried and sometimes flawed decisions in drawing the specific boundaries for the Urban Areas and the Scenic Area as a whole, depending on information that was sometimes inaccurate or inadequate. Preservationists have a list of additional areas that should be protected, such as

162 Burdoin Mountain northeast of White Salmon (outside the Scenic Area) and a prominent waterfront peninsula included within the Urban Area of Lyle, Washington. There are also areas that many think should have been left open for development, including land to the east of the industrial city of Washougal, Washington, property owned by the Port of The Dalles, and the rural community of Corbett, which includes twenty businesses as well as several hundred houses. Boundaries were a significant issue during the development of the Management Plan and the Gorge Commission postponed all active consideration until after the plan had been adopted. The Scenic Area Act gives the commission authority to make minor shifts between the two management areas and to expand Urban Areas, but more substantial changes would require congressional consideration.

Debates about lines on the landscape point up one of the problems with abstract rule making. Initial planning and zoning by outsiders under severe time constraints is likely to produce errors. Some result from a lack of adequate local knowledge, others from the need to produce zones at a gross scale. Landscape experts criticize the Pinelands plan, for example, because it does not recognize half a dozen subregions with distinct socioeconomic and natural characters.

More broadly, however, the problem is a basic difference between the goals of regulation and those of place making. The exact location of a boundary line matters very much to local people who are deeply familiar with the landscape. It is far less important to regulators who realize that every zoning boundary is partly arbitrary, and whose chief concern is not the precise categorization of properties but rather the appropriate size of the zones. Each side thinks that the other is missing the key point.

Rowena

An example of problems with the Management Plan is the designation for Rowena, Oregon, for limited residential and no commercial development. Rowena is an area with a new state park, adjacent upscale housing along the waterfront, and an older rural center on the inland side of I-84. The waterfront at Rowena was cut off from most access by the Union Pacific rail tracks and was minimally developed in the early 1980s. Opinions differ whether all development should have been restricted in this area, whether the old townsite was a natural site for more intense rural development, or whether new retailing might go on the waterfront. Wasco County already had a local gorge overlay in place to control development and wanted the commission to recognize Rowena as a small community. Wasco County Judge John Mabrey believes it should have been designated an Urban Area, although its own school and firehouse have been gone since the 1940s. Environmental activists such as Chuck Williams believe that development should have been further restricted, either to allow more public access or for protection as a natural area. A different view comes from Tyler Keyes, a windsurfer and a developer of the upscale housing, who sees his action as providing significant benefit to the area. When he bought his original parcel, the park not exist. The boardsailors helped make the park a reality and the new development in the area has added to both the aesthetics and the tax base of the area.

163

Residents of the Scenic Area say that the Management Plan is riddled with errors in the classification of specific parcels, usually in applying stringent open space zoning inappropriately. Scenic Area planners were careful to incorporate local knowledge by holding community workshops, using local environmental groups to help with inventories, and hiring consultants from the Pacific Northwest. Wary about the need to be able to defend land use classifications in court, the commission made numerous adjustments in response to citizen comments. Nevertheless, local residents will never consider outside professionals to be truly knowledgeable about local problems. Managers continue to get no credit for getting most things right but plenty of blame for getting anything wrong.

Land Adjustment

For Portlanders, the story of the Scenic Area is the protection of sweeping vistas from I-84, Washington 14, or the Scenic Highway. For residents of the core counties, the story is also the pain experienced by small landowners who have seen their land rezoned from five-acre residential to forty-acre minimum lot size or open space. Critics talk about neighbors who had planned to finance their retirement by selling their property or widows who were financially devastated by the Management Plan. Through telling and retelling these stories take on their own life as local myths; their factual basis is less important than their ability to articulate common fears. One of the main problems is the absence of any purchase provisions in the General Management Area. Another is strict interpretation of restrictions on use. Considerable local sentiment supports allowing case-by-case exemptions for long-standing property owners who are facing increased limits on the use of their land.

In contrast, gorge residents have little sympathy for Californians or other outsiders who want to make a quick profit or for large landowners who are presumed to have the political clout to be protected or bought out at an attractive price. Many residents and some gorge commissioners think that land acquisition by the Forest Service has focused too much on large blocks of land, to the economic detriment of the owners of small parcels; to leave two- or three-acre parcels in

164

areas restricted to agriculture or forestry looks to many like a taking.

Beginning in 1992, the Forest Service faced mounting criticism that it was rapidly using up its $40 million authorization for land acquisition without clear priorities. The purchase and exchange or "land adjustment" program had operated as an independent entity since 1986, with little connection to the Forest Service and Gorge Commission planning efforts. Instead, the Forest Service had usually acted on offers from willing sellers. The result, said Gorge Commission staff, was that "lands acquired by the Forest Service have not clearly reflected the standards of the Act or the land use designations and guidelines in the Management Plan."

From 1986 through June 1996, the Forest Service paid $33.3 million to acquire 7,398 acres in Oregon (for $9.9 million) and 19,572 acres in Washington (for $23.4 million). Many of the larger acquisitions came in the first years of the program, when large, sophisticated landholders offered to sell. More than half of the total was in Skamania County, location of large tracts of private timberlands. Apart from the Trust for Public Land, which sold 6,300 acres for $8.7 million through 1992, the largest sellers were timber companies.

Critics of the Forest Service have two technical concerns. One is the worry that soaring prices have made it impossible to acquire as much land as originally anticipated. Said Chuck Williams, "We could have had a Mercedes for the price of a Volkswagen. Now we have to pay Mercedes prices for a VW." This in turn fuels the fear that sensitive and/or highly restricted parcels will therefore go unacquired, opening the door to takings litigation. These fears are substantiated by the experience in the Tahoe area, where the Forest Service also operated on a willing-seller basis that did not promote protection goals.

Late in 1992, the Forest Service began to develop a procedure for selecting and prioritizing eligible parcels. It offered a preliminary draft of its Land Adjustment Strategy in May and a fuller draft in October 1993. Criteria for establishing eligibility of a parcel for adjustment include open space designation; parcel size under 40 acres; sensitivity of resource; inconsistent quarries and landfills; recreation sites; and potential for enhancement. Criteria for prioritizing eligible lands are the possibility of reasonable economic use; existence of a threat to the land; and significance of the land. Criteria to

165

refine the ranking of most needed lands include enhancement potential; consolidation of holdings; value; and hardship to owner.

Gorge Commission staff and commissioners responded that the land acquisition strategy was too complex, and came too late to guide the bulk of the purchases. Doherty suggested that the Forest Service focus on parcels that are vital to preserving land use designations, precluding litigation, and protecting sensitive resources. The implication is that land adjustment should take individual hardship into account and focus on two types of properties. One type is the thirteen thousand acres of privately held SMA land designated as open space—land essential for meeting basic plan goals. The other type is vacant, undevelopable parcels of fewer than forty acres, the resolution of which is highly important for the political leadership of the gorge counties.

Gorge Commission debate about this issue provided the backdrop for a political bombshell in April 1994, when commissioner Kathleen Butcher (Skamania County) filed a Freedom of Information Act request for current information on Forest Service purchases. The Klickitat County Commission had recently called for a General Accounting Office audit on the purchase program. The other gorge commissioners backed Butcher's request, having passed a resolution asking for similar information.

Although the two management agencies patched up this rift, it suggested a weakness in the Scenic Area's bureaucratic partnership. Behind the clash is the suspicion that the Forest Service offered sweetheart deals for large landowners and backdoor access for the Trust for Public Land, excluding small property owners and ignoring locally significant places. The Trust for Public Land, which has positioned itself to be an active player in gorge land acquisition, worries that an explicit policy may be a mistake because it will generate political opposition. It also worries that the time required for detailed inventories and rankings might render the whole approach moot. By implication, the Trust would prefer that the Forest Service quietly and quickly work from its own shopping list.

166　　Land purchases also fuel county officials' budgetary worries. Forest Service acquisitions under the Scenic Area legislation have removed twenty thousand acres of private land from the county tax rolls (including eight thousand acres valued at $4 million in Skamania County alone). The Act authorized a total of $2 million for payments to local governments to compensate for the resulting decline in property taxes; the payments are expected to continue through 1999. Nevertheless, county officials still wonder where ongoing funding will come from, especially as they face declines in shared revenues from timber sales. As tourism increases, counties will bear major expenses associated with sheriff patrols, search and rescue, litter, accidents, and parks. They see increased planning costs and potential litigation costs.

In mid-1996 it was clear that the acquisition program had painted itself into a corner. Forest Service staff scrambled to explain how there had been nothing wrong with its earlier willing-seller policy though nearly a hundred parcels remained on its high-priority list. With $6.7 left, the price tag for the high-priority list was substantially over $25 million. Opponents of the Scenic Area have swamped the Forest Service with offers to sell their SMA lands. If the Forest Service is unable to accept a legitimate offer within three years, the parcel automatically shifts to a GMA farm or forest designation, potentially undermining the more stringent SMA protection. Although the Friends of the Gorge have repeatedly returned to Congress to ask for additional purchase funds, the likelihood of extra appropriations to relieve the Forest Service dilemma is small.

Stick First, Carrot Later

The Scenic Area Act explicitly started the management process with the stick of Interim and General Management Plans, with their new regulations and limitations on the use of private land. Earmarked economic development funds for the conference and interpretive centers and open-ended economic development funds were to be available following adoption of county implementing ordinances. In fact, the first earmarked funds did not arrive until 1994, and county arguments with the Gorge Commission further delayed most of the open-ended funding. An unsurprising result has been anger in the gorge that the federal government has broken its promise.

Nevertheless, the gorge management agencies are slowly moving into their post-planning roles. The commission is expected to evolve into an appeals court for land use decisions and a catalyst for the enhancement of gorge resources. The Forest Service will function as an economic development agency.

167

Pat Bleakney

(Photo: Hood River News)

Pat Bleakney's leadership in forming the Gorge Trust is an example of the thoughtful accommodation of gorge residents to the conservation process. A rancher with 6,000 acres in Klickitat County, Bleakney was an early opponent of the Scenic Area who traveled to Washington to testify against the legislation. As Klickitat County's first appointee to the Gorge Commission, he pushed for greater reliance on county planning and was one of three commissioners to vote against the Management Plan. In the 1990s, health problems forced him to sell his gorge property to the Washington Department of Natural Resources and to move to Vancouver. However, he remained interested in building local awareness of and responsibility for better managing the gorge as a middle way between the bureaucracy of the Management Plan and the adamant resistance of the property rights movement. Bleakney's involvement in gorge management has given him a much stronger awareness of limitations on the use of natural resources. As he now says, the only thing worse than planning is no planning at all.

Late in 1992, the Gorge Commission received a grant from the Oregon Community Foundation to develop a "New Approaches" proposal to flesh out the Management Plan. The ideas that emerged were an elaboration on the idea of a land trust. Commissioners strongly, although not unanimously, thought that their work could be effectively supplemented by an independent, nonprofit entity that could acquire and manage land in the General Management Area and serve as a focus for education and action by conservation-minded gorge residents.

168

The first steps came in May 1995 with the incorporation of the Gorge Trust as a bistate nonprofit corporation. With an interim board chaired by former gorge Commissioner Pat Bleakney, the Gorge Trust hoped to build local acceptance of the Scenic Area, to further the protection of the most sensitive natural areas through private stewardship as well as regulation, and to facilitate the transition to a diversified but increasingly information-based economy. Depending on its success in fund raising, the Trust anticipates projects in land conservation, sustainable development, education, and local community partnerships.

In the post-planning stage of the Scenic Area, the Forest Service will revert to one of its well-established roles as a recreation development agency. The Scenic Area Act authorizes $10 million for recreational projects. The first is the Doetsch Ranch multi-purpose day-use recreation area along a mile of riverfront near Washington's Beacon Rock State Park ($1.63 million). Several projects are planned at entrances to the gorge: Steigerwald Lake Gateway in Washington and Sandy River Delta, The Dalles Riverfront Trail, and Memaloose Campground in Oregon. Additional Forest Service projects not dependent on Scenic Area funding include new trails at Multnomah Falls and Husum Riverfront Park on the White Salmon River.

A second $10 million was authorized for regional economic development. Allocation of the funds requires an elaborate committee structure under the aegis of the Oregon Department of Economic Development and Washington Department of Community Development. Two years of meetings went into creation of a twenty-two-member Bi-State Advisory Council and completion of a Bi-State Economic Development Plan in November 1993. The Bi-State Council will advise separate Oregon and Washington investment boards. The Gorge Commission will certify that proposals are consistent with the Management Plan and land use ordinances and the state investment boards will decide which projects to fund. The funds are not available until counties have approved ordinances and Congress makes appropriations. By reserving some of the money for revolving loan funds, the states will ensure that counties that are slow to get on board are not completely left out.

As the economic development dollars dribble into the gorge economy they will represent the power of established governmental entities to foreclose innovative approaches to community development. The bureaucratic allocation procedures amount to patronage for state economic development departments and local governments. Left by the wayside is an innovative proposal from real estate consultant Will Macht to use the entire amount to capitalize a gorge development bank. The independent locally based board of

169

such a bank might have used the funds as seed money for projects to build local community development capacity and to ease and direct the economic transition. Instead, Congress transformed the original idea into the earmarked funds for economic and recreational development and the conference center and interpretive center.

Despite lost opportunities, it is important to remember that broader market forces have dwarfed the direct measures associated with the Scenic Area. The industrial structure in the gorge was in rapid transition throughout the 1980s, and the Act is an effort to promote rationality in that transition. Within this context, the Scenic Area has begun to reallocate economic activities and benefits, creating a new mix of winners and losers.

Few local residents are willing to boast publicly of profits from escalating property values. They focus instead on rising property tax rates and on those properties outside the Urban Areas where land values may have declined. Nevertheless, the Scenic Area certainly has the potential to increase the value of some property by restricting the land available for development. As would any rezoning, the Scenic Area regulations have shifted the pattern of real estate development, offering the potential of windfall profits on some properties and undercutting the market value of others. Rising values are real, particularly in the Urban Areas, but also for some land in the management areas, even when uses are restricted.

Taken together, the four counties in the heart of the National Scenic Area now have a spread of industries quite similar to the states of Oregon and Washington. Over the past thirty years, the consistent thread has been the decline of large-scale manufacturing and the simultaneous growth of services. New industrial uses are now confined to the Urban Areas where they will have to compete for land with recreational and tourism facilities, which are already pressuring older manufacturing in places such as the Hood River waterfront, redrawing the dividing line between the old and new economies.

170

The Promise of Planning

The multiplicity of planning steps and development projects involved in putting the Scenic Area into operation were intended to offer residents a variety of points of attraction and attachment. Instead, the complexity of the implementation process has given opponents of the Scenic Area a series of defensive positions from which to contest its advance. Some of the issues were predictable in 1986: land acquisition, boundaries, allocation of economic development funds, extension of Oregon-style land use regulation.

Given substantial local opposition, the Gorge Commission and its staff were destined to face sharp criticism no matter what they decided or how forthcoming their procedures. Local residents have strong memories, and will resent the Interim Guidelines and the first Gorge Commission long after the regulations and personnel have changed. The current commission gets little credit for smooth implementation of the Management Plan. Property owners flooded the commission with development applications in the first years of the Scenic Area. There were 299 applications in the peak year 1989. As initial panic about the Scenic Area fades and the counties take up review responsibilities, the commission's annual application load has fallen below one hundred, with a 98 percent approval rate.

The Scenic Area is also doing well in the sensitive area of cultural resource protection. Only a small fraction of the Scenic Area has been thoroughly surveyed for historical artifacts and archeological sites. Public conflicts have arisen over issues outside the purview of the Management Plan, such as in lieu fishing sites for traditional sites drowned by federal dams or a Native American camp-in in 1994 to protest an upscale subdivision within the Lyle Urban Area that reduced access to riverfront fishing sites. Meanwhile, the commission has quietly reviewed development applications for impacts on cultural resources and suggested changes to appropriate development plans.

Hostility to the Scenic Area continues in part because local opponents attribute more unity and power to the commission and the Friends than they actually have. Similarly, in the case of Lake Tahoe, activists on both sides of a controversy tended to question the legitimacy and reasonableness of their opponents' motives and also saw "their opponents to be more powerful and themselves less powerful, than is probably the

171

case." There is evidence of a similar mismatch of perceptions and reality in the gorge, as each side misconstrues the other's influence and attributes self-serving motives.

Local residents have been more cautious in their acceptance than the framers of the legislation hoped. From the Portland viewpoint, many gorge residents have been less pragmatic and more stubborn than expected. The residents themselves characterize their noncooperation as determined and principled. The delay in the arrival of federal economic development funds is in part a reason for local reluctance, in part an excuse. More broadly, continued disagreement over the basic structure of the Scenic Area as a regulatory system has kept the arguments of the mid-1980s fresh. Local officials and opinion leaders in the middle and east gorge assume that the intent of the Scenic Area Act was regional-local partnership and lament its failure. Advocates of scenic preservation, in contrast, have always defined partnership as an undesirable compromise with the interests and political forces that the Act was designed to neutralize. These strikingly different conceptions promise continued conflict.

Many (but not all) residents of the Scenic Area remain convinced that the regulatory structure is basically illegitimate because there was no problem that required intervention. Members of the Friends look at Skamania and Clark county subdivisions, I-84 truck stops, and factory outlet malls at the entrance to the gorge as the first stages of a mighty flood of trashy development that was stemmed in the nick of time. Residents may look at the same things and see isolated investments rather than a pattern of threats. They contend adamantly that their knowledge and care would have sufficed to prevent serious degradation. They would agree with Mary Lou Braden that "those who have invested in the gorge because they love its scenic areas would not defeat their own interest by destroying that beauty" and with the *Hood River News* that "gorge residents have been responsible stewards of the property within the scenic area. That's the main reason the area remains worthy of continued attention." For residents who share these views, the Scenic Area is an insult, not an ally against powerful forces of change.

172

To date, only a minority of gorge residents approach the Scenic Area as an opportunity to transcend the century-long debate between Portlanders and gorge communities and think proactively about a larger regional future. Growth *is* happening in the gorge, and many residents *are* unprepared for its consequences. The attractiveness of sailboarding for observers as well as participants, the general push for tourism, and the growth of the Portland-Vancouver metropolitan area have placed strong development pressures on the communities lining the Columbia River. Before the Scenic Area, the "black ice curtain" of dangerous winter travel was the major barrier to exurban sprawl. Gorge commissioner Sally Newell of Underwood, Washington, puts the central issue clearly: "When greed meets desire, some local officials have a hard time turning away the bulldozers. Since greed and desire have met here with increasing frequency in the past few years, these folks should be glad the act passed when it did."

As we evaluate the implementation process, we agree with Pat Schroder, then the mayor of White Salmon, who commented in 1993 that potentially the most important accomplishment of the National Scenic Area can be to help residents recognize the value of what they have and awaken them to the need to actively shape their community futures. Without a regional vision for economic change, the gorge will continue to evolve into an economic annex of metropolitan Portland-Vancouver. Without local leadership that moves beyond the specific concerns of city and county governments, the future of the gorge will continue to be decided in Portland, Salem, Olympia, and Washington. If gorge residents dislike the Scenic Area vision as shaped by Portland-based organizations and activists, their challenge is to use the Scenic Area program as a means to shape an equally compelling alternative.

CHAPTER 7

Whose Gorge Is It?

"We are responsible for imagining our way into a just society, and an economy based on our own labor and inventiveness rather than continued deep plowing of the pastures of heaven."
     William Kittredge, 1996

Folks in Hood River are accustomed to waking to the perpetual battle between the warmth of the rising sun and looming clouds churning in on the west wind. For hints about the day's outcome in the battle of the elements, they can dial 386-1336 for the KIHR and K-105 Weather and Information Line. The touch-tone options encapsulate the dynamics of the changing gorge. After pressing 1 for the weather, windsurfers can plan their day by pressing 2 for the "K105 gorge wind report" and scope out their evening by pressing 3 for the "what's happening report with live entertainment around town." People who still depend on the old economy have the option of pressing 5 for "the current fruit-frost forecast."

The same diversity that requires this unusual phone menu also fuels sharp and angry confrontations. On May 7, 1996, the city council room in Bingen, Washington, erupted in chaos as a former council member (and restaurant owner) stood in the audience to denounce a newly appointed member for negative remarks about environmentalists and windsurfers. "I don't like environmentalists because they take jobs away from people," said the new council member. The two men scuffled several times before police hustled the angry citizen from the room. Two years earlier, a Hood River Port Commission hearing had elicited a similar confrontation. "This is no longer your town; this is our town," a windsurfer told the tense meeting on May 10, 1994. The specific issue was whether to allow a new motel on undeveloped land along the Columbia River adjacent to downtown Hood River. On one side were members of the gorge's economic establishment who hoped to tap the flow of tourist dollars for long-time residents through real estate development and service jobs. On the other side were advocates of the windsurfing business whose preference was unencumbered waterfront space as a community amenity. Tempers flared, gavels pounded, an edgy crowd spilled out the doors with the question unresolved.

These feelings reflect some of the social and economic tensions that have been mounting in the Columbia River gorge over the last decade. The gorge is very much a region in economic and social change, and the National Scenic Area is central to this transformation. The Act was designed to help manage and guide change . . . and perhaps to accelerate it. In taking on these tasks, the Forest Service and Gorge Commission have found themselves in the middle of deep divisions and bitter controversies within the gorge itself and between gorge and Portland interests.

In writing about this political bargain and planning experiment, we have chosen our title with care. The Columbia River Gorge National Scenic Area is not the *only* prototype for the New West, but it is an important and valuable model. The gorge in the late 1990s is emerging as an example of the New West, with the possibilities and problems that accompany fundamental change.

Maintaining the Greenline Balance

As developed in Western Europe, a greenline park is a compromise that tries to combine the multiple goals of maintaining a working landscape and protecting local economic opportunity in the midst of measured scenic preservation. The Columbia River Gorge National Scenic Area is a greenline program in this sense. Congress defined the Scenic Area to include substantial areas of farm and rural residential development. A land use inventory in 1986 found 2,927 houses within the Scenic Area but outside designated Urban Areas, three-quarters in Skamania, Klickitat, and Multnomah counties. The legislation recognized the character of the area by attempting a balance between the potentially contradictory goals of accepting the gorge as a developed and populated working landscape and making scenic preservation a priority in future decisions. The balance was to be implemented through such policies as limited and voluntary property transfers, maintenance of existing housing, and acceptance of a measure of local control and participation in implementation.

175

The greenline approach is appropriate for, far more than its possible models around the United States, the National Scenic Area deals with the social landscape rather than the natural environment. In several comparable cases, regulatory effort has centered on the protection of a *measurable* natural resource. The underlying purpose at Lake Tahoe, for example, is to preserve the purity and clarity of the lake itself. The ecological justification for regulation of the Pine Barrens is to protect the quality of surface and sub-surface water. The Cape Cod National Seashore protects specific dune, marsh, and pond areas. The original reason for an Adirondack Park was to protect water quality and flow, although regulations now deal with both aesthetic impacts of development and generic environmental concerns such as wetlands.

The Columbia River Gorge is even less pristine than the Adirondacks. Timber harvest, fishing, grazing, farming, and the operation of huge dams have drastically altered its natural systems. Human action has so modified the gorge's forests and fish runs that they can only be managed, or perhaps restored, not "preserved." The key environmental resource that remains relatively unaltered is scenery. Like their counterparts in the Adirondacks, gorge regulators face the task of selling a nebulous aesthetic judgment to local people who may not share it, indeed of transforming that aesthetic and moral judgment into public policy. The judgment, held by many urban supporters and by some rural residents, is that the natural and/or pre-European environment is more attractive and meritorious than the European-American built environment. Nature may also seem an element of stability that counterbalances an uncertain and intimidating future. Certain elements of the built environment, such as the Columbia River Scenic Highway, are seen as acceptable because of their "sensitivity" (itself an aesthetic judgment), but the bias built into the planning process is that anything new should be unobtrusive.

In this context, critics charge that the Gorge Commission never took the greenline idea seriously. Rather than trying to work out avenues of cooperation with rural residents, the commission leadership from the start devised a top-down regulatory approach to resource protection. Joan Smith, a politically savvy Portlander who served on the pre-1986 Oregon Gorge Commission, complained about the "elitist lack of trust" in the Management Plan. Gorge commissioner Nancy Sourek, from Skamania County, cites the frustrating indifference to the possibilities of a "living landscape" approach that might have adapted management controls to the character of subregions. Gorge residents could scarcely be comforted by the Friends member who told the Gorge

176

Commission that "the beautiful gorge belongs to everyone in the United States, just like Yellowstone Park," or by a 1992 profile of Nancy Russell in a national magazine that carried the title "You Own the Columbia River Gorge" (admittedly not Russell's own words).

Meanwhile, the Friends of Columbia River Gorge have brought a series of lawsuits that challenge Gorge Commission and county regulations, apparently unwilling to let the carefully balanced regulatory process work itself through with local residents increasingly in control of decisions. The Friends have been vigilant against accommodation with local interests on both procedural and aesthetic issues and remain worried that residents in the gorge will take every opportunity to undermine the Scenic Area. They remain concerned that "flexibility" is not just a solution for a few hardship cases, but a code word for an endless string of land division and development requests that will subvert the intent of the Scenic Area.

Gorge Creep

Communities adjacent to the Scenic Area have begun to worry about what one economic development professional calls "gorge creep." The Gorge Commission has commented on the location of a foundry in the Urban Area of Dallesport and on the expansion of an aluminum plant near Goldendale, well outside the Scenic Area. Though they had no authority to control activity in either instance, they commented on potential air pollution effects within the gorge. Environmentalists also resisted a $40-million electricity co-generation facility planned for a site adjacent to the SDS sawmill and plywood plant in Bingen, one of the Urban Areas exempt from Scenic Area regulation.

Gorge creep, with a slightly different emphasis, can also be seen in social changes in communities outside the Scenic Area. Weekending Portlanders can now buy espresso and Italian ices in Trout Lake, Washington, in the shadow of Mount Adams, and enjoy high tea in a historic home in Parkdale, Oregon, at the end of the Mount Hood Railroad. Both towns lie in the Hood-Adams recreation corridor. Trout Lake is the scene of confrontation over the need for strong, enforceable planning and land use regulation outside the Scenic Area. New residents want to see restrictions on

177

potentially detrimental growth, while the Klickitat County
Commission is described as unwilling to take strong action to
control development.

Battling Over Bridal Veil

The continuing conflict of greenline goals has been
epitomized in the 1993-94 battle over a handful of
rundown houses at Bridal Veil, Oregon. Located in the
western end of the gorge, settlement at Bridal Veil dates from
the 1880s. A small company town housed workers who milled
logs that rode a two-mile flume from Larch Mountain.
Although logging operations ended in the 1940s, the Bridal
Veil plant continued to manufacture wooden boxes until 1960.
After that time, a series of private investors owned the townsite
with unrealized plans for real estate developments such as
vacation homes or a motel. Meanwhile, the dozen slowly
deteriorating houses provided low-cost rental housing within
range of jobs in Portland and the gorge. To several Portland-
based members of the Gorge Commission, Bridal Veil and
other hamlets within the GMA were "mistakes" that might well
be "erased" through land use restrictions.

The opportunity came when the Trust for Public Land (TPL)
purchased the property in 1991. The Trust used a large
donation from a prominent Portland industrialist with the
understanding that the site would be cleared and returned to
something like its natural state, with trail access to Bridal Veil
falls and restoration of salmon spawning grounds. The Trust's
eviction of Bridal Veil residents and its demolition plans
elicited strong local protests and triggered a review of the
eligibility of the site for protection as a historic resource by
Multnomah County.

Preservation consultants working for the TPL argued that
each house had been altered so extensively that it had lost its
value as a historic resource, but many historic preservation
activists agreed with the contrary argument that the entire
townsite had historical value as the last surviving lumber town
in Multnomah County. Although we agree with the second
position, the merits of the historic designation are less
important than the motivations of the actors.

On one side were an ad hoc assortment of historic
preservationists, gorge residents with an interest in preserving
housing options, and other local residents with grand schemes

178

for a logging history interpretive center. On the other side was the Oregon office of the TPL, directed by Bowen Blair, former executive director of the Friends of the Columbia Gorge; Nancy Russell was also an important influence. The Trust's argument against preserving a residential community depended on culturally loaded aesthetic judgments. The Bridal Veil renters were said to be transient short-termers rather than members of a real community (although one 1991 resident said she was the fourth generation of her family to live in the area). The houses were described as "ugly," "derelict," and "shack-town clutter" (the latter by John Yeon, the long-time gorge preservationist who owned extensive lands across the river). Russell called the idea of an interpretive center "a lumber mill Disneyland." The conflict was clearly one of differing values and social agendas between urban and rural Oregonians—an encapsulation of the tension between Portland and local visions for the gorge, between New West transition and Old West continuity.

House in Bridal Veil, Oregon, 1996. (Photo: authors)

To remove a somewhat scruffy but affordable community because it is unsightly sets a questionable precedent. It has looked to many observers as if Portland preservationists are trying an end run around the Scenic Area's greenline compromise. "They have moved in with the stated intent of destroying what is here and replacing it with something else of their own devising," said one long-term opponent of the Scenic Area.

179

The Columbia River Gorge and the Stress of Modernization

This study has analyzed the Columbia River Gorge National Scenic Area as part of the transition from a resource to a service economy in the American West. This economic transition, and the associated social changes, constitute a fundamental reshaping of the Old West of resource harvesting. In the language of social science, the gorge is experiencing the process of modernization, with its large-scale organizations, long-distance relationships, and bureaucracies. In the ongoing drama of Western history, the beneficiaries of nineteenth-century conquests find themselves sharing authority and control with newcomers who draw their power from external connections. Modernization is thus the latest step in the process by which North American resource regions have been incorporated into the systems of Euro-American and now global capitalism.

In substance, the Scenic Area envisions a change in the relationships between gorge communities and their regional environment. The traditional relationship has been one of easy movement from town to hinterland for organized and casual economic uses ranging from logging and running cattle to hunting and wood cutting. The new regulations draw a much sharper boundary between old communities, their economies, and the surrounding scenery, which they declare off limits. A systematic approach to enforcement devalues local knowledge and local use patterns in favor of uniform abstract standards.

We can also ask who gets to define the Columbia River gorge as a place. Who gets to prioritize the region's important and essential features? Who gets to arbitrate among conflicting futures? The answer in part, of course, is "outsiders." The Scenic Area legislation originated in the growing spatial reach of Portland and involves the use of federal and state authority to override local preferences. The increasingly complex procedures and rules for managing the gorge disregard local knowledge in relation to abstract expertise. Regulation itself is a networked, professionalized, urbanized style of management compatible with the skills and orientations of New Westerners.

180

Local residents fear that the result will be to turn the beauty of the gorge into an exhibit. One commented angrily that the goal of the Friends of the Columbia Gorge is to erect barricades at the entrances to the gorge and "only let people in on foot for an hour at a time." Another complains that the

Scenic Area "pours lucite overeverything." A third fears that outsiders are trying to create an artificially timeless "snapshot" that freezes change (a phrase actually used by Art DuFault, the first Scenic Area manager for the Forest Service). Also strong is the related belief that local residents will bear all the costs of the Scenic Area against their will. The frustrations of gorge property owners and their anger at being told they are incompetent to take care of the place they live are both potent forces.

Large-scale Management and the Values of Place

Within the gorge itself, increasing complexity will tend to favor large organizations and large capitalists over small landholders. Developers can figure out the rules more effectively than can local residents who want to build on their three-acre parcel. Major landowners like SDS Lumber or sophisticated organizations like the Trust for Public Lands are in a good position to work effectively with the Forest Service. Environmental interest groups, including Indian tribes, have more clout than individual hunters and fishers unless they are themselves organized for lobbying and advocacy.

Will this change in scale of management protect the gorge or actually encourage its destruction? Local residents frequently claim to be better stewards of the land than large bureaucracies. A favorite local example is the unchecked spread of noxious weeds on public lands to the detriment of adjacent ranchers. Another is management of the open grasslands atop the cliffs of the Rowena Plateau in the drier eastern end of the gorge, which produce fantastic wildflowers in early summer. The Nature Conservancy in the late 1980s purchased the 230-acre site from a cattle rancher, fenced it, and designated it as the Governor Tom McCall Preserve. It is highlighted as one of the scenic spots of the gorge, with signs and trails leading visitors through the fields. Are people gently passing through to enjoy the beauty, or are they trampling it beyond recovery? Could this precipitous area be better protected if it were pastureland? In the past it was unprotected, unknown except to a few, and apparently thrived.

The recreationists who crowd Hood River and the central gorge produce similar results, including congested traffic, skyrocketing housing prices, rapid jumps in rentals for

181

importance of regional roots and affiliation, long-term local residents may have a truer and more meaningful relationship with their home ground than do flighty cosmopolitan newcomers. However, we need to be cautious in accepting these neoregionalist claims, for political analysis shows time and again that local place makers with neoregionalist values are not necessarily the folks in charge. Local leadership on American resource frontiers has usually gone to men on the make. The growth coalitions and courthouse cliques that have dominated local governments in small towns and rural counties have consistently overridden the claims of place. They may sometimes appropriate the rhetoric of a land ethic, but as a tool for protecting autonomous decision making rather than as a goal in itself.

The other weakness of insulated communities is the sharp boundaries that they have tended to draw between insiders and outsiders, between accepted and unacceptable members. From the 1920s through the 1940s, for example, European Americans in Hood River County were leaders in efforts to exclude and disfranchise Japanese Americans. European-American residents of the Columbia Gorge have also been eager to dispossess Native Americans from lands and fishing grounds in the name of economic development—memorably with the construction of The Dalles Dam and the drowning of the historic salmon fishing site at Celilo Falls.

Networked New West communities offer the opposite strengths and weaknesses. They are far more *open* as social and economic environments. They more easily accept and accommodate conflicting values and new enterprises. They are easy places to be a newcomer. However, they face the criticism of superficiality and the fear that they treat places as disposable consumer products.

The Pace of Change

Change is inevitable in the Columbia River gorge. In a very real sense, the Scenic Area was emergency intervention, coming just before revival of the Pacific Northwest economy in the late 1980s. By the mid-1990s, demographic planners expected another half-million people in the greater Portland area within two decades. In the midst of this regional boom, education, volunteerism, and small-scale stewardship by individual landowners would not have been enough to stem the tide of development. Louie Pitt, of the Confederated Tribes of Warm Springs, puts the situation bluntly: until *all* residents develop a sense of heritage and

185

close relationship with the land, artificial measures such as the Scenic Area are necessary to protect the gorge.

Change has come in different ways in different parts of the gorge. In recent statewide elections voting patterns in Hood River and Wasco counties were closer to those in the Portland suburbs than those in eastern Oregon. In a 1996 election for the U. S. Senate, Portland Democrat Ron Wyden narrowly defeated Pendleton Republican Gordon Smith. Wyden ran strongly in metropolitan Portland and came within one or two percentage points of winning Hood River and Wasco counties, while in eastern Oregon Smith ran up two-to-one margins. Hood River and Wasco counties similarly voted with the metropolitan area and against eastern Oregon in 1990 on Ballot Measure 5 (they favored property tax limitation), in 1992 on Ballot Measure 9 (they opposed restrictions on gay rights), and in 1994 in the gubernatorial contest, favoring Democrat John Kitzhaber over Republican Denny Smith.

In contrast, Klickitat County in 1995 retained a leadership that viewed tourism as a nuisance rather than an opportunity, though even within that one county, the adjacent towns of White Salmon and Bingen are substantially different in political goals and style. Skamania County has been eager to enjoy the economic benefits of the legislation. Wasco County is caught between eagerness for economic benefits and fear of losing its "western" ambience. Multnomah and Clark county governments have paid little attention to the Scenic Area, while their urban residents treat the gorge as weekendland.

Intergovernmental Juggling

The National Scenic Area raises a complex of issues of intergovernmental relations. It involves both "horizontal" state/state coordination and "vertical" coordination among federal and state agencies and local governments. Although we have noted some of the problems of bistate coordination, we have chosen to emphasize problems related to the assignment of responsibilities among local governments and translocal agencies, which we believe are the most problematic for the Columbia River gorge. They are also the most common problems for land use planning and economic development planning nationwide. The allocation of responsibilities among different levels of government involves fundamental political and cultural values.

In contrast, state-to-state coordination is a more tractable problem of political interests. The United States has developed

186

a variety of multi-state forums in which states can work out compromises between differing economic interests and political agendas. Examples range from the Colorado River Compact to the New England River Basin Commission to the Northwest Power Planning Council. The Columbia River Gorge Commission, created through a bistate compact to mediate between Oregon and Washington interests, is one more example of such a forum.

One result of the tensions between local and national interests in the gorge was the partial failure of the nationalization strategy. The impetus for the national legislation was a *regional* concern and its details were the results of *regional* political compromises. The resulting Scenic Area Act was less strongly centralized than many advocates of a federal role had hoped. The first interest in a strong federal role in management emerged during the late 1970s, when the Carter administration was pursuing an activist park development strategy. Legislative and implementation decisions, however, came during the Reagan and Bush administrations—bad years for efforts to expand federal environmental responsibilities. We can see the temper of the times in the legislation itself, shaped in part by the reluctance of the Forest Service to directly regulate private land. The Reagan administration's approach to federal land policy is also apparent in the response of Forest Service headquarters to the Interim Guidelines and in the secretary of agriculture's back-handed concurrence with the Management Plan. The architects of the Scenic Area expected the Forest Service to guard environmental values while the Gorge Commission represented local property. In fact, the commission was the stronger environmental guardian in the first decade.

The Scenic Area builds on Oregon's system of land use planning through regulation; Washingtonians who have complained about the imposition of Oregon planning are right. The Management Plan takes important ideas from Oregon's statewide planning goals. It functions as a comprehensive land use plan to be implemented through zoning regulations. In this way it differs from the Pinelands and Adirondack programs, which depend more heavily on case-by-case review of development permit applications. In comparison with its counterpart agencies in the East, the Gorge Commission is more rigid but less powerful. It imposes detailed and specific land use regulations, but is expected to rely on local implementing ordinances and local officials for enforcement.

187

Evaluating the Management Plan

What about the Management Plan itself several years after adoption and approval? Has it come up to the expectations of environmentalists? Is it as intrusive and misguided as many local residents claim? It is a decade too soon for sure answers, particularly because everyone interested in the Scenic Area recognizes a lack of systematic data on Scenic Area impacts. In 1996, Forest Service and Gorge Commission staffs began to pull together a long-term monitoring effort. They expect to assess the economic and environmental impacts of the Scenic Area, including the fifteen hundred developments approved since 1986, and to evaluate whether implementing ordinances are working as expected. However, we can test the results to date against the four goals of the Gorge Commission's own 1988 Vision Statement:
- stewardship of the gorge;
- leadership for implementation of the National Scenic Area;
- partnership with communities, tribal governments, and agencies;
- and a vision of the gorge as a single region.

As a development regulation program, the Scenic Area has substantially accomplished its explicit stewardship goal. Environmentalists have criticized the Management Plan for giving too much away, but it is likely that the tradeoff is minimal political acceptability and good legal defensibility. The Scenic Area is legally sound. The entire Scenic Area apparatus, the planning process, and the Management Plan have all weathered challenges in state and federal courts. There is agreement on all sides that a major flaw was the different treatment of the SMAs and GMAs in relation to land acquisition, providing for federal purchase or exchange in the former but not the latter. In general, however, advocates of scenic protection have gained a law and Management Plan that substantially limit land development in favor of preserving natural and cultural resources.

188 The results are less favorable if stewardship is seen as a social commitment rather than a management process. The Scenic Area Act created incentives that have been useful in securing the cooperation of large landowners and local governments, but offered little to help small property owners. The Gorge Commission needs more management tools for encouraging small property holders to become involved in cooperative management of forests and streams. It also faces the simple problem that it cannot afford to be proactive. For nearly a decade its annual funding has fluctuated around $500,000, compared with $3 million or more for the Tahoe and Pinelands programs. A tight budget means a small staff that necessarily concentrates on the immediate work of reviewing development applications to the neglect of efforts to foster grassroots stewardship—surely a result opposite the goal of fiscally conservative budget cutters. In short, the managers of the Scenic Area have not yet had time or resources to work at crafting a conservation ethic that spans local social differences. With changing leadership at the Gorge Commission and a new Gorge Trust beginning to afford consideration to alternative voices, however, we are hopeful that it will be possible to accommodate locally based stewardship within the regulatory process.

The commission provided strong leadership in the narrow sense of forging ahead and doing the job of creating and implementing a Management Plan. In so doing, however, it created very few followers and only a limited number of partners. It has worked well and creatively with the four Columbia River tribes as genuine partners. Many non-Indian residents and county officials, in contrast, continue to complain about the lack of partnership between Gorge Commission and local governments. These complaints range from lack of respect for pre-1986 planning to lack of concern about the impacts of the Scenic Area on county responsibilities and budgets.

The political legacy of the planning process is dissatisfaction among environmentalists *and* local residents, who can look at the same institutions and processes and see very different creatures. The Friends wanted a powerful agency to take care of the gorge. Instead they got a mixed management system that requires constant monitoring in county seats as well as Gorge Commission and Forest Service offices. It is a nerve-wracking situation for environmentalists (and the four tribes), who do not trust local residents to consistently make acceptable decisions. Many gorge residents however would be puzzled by the idea of the gorge planning system as a fragile institution threatened by local appropriation. To them the new bureaucratic apparatus looks monolithic, threatening, and confusing.

189

The fourth of the 1988 goals was to create a sense of the gorge as a single region tied together rather than separated by the Columbia River. Here too the results are mixed. The Scenic Area legislation promoted a regional consciousness by creating the first gorgewide institutions, but it undermined that consciousness by incorporating county governments as participants. The Management Plan has brought common land use procedures to both sides of the river, but it has angered many Washingtonians in the process. In larger regional terms, it remains clear that the Scenic Area continues to represent the ascendancy of Portland. As economic transition proceeds, individuals and groups with the sophistication and resources to deal with the Gorge Commission and Forest Service will have the advantage in shaping a New West out of the Old.

Gorge residents too, of course, can utilize the new bureaucratic system for resource economy goals. Ranching and logging industries have long known how to work with the Bureau of Land Management and Forest Service to the benefit of local economic interests. Landowners who have flooded the Forest Service with offers to sell SMA lands (in the hope that failure to complete the transaction within three years will kick their land into a less limiting classification) are just as sophisticated as the Friends of the Columbia Gorge. Local governments in the gorge are also more astute than urban environmentalists may credit. Nevertheless, gorge residents still face the possibility of being squeezed by the fund-raising, litigating, and public relations capacities of Scenic Area advocates.

This being said, we argue that the Scenic Area is likely to temper the economic transition and perhaps ease its pain. The creation of a new institutional forum for debating regional issues should make backroom deals more difficult and provide the opportunity to air new ideas. Thoughtful discussion of economic change may help gorge communities move beyond the tourism industries envisioned in the legislation and position themselves to attract some of the higher wage industries and jobs of the post-industrial economy. The land use regulations themselves are likely to discourage megadevelopers. In these ways, the Scenic Area speaks to and balances the needs of a variety of interests and residents. It **190** tries to fend off the dangers of the rapid shift from a natural resource economy to a tourist economy that historian Hal Rothman calls a "devil's bargain." It meets the call of tough-minded environmentalists such as Charles Wilkinson for adequate standards and procedures to deal with the disputes that are inevitable in a dynamic society. Despite our criticisms, we believe that the Columbia River Gorge and its people are better off with the National Scenic Area than without.

To summarize, we see in the Columbia River gorge a process of market penetration and economic diversification in the shadow of Portland, including a substantial role as a metropolitan recreation zone. Proximity to Portland has meant investment and economic development since the nineteenth century, but has also brought less welcome metropolitan agendas. Economic use has been followed in the late twentieth century by regulatory intervention, again driven from metropolitan Portland. We have characterized the process as a painful transition between Old West and New West, using these terms as shorthand for sets of values and behaviors associated with different types of economic activities and, consequently, different uses for natural resources. Old and New Wests also represent different styles of living in the landscape, based on different ways of making a living.

Old and New Visions of the West

The contest between old and new visions for the gorge has played itself out in debates and political battles over creating and implementing the National Scenic Area, a complex system for managing land development and economic change. We have characterized the content of these debates as choices between place making and rule making. The Columbia River Gorge National Scenic Area seems to shift authority from locally knowledgeable leaders to external (or at least externally oriented) bureaucracies and impose specific guidelines and standards on previously vague and flexible decisions.

On closer examination, however, it is not clear that the dichotomy is so precise. We need to be reminded that the American system of private property rights, central to the Old West economy and society, is itself a regulatory system. It tells people what they can and cannot do, and enforces those rules with a massive legal and administrative bureaucracy. And the regulators themselves often claim to be working as place makers—protecting place with more powerful tools than previously available, and with a broad understanding of how a specific place fits into a larger whole. At the extreme, they argue that they are rescuing places from people who claim to love but really exploit them.

191

The Scenic Area is thus an effort to shift the *scale* and *scope* of place making from town and county to a larger region, in effect redefining the locality to which residents give loyalty. The Scenic Area program tries to find common interests among multiple jurisdictions and subregions. It is a way to build new regional institutions, foster regional cooperation, and pool resources—all in the interest of giving the people of the gorge a greater capacity to shape their own future in competition with similar regions around the continent. One of the problems during the first decade of the Scenic Area has been the simple fact that it has been easier to see and envision the gorge as a single place from the outside than from the inside.

It is our hope that the Columbia River Gorge National Scenic Area proves in the long run to be a tool that residents can use to plan thoughtfully for their own future. We agree with gorge commissioner George Rohrbacher, from Klickitat County, who writes that "in the not too distant future, I believe the scenic act will be a very valuable tool for gorge residents to use to protect us from *them*!" (referring to Portlanders and their need for a bedroom community and playground). In the late 1970s and early 1980s, environmental advocates in the gorge lacked the political capacity to control place-making decisions. Centralization of decisions and regulation under federal sponsorship was the only practicable alternative to local business as usual—and may have empowered gorge residents by making them more conscious of the special values of their home territory. With the Scenic Area program as a starting place, it may now be time to revisit the possibilities of place making with both old and new gorge residents in the lead and Portland environmentalists in supporting roles.

At the end we return to the contrast between two Wests. The New West carries the burdens of *replacement* in many cases. It means new people, new technologies, new businesses and industries pushing aside the old in the creative destruction of capitalism. The Denver-based "Center for the New West," for example, has appropriated the term for a think tank that has used backing from the telecommunications company U.S. West to study tourism, immigration, telecommuting, and the information economy as sources of a New Western boom.

But the rise of a New West does not have to imply replacement only. It can also involve a deepening appreciation

192

of economic and social variety. It has the potential to be synthesis rather than antithesis. Just as thoughtful Northwestern writers such as John Keeble, Craig Lesley, and David James Duncan struggle to understand and express the complexity of a modernizing region, the greenline concept and the Scenic Area itself are efforts to value the Old West within frameworks created by the powerful presence of the New West.

The New West is not going away any time soon. Urbanization and bureaucratization have been transforming the West for more than a century and will continue to be driven by the growing power of a global economy—a complex of forces that far outweighs the resistant power of individual communities. "Tourism and the educated are in the saddle," writes Oregonian-turned-Montanan William Kittredge, "and they are going to be."

The choice in places like the Columbia Gorge lies between reaction or adjustment. The Old West can respond to the New West antithetically, with angry localistic nostalgia, property rights fundamentalism, and antigovernment militias. Or it can use new tools and opportunities to synthesize and integrate the best of the twenty-first century into healthy communities that develop their futures in partnership with metropolitan interests. Kittredge and other thoughtful Westerners have repeatedly reminded us of the importance of finding a middle ground from which to move forward. We need to invent a new story, says Kittredge, a story about reciprocity and resolution: "We have to talk things out, searching for accord, however difficult and long-winded the undertaking. . . . Our future starts when we begin honoring the dreams of our enemies while staying true to our own." Within the limits of its far less eloquent vocabulary of planning and growth management, the Columbia River Gorge National Scenic Area is a serious and promising response to this challenge.

Sources

General sources

The documentary core of the research is drawn from a series of formally issued planning reports dating from the 1930s to the 1990s. These documents have been published by such agencies as the Pacific Northwest Regional Planning Commission, the U. S. Forest Service, the National Park Service, the Columbia River Gorge Commission, and a number of planning consultants. We have supplemented these documents with the records of public hearings about issues of gorge management and legislation, with the minutes and administrative memoranda of the Columbia River Gorge Commission, and with administrative documents of the U. S. Forest Service.

We have also drawn on a scattered secondary literature dealing with the history and character of the gorge and its features. A handful of this work has been produced by professional historians such as William Lyman, Ronald Fahl, Paul Hirt, and William Willingham. Some is the work of historic preservation consultants and professionals. Much of the rest is the work of local history amateurs and journalists who have been taken by the attractions of the gorge. Outstanding within this broad category is Chuck Williams, *Bridge of the Gods, Mountains of Fire: A Return to the Columbia Gorge* (New York: Friends of the Earth, 1980). Two recent books on the Columbia River provide historical and regional context for the Scenic Area: Richard White, *The Organic Machine: The Remaking of the Columbia River, of Indians and Whites, Salmon, Energy, and Hanford* (New York: Hill and Wang, 1995) and William Dietrich, *Northwest Passage: The Great Columbia River* (New York: Simon and Schuster, 1995). A valuable source of detailed information is Gordon Mathews Euler, "The Politics of Scenery: Scenic Resources Management in the Columbia River Gorge National Scenic Area as a Case Study" (Ph.D. dissertation, Portland State University, 1996).

Aspects of gorge politics, economic change, and implementation controversies have been traced in the Portland-Vancouver metropolitan newspapers (*The Oregonian* and the Vancouver *Daily Columbian*) and gorge community newspapers (*Hood River News, Skamania County Pioneer, Gorge Weekly, The Dalles Reminder*).

The development of the gorge as an economic and social region can be profiled with data from a number of state and federal agencies. Key sources include federal census reports on population and economic activity, federally compiled employment data published in *County Business Patterns*, and state data on timber harvests.

In 1989 we conducted individual or team interviews with a number of the key actors in the development and initial implementation of the legislation. We tried to include representatives of federal agencies, environmental lobbyists, and congressional staffers. These persons included Emily Barlow, staff to Senator Robert Packwood; Richard Benner, executive director, Columbia Gorge Commission; Art DuFault, U.S.D.A. Forest Service, National Scenic Area director; Katherine Jesch, U.S.D.A. Forest Service, National Scenic Area staff; Nancy Russell, Friends of the Columbia Gorge; Paulette Carter Bartee, executive director, Friends of the Columbia Gorge; Mike Salsgiver, staff to Senator Mark Hatfield.

We also used a formal open-ended questionnaire to conduct interviews during 1992-93 with nearly thirty opinion leaders in the Gorge communities. They included Austen Abrams, managing editor, *The Dalles*

Chronicle; Frank Backus, forester, SDS Lumber; Sverre Bakke, Klickitat County Commissioner; Melissa Carlson-Price, Skamania County Commissioner; Bob Chamberlain, forester, SDS Lumber; Stuart Chapin, former Columbia Gorge Commissioner (Washington gubernatorial appointee), White Salmon, Washington; Jonathan Doherty, Executive Director, Columbia Gorge Commission; Lorretta Ellet and Vance Ellet, major landowners, The Dalles; Vicki Ellet, realtor, The Dalles; Scott Hege, executive director, Port of The Dalles; Tyler Keyes, real estate developer, Rowena, Oregon; Tom Koenninger, vice-president & editor, *Daily Columbian*, Vancouver; John Mabrey, Wasco County Judge; Ed McLarney, former Skamania County Commissioner, former owner *Skamania County Pioneer*; Jack Mills and Kate Mills, civic activists, Hood River; Tom Reynolds, attorney, White Salmon, Washington; George Rohrbacher, Klickitat Economic Development Organization; Jerry Routson, Chair, Hood River County Commission; Pat Schroder, Mayor, White Salmon, Washington; Linda Sokomano, civic activist, Vancouver; Dan Spatz, managing editor, *The Dalles Reminder*; Paul Spies, director of corporate planning, Columbia Aluminum; Dennis White, co-founder Columbia Gorge Coalition, Trout Lake, Washington; Joe Wrabek, co-founder Columbia Gorge United, Cascade Locks, Oregon; Chuck Williams, author, co-founder Columbia Gorge Coalition, Mosier, Oregon.

In 1995 we returned for additional interviews to pursue ongoing issues of implementation and economic development with RaeLynn Atay, editor, *Skamania County Pioneer*; Lauri Aunan, executive director, Friends of the Columbia Gorge; Barbara Bailey, former Columbia Gorge Commissioner, The Dalles, Oregon; Pat Bleakney, former Columbia Gorge Commissioner, Klickitat County; Johnny Jackson, chief, Klickitat tribe; Will Macht, real estate development consultant, Hood River, Oregon; Louie Pitt, Jr., Columbia Gorge Commissioner (Oregon gubernatorial appointee), Warm Springs, Oregon; Kristine Olson Rogers, former Columbia Gorge Commissioner, Multnomah County; Nancy Sourek, former Columbia Gorge Commissioner, Skamania County; Bob Thompson, Chair, Columbia Gorge Commission, Brush Prairie, Washington.

Sources for Introduction

A sampling of early guidebooks and descriptions include Leo Samuel, *Portland and Vicinity: Willamette Valley, Columbia River, Puget Sound* (Portland: L. Samuel, 1887); William Lyman's fine book *The Columbia River: Its History, Its Myths, Its Scenery, Its Commerce, Including a Section on the River Today* (New York: G. P. Putnam's Sons, 1909); M. C. George, *The Columbia Highway: Through the Gorge of the Columbia River with Geologic Interpretations, Former Indian Tribes, Topographic, Historic, Climatic, and Other Interesting Features* (Portland: James, Kerns, and Abbot, 1923); and *The Columbia River Gorge and Mount Hood* (Union Pacific Railroad, undated). Many nineteenth-century descriptions talked about the "middle river" rather than the gorge, referring to the portion between The Cascades (now the Cascade Locks area) and the falls at The Dalles, a stretch served by a separate set of steamboats connected by portage railroads to downriver and upriver shipping.

195

The greenline idea is discussed in Marjorie Corbett, ed., *Greenline Parks: Land Conservation Trends for the Eighties and Beyond* (Washington: National Parks and Conservation Association, 1983); Charles E. Little, *Green-Line Parks: An Approach to Preserving Recreational Landscapes in Urban Areas* (Washington: Library of Congress, Congressional Research Service, 1975); and Stephen C.

Harper, Laura L. Falk, and Edward W. Rankin, *The Northern Forest Lands Study of New England and New York* (Rutland, VT: U.S.D.A. Forest Service, 1990).

For a discussion of the possibilities and problems of place-based politics, see Daniel Kemmis, *Community and the Politics of Place* (Norman: University of Oklahoma Press, 1990); Paul Niebanck, "The Shape of Environmental Planning Education," *Environment and Planning B: Planning and Design*, 20 (1993): 511-18; and Charles Wilkinson, "Toward an Ethic of Place," in *The Eagle Bird: Mapping a New West* (New York: Pantheon, 1992).

Comparator cases are discussed in Charles H. W. Foster, *The Cape Cod National Seashore: A Landmark Alliance* (Hanover, NH: University Press of New England, 1985); Charlotte E. Thomas, "The Cape Cod National Seashore: A Case Study of Federal Administrative Control over Traditionally Local Land Use Decisions," *Boston College Environmental Affairs Law Review*, 12 (Mid-Winter 1985): 225-72.

Richard Liroff and G. Gordon Davis, *Protecting Open Space: Land Use Control in the Adirondack Park* (Cambridge, MA: Ballinger, 1981); Michael K. Heiman, *The Quiet Evolution: Power, Planning and Profits in New York State* (New York: Praeger, 1986); Holly Nelson and Alan J. Hahn, *State Policy and Local Influence in the Adirondacks* (Ithaca, NY: Cornell University Center for Environmental Research, 1980); Alan J. Hahn and Cynthia D. Dyballa, "State Environmental Planning and Local Influence," *Journal of the American Planning Association* (July 1981): 324-35; Richard Booth, "New York's Adirondack Park Agency," in David J. Brower and Daniel S. Carol, eds., *Managing Land-Use Conflicts: Case Studies in Special Area Management* (Durham, NC: Duke University Press, 1987).

Robert J. Mason, *Contested Lands: Conflict and Compromise in New Jersey's Pine Barrens* (Philadelphia: Temple University Press, 1992); Jonathan Berger and John W. Sinton, *Water, Earth, and Fire: Land Use and Environmental Planning in the New Jersey Pine Barrens* (Baltimore: The Johns Hopkins University Press, 1985); Beryl Robichaud Collins and Emily W. B. Russell, eds., *Protecting the New Jersey Pinelands* (New Brunswick, NJ: Rutgers University Press, 1988); Richard M. Hluchan, "Overview of Pinelands Preservation Plan," *New Jersey Lawyer* (August 1983): 21-25; Kevin J. Rielley, Wendy U. Larsen, and Clifford L. Weaver, "Partnership in the Pinelands," in Charles C. Geisler and Frank J. Popper, eds., *Land Reform, American Style* (Totowa, NJ: Rowman and Allanheld, 1984); Richard F. Babcock and Charles L. Sieman, *The Zoning Game Revisited* (Cambridge, MA: Lincoln Institute of Land Policy, 1985); Daniel S. Carol, "New Jersey Pinelands Commission," in Brower and Carol, *Managing Land-Use Conflicts*; R. J. Lilieholm and J. Romm, "Pinelands National Reserve: An Intergovernmental Approach to Nature Preservation," *Environmental Management*, 16: 3 (1993): 335-43.

Douglas H. Strong, *Tahoe: An Environmental History* (Lincoln: University of Nebraska Press, 1984); W. Turrentine Jackson, *Environmental Planning Efforts at Lake Tahoe: The Evolution of Regional Government, 1963-68* (Davis: Institute of Governmental Affairs, University of California, 1974); Bradley R. Mozee, "Government Regulation of Ski Resort Development in the Lake Tahoe Region," *Stanford Environmental Law Journal*, 11(1992): 68-113; Wayne D. Iverson, Stephen R. J. Sheppard, and R. Andrew Strain, "Managing Regional Scenic Quality in the Lake Tahoe Basin," *Landscape Journal*, 12 (1993): 23-39; Richard J. Fink, "Public Land Acquisition for Environmental Protection: Structuring a Program for the Lake Tahoe Basin," *Ecology Law Quarterly*, 18 (1991): 485-557.

196

Several other possible comparison cases appear to lack a substantial analytical literature. These include the Golden Gate National Recreation Area, the Santa Monica Mountains National Recreation Area, the Lower St. Croix National Scenic River (Minnesota-Wisconsin), and the Sawtooth Mountains (Idaho) management program of the U.S.D.A. Forest Service.

Sources for Chapter 1

For patterns of regional urban growth and influence, see Kirkpatrick Sale, *Power Shift: The Rise of the Southern Rim and Its Challenge to the Eastern Establishment* (New York: Random House, 1975); Carl Abbott, *The New Urban America: Growth and Politics in Sunbelt Cities* (Chapel Hill: University of North Carolina Press, 1987) and "The Metropolitan Region: Western Cities in the New Urban Era," in Gerald Nash and Richard Etulain, eds., *The Twentieth Century West* (Albuquerque: University of New Mexico Press, 1990); Peter Hall and Anne Markusen, eds., *Silicon Landscapes* (Boston: Allen and Unwin, 1985); Everett Rogers and Judith Larsen, *Silicon Valley Fever: Growth of High-Technology Culture* (New York: Basic Books, 1984); Peter Hall et al., *The Rise of the Gunbelt* (New York: Oxford University Press, 1991).

The character of the emerging New West is discussed in Ed Marston, ed., *Reopening the Western Frontier* (Washington: Island Press, 1989); Frank Popper, "The Strange Case of the Contemporary American Frontier," *Yale Review*, 76 (Dec. 1986): 101-21. Also see publications of the Denver-based Center for the New West, which has defined itself as a think-tank for the new information-based economy.

The urban dimension of Western environmental politics is discussed in Samuel Hays, *Beauty, Health and Permanence: Environmental Politics in the United States, 1955-1985* (New York: Cambridge University Press, 1987); Kathleen Ferguson, "Toward a Geography of Environmentalism in the United States" (MA thesis, California State University, Hayward, 1985); Thomas A. Wikle, "Geographical Patterns of Membership in U.S. Environmental Organizations," *Professional Geographer*, 47 (Feb. 1995): 41-48; Frank J. Popper, *The Politics of Land-Use Reform* (Madison: University of Wisconsin Press, 1981); Michael Heiman, *The Quiet Evolution: Power, Planning, and Profits in New York State* (New York: Praeger, 1988).

The development of Western tourism is treated in Earl Pomeroy, *In Search of the Golden West: The Tourist in Western America* (New York: A. A. Knopf, 1957); John Jakle, *The Tourist: Travel in Twentieth Century North America* (Lincoln: University of Nebraska Press, 1985); Kevin Starr, *Americans and the California Dream* (New York: Oxford University Press, 1973); Drake Hokanson, *The Lincoln Highway: Main Street Across America* (Iowa City: University of Iowa Press, 1988); and Quinta Scott and Susan Croce Kelly, *Route 66: The Highway and Its People* (Norman: University of Oklahoma Press, 1988). Richard White, *Land Use, Environment and Social Change: The Shaping of Island County, Washington* (Seattle: University of Washington Press, 1980) describes growing recreational use of one part of the rural Northwest.

197

The most comprehensive sources on the history of the Columbia River Highway are its National Register nomination, prepared by Dwight Smith, Oregon Department of Transportation, 1983, and Ronald J. Fahl, "S. C. Lancaster and the Columbia River Highway: Engineer as Conservationist," *Oregon Historical Quarterly*, 74 (June 1973): 101-44. Also useful are Oral Bullard, *Lancaster's Road: The Historic Columbia River Scenic Highway* (Beaverton, Oregon: TMS Book Service, 1982); Alice

Benson Allen, *Simon Benson: Northwest Lumber King* (Portland: Binford and Mort, 1971); C. Lester Horn, "Oregon's Columbia River Highway," *Oregon Historical Quarterly*, 66 (Sept. 1965): 249-71; and Diane Ochi, *Columbia River Highway: Options for Conservation and Reuse* (Seattle: U. S. National Park Service, 1983).

Details about the development of the gorge are found in Fred Lockley, *History of the Columbia River from The Dalles to the Sea* (Chicago: S. J. Clark Publishing Co., 1928) and *History of Hood River County, Oregon, 1852-1982* (Hood River: Hood River County Historical Society, 1982). Recreational development more specifically is described in National Register Nomination for Vista House, by Paul Hartwig, Oregon State Highway Division, 1964; National Register Nomination for Multnomah Falls Lodge, by Jonathan Horn and Mary Stuart, Mount Hood National Forest, 1980. Also see Thomas Cox, *The Park Builders: A History of State Parks in the Pacific Northwest* (Seattle: University of Washington Press, 1988).

The debate over the management of Bonneville Dam is discussed in Charles McKinley, *Uncle Sam in the Pacific Northwest* (Berkeley: University of California Press, 1952), 157-62; Philip Funigiello, "The Bonneville Power Administration and the New Deal," *Prologue*, 5 (Summer 1973): 89-97; William F. Willingham, *Water Power in the Wilderness: The History of Bonneville Lock and Dam* (Portland: U. S. Army Corps of Engineers, 1988).

A number of manuscript collections contain material about Portland's interests in the gorge. These include the papers of the Governor's Committee for a Livable Oregon, Manuscript Collection 2537, Oregon Historical Society; Columbia Gorge Preservation Committee, Manuscript Collection 661B, Oregon Historical Society; Oregon Environmental Council Papers, Manuscript Collection 2386, Oregon Historical Society; Multnomah County Roadmaster papers, Manuscript Collection 2607, Oregon Historical Society; Portland Chamber of Commerce Papers, University of Oregon; Portland Parks Bureau Papers, Archives and Records Center, City of Portland.

Economic development studies include Robert Ormond Case, *River of the West: A Study of Opportunity in the Columbia Empire* (Portland: Northwestern Electric Company and Pacific Power and Light Company, 1940); Ivan Bloch and Associates, *Industrial Plant Sites of Cascade Locks, Hood River County*, for the Port of Cascade Locks, June 1964; U.S.D.A. Forest Service, *Columbia Gorge Recreation Study* (1964); Joseph D. Meyers, *A Plan for Development of the Oregon Mid-Columbia River Waterfront, Prepared for the Mid-Columbia Planning Council* (Salem: Oregon Department of Commerce, 1966); Douglas C. Couch, *Mid-Columbia Park and Open Space Plan* (The Dalles: Mid-Columbia Economic Development District, 1974); J. Jeffrey Murtaugh, *Industrial Site Survey: An Economic Analysis of the Supply, the Potential, and the Demand for Industrial Land in the Mid-Columbia* (The Dalles: Mid-Columbia Economic Development District, 1976).

198

Sources for Chapter 2

This chapter explores both long-term and short-term changes in the economy of the Columbia River Gorge by focusing on the four counties which are the heart of the National Scenic Area—Klickitat and Skamania counties in Washington and Hood River and Wasco counties in Oregon. Clark County, Washington, and Multnomah County, Oregon, are included as appropriate, but county-wide statistics for these areas are so dominated by the urban functions of Portland and Vancouver that they tell little about the National Scenic Area.

The four primary gorge counties are heavily oriented to the Columbia River. The bulk of their development lies along the river and its small tributaries, forced in part by topography, in part by limited water resources, in part by patterns of federal land ownership. As a result, roughly 75 percent of their 63,500 residents live within the Scenic Area boundaries. County-wide data are therefore a reasonable measure of what is happening in the National Scenic Area.

Analysis of long-term trends in population and industrial employment data draw on the decennial census of population. Statistics on farm acreage, farm size, and agricultural land value come from the U.S. Department of Commerce, *Census of Agriculture* for 1992. Other employment data come from the U. S. Department of Commerce's *County Business Patterns.* This annual publication summarizes information on jobs eligible for FICA, excluding all self-employed, all government workers and railroad workers, and certain other classes. Thus it is an incomplete measure but provides comparable annual data. Information on second homes is from the U.S. Census of Housing, *General Housing Characteristics.* In 1980 this source reported 298 dwelling units in the four counties vacant and "held for occasional use." In 1990, the same source reported 1,593 vacant units "held for occasional, seasonal, and recreational use." Housing for migrant farm workers is reported separately.

Other general economic data came from the Oregon Employment Division (unemployment levels); Office of Research and Data Analysis, Washington Department of Social and Health Services (food stamp and AFDC recipients); and Research and Statistics Unit, Adult and Family Services, Oregon Department of Human Resources (food stamp and AFDC recipients); County Treasurer's offices in the four counties (county budgets and timber revenues); and Mid-Columbia Economic Development District (large employers).

The pioneer passage of the gorge is the topic of G. Thomas Edwards, "The Oregon Trail in the Columbia Gorge, 1843-1855: The Final Ordeal," *Oregon Historical Quarterly* 97 (Summer 1996): 134-75.

The history of early navigation is discussed in Randall V. Mills, *Stern-Wheelers Up Columbia: A Century of Steamboating in the Oregon Country* (Palo Alto: Pacific Books, 1947); Fritz Timmen, *Blow for the Landing: A Hundred Years of Steam Navigation on the Waters of the West* (Caldwell, ID: Caxton Printers, 1973); and Dorothy Johanson and Charles Gates, *Empire of the Columbia* (New York: Harper and Row, 1967). Current river traffic data are found in U.S. Army Corps of Engineers publications: *Waterborne Commerce of the United States*, Part 4, (New Orleans, 1993), "Report of Commerce for Willamette, Columbia and Snake Rivers" (Portland 1988); and Lockmaster's Report for Bonneville Lock.

Other aspects of the nineteenth-century economy are discussed in Fred Lockley, *The History of the Columbia River Valley from The Dalles to the Sea* (Chicago: S. J. Clarke Publishing Co., 1928); Ivan Donaldson, *Fishwheels on the Columbia* (Portland: Binford and Mort, 1971); and Francis Seufert, *Wheels of Fortune* (Portland: Oregon Historical Society, 1980).

For the context of national forest harvest policy, consult Paul W. Hirt, *A Conspiracy of Optimism: Management of the National Forests since World War II* (Lincoln: University of Nebraska Press, 1994) and Charles F. Wilkinson, *Crossing the Next Meridian: Land, Water, and the Future of the West* (Washington, DC: Island Press, 1992). Timber harvest data for

199

Oregon, Washington, and the four counties are compiled by the Oregon
Department of Forestry and Washington Department of Natural
Resources.

Outstanding sources on the role of Japanese immigrants in the
development of agriculture are Lauren Kessler, *Stubborn Twig: Three
Generations in the Life of a Japanese-American Family* (New York:
Random House, 1993) and Linda Tamura, *The Hood River Issei: An Oral
History of Japanese Settlers in Oregon's Hood River Valley* (Urbana:
University of Illinois Press, 1993).

We learned about the contemporary gorge economy from interviews
with officials of SDS Lumber, Columbia Aluminum, and the Port of
Skamania County among other interviewees; from articles in gorge
newspapers; from Kathleen S. Morse and Randall S. Anderson, *Tourism
in the Columbia River Gorge* (Seattle: University of Washington Sea Grant,
1988); and from Samuel V. Lankford, *An Analysis of Residential
Preferences, Attitudes and Opinions toward Tourism and Rural Regional
Development in the Columbia River Gorge* (Ph.D. dissertation, University
of Oregon, 1991). Ann Markusen, *Regions: The Economics and Politics of
Territory* (Totowa, NJ: Rowman and Littlefield, 1987) describes product
cycle theory as a framework for understanding industrial transition.

Sources for Chapter 3

Essential to understanding the political background and arguments
about gorge protection are Bowen Blair, Jr., "The Columbia River Gorge
National Scenic Area: The Act, Its Genesis and Legislative History,"
Environmental Law, 17 (1986-1987): 863-969. The key National Park
Service documents that ignited the simmering controversy are *Draft
Study of Alternatives, Columbia River Gorge* (November 1979) and *Study
of Alternatives, Columbia River Gorge* (April 1980). Much of the
discussion is drawn from regional and gorge newspapers (*The Oregonian*,
Skamania County Pioneer, Vancouver *Daily Columbian*) and from
testimony before congressional committees. Important hearings were
held by the Subcommittee on Public Lands and Reserved Water, Senate
Committee on Energy and Natural Resources (March 25, 1983, November
8, 1984, and June 17, 1986) and the Senate Committee on Commerce,
Science and Transportation (Feb. 10, 1983).

Thomas Rudel discusses the context of rural land use planning in
Situations and Strategies in American Land-Use Planning (Cambridge,
England: Cambridge University Press, 1989). Background on religiously
based property rights ideology is found in James Aho, *The Politics of
Righteousness: Idaho Christian Patriotism* (Seattle: University of
Washington Press, 1990).

Among the key actors, the ideas of Chuck Williams are accessible in
his book *Bridge of the Gods, Mountains of Fire: A Return to the Columbia
Gorge* (New York: Friends of the Earth, 1980). A good profile of Nancy
Russell is R. Gregory Nokes, "Nancy Russell: Protector of the Columbia
Gorge," *The Oregonian*, March 29, 1994. Charles Cushman is described
in Rob Eure, "Fiery Defender of Property Rights," *The Oregonian*, January
1, 1995 and Margaret Knox, "The World According to Cushman,"
Wilderness, 56, 200, Spring 1993.

200

Sources for Chapter 4

The text of S. 627 is included in the report of hearings by the U.S. Senate, Committee on Energy and Natural Resources, 1983. The text of S. 2055 is included in the reports of hearings by the same committee in 1986. All references to changes in S. 2055 are taken from the *Columbia River Gorge National Scenic Area Act*, Public Law 99-663-November 17, 1986.

Senator Packwood described his goals in "The Columbia River Gorge Needs Federal Protection," *Environmental Law*, Volume 15, 1984. Other law journal reviews include Gary Myers and Jean Meschke, "Proposed Federal Land Use Management of the Columbia River Gorge," *Environmental Law*, 15 (Fall 1984): 71-113 and the valuable and detailed summary in Bowen Blair, "The Columbia River Gorge National Scenic Area: The Act, Its Genesis and Legislative History," *Environmental Law*, 17 (Summer 1987): 863-969. The formal positions of interested organizations and the often eloquent testimony of individuals are included in the records of the 1983, 1984, and 1986 hearings of the Senate Committee on Energy and Natural Resources and 1983 hearings of the Senate Committee on Commerce, Science, and Transportation.

Portland's metropolitan newspaper, *The Oregonian*, thoroughly covered the legislative process. The colloquies that satisfied Senator Wallop and Senator McClure are in U.S. Congress, *Congressional Record-Senate*, Vol. 132, Part 20, 99th Cong., 2nd Sess., pp. 29506-10.

Sources for Chapter 5

Background on the slowly changing character of the Forest Service is found in Julia Wondolleck, *Public Lands Conflict and Resolution: Managing National Forest Disputes* (New York: Plenum Press, 1988). We also drew on 1987 interviews with the Forest Service's first Scenic Area staffers Art DuFault and Katherine Jesch.

Central to this chapter is comparative analysis of successive planning documents: Columbia River Gorge Commission, *Preliminary Draft Management Plan for General Management Areas*, December, 1990; Columbia River Gorge Commission and U.S.D.A. Forest Service, *Final Draft Management Plan for General and Special Management Areas*, July 1991; and Columbia River Gorge Commission, *Management Plan for the Columbia River Gorge National Scenic Area*, October 15, 1991. Comments about the various drafts of the Management Plan are contained in binders housed in the Columbia River Gorge Commission office in White Salmon, Washington. They are grouped by individual or by organization of origin, such as Nature Conservancy, Friends of the Columbia Gorge, National Wildlife Federation, Wilderness Society, Gorge Audubon Society, Sierra Club, Oregon Natural Resources Council, Native Plant Society of Oregon, Columbia Gorge Boardsailors' Association, Columbia Gorge United, and gorge businesses.

These documents and comments are supplemented with various Forest Service and Gorge Commission materials, including minutes of commission meetings, annual reports, the Commission's *GMA Gorge Planning Update*, internal memoranda, and interviews with commission staffers Richard Benner, Allen Bell, James Johnson, and Brian Litt. The planning process is chronicled in *The Oregonian* and in gorge community newspapers. A critical external perspective is found in the Columbia Gorge Coalition's newsletter *Gorge Winds*.

Two specific dimensions of gorge planning and protection are discussed in Kristine Olson Rogers, "Native American Collaboration in Cultural Resource Protection in the Columbia River Gorge National Scenic Area," *Vermont Law Review* 17(3): Spring, 1993 and Gordon Mathews Euler, "The Politics of Scenery: Scenic Resources Management in the Columbia River Gorge National Scenic Area" (Ph.D. dissertation, Portland State University, 1996).

Sources for Chapter 6

This chapter interweaves the reactions of opinion leaders living within or near the gorge with an analysis of several implementation issues. Where the previous chapter looked over the shoulders of Forest Service and Gorge Commission planners, we now shift point of view to that of gorge residents; some of the same issues appear in a different light. We used a formal, open-ended questionnaire to conduct over thirty interviews in 1992-93 and 1995. The interviewees include environmentalists active in creation of the Scenic Area, a county commissioner or county judge from each of the four counties at the heart of the gorge, major landowners, newspaper editors, representatives of local businesses, and economic development officials. We asked about their perceptions of the Gorge Commission and the planning process. We also asked them to name the best and the worst features of the Act, comment on its effect on the local economy, and say whether the Act has held any surprises. Their open-ended responses indicate the issues in the forefront of people's minds as the new regulatory regime is put in place. For Tables 6.1 and 6.2 we grouped the interviewees into four categories:

(1) Portland/Vancouver: Persons living in the Portland metropolitan area: Tom Koenninger, Kris Olsen Rogers, Linda Sokomano, and Bob Thompson.

(2) Residents by Choice: Persons living in Hood River, Skamania, Klickitat or Wasco counties who moved there from elsewhere: Raelynn Atay, Barbara Bailey, Stuart Chapin, Scott Hege, Tyler Keyes, Will Macht, Jack Mills, Pat Schroder, Nancy Sourek.

(3) Local, New Generation: Persons living in the four-county Gorge area who are part of the newer generation of leadership: Sverre Bakke, Melissa Carlson-Price, Vicki Ellett, Louie Pitt, Tom Reynolds, George Rohrbacher, and Dan Spatz.

(4) Local, Old Generation: Persons in the four-county area with a long history of participation in local businesses or politics prior to adoption of NSA: Austen Abrams, Pat Bleakney, Bob Chamberlain (and Frank Backus), Lorretta Ellett (and Vance Ellett), Chief Johnny Jackson, John Mabrey, Ed McLarney, Jerry Routson, Dennis White, Chuck Williams, and Joe Wrabek.

We also draw on coverage in the *Hood River News*, *The Oregonian*, *Goldendale Sentinel*, *The Dalles Chronicle*, Vancouver *Daily Columbian*, and *Skamania County Pioneer*; on Gorge Commission minutes and staff memos; on Forest Service documents about land acquisition plans; and on Cascade Planning Associates, *Columbia Gorge National Scenic Area: Existing Land Use Inventory* (July 1988). The discussion of perceptions of opponents draws on Paul Sabatier, Susan Hunter, and Susan McLaughlin, "The Devil Shift: Perceptions and Misperceptions of Opponents," *Western Political Quarterly*, 1986.

Sources for Chapter 7

For arguments and documentation about Bridal Veil, see Heritage Investment Corporation, "Bridal Veil, Multnomah County, Oregon: Historical and Architectural Evaluation," prepared for The Trust for Public Land (August 20, 1992) and Sharr Prohaska, "History of the Development of Bridal Veil, Oregon and the Bridal Veil Lumbering Company," prepared for Multnomah County (June 1992).

Lawrence Watters, "The Columbia River Gorge National Scenic Area Act," *Environmental Law*, 23 (4): 1127-42 discusses legal challenges to the Scenic Area.

Recent analyses of changes in the larger Northwest economy are Ray Rasker, *A New Home on the Range: Economic Realities in the Columbia River Basin* (Washington, DC: The Wilderness Society, 1995); Tom Power et al., *Economic Well-Being and Environmental Protection in the Pacific Northwest: A Consensus Report by Pacific Northwest Economists* (1996). These can be placed in the context of William Robbins, *Colony and Empire* (Lawrence: University Press of Kansas, 1994), which interprets Western regional change in terms of global capitalism.

Good introductions to a large rural studies literature on the dynamics of rural social and economic change are Art Gallaher, Jr., "Dependence on External Authority and the Decline of Community," in Art Gallaher, Jr., and Harland Padfield, eds., *The Dying Community* (Albuquerque: University of New Mexico Press, 1980), 85-108; Daryl Hobbs, "Social Organization in the Countryside" and Mark Drabenstott and Tim R. Smith, "Finding Rural Success: The New Rural Economic Landscape and Its Implications," both in Emery Castle, ed., *The Changing American Countryside* (Lawrence: University Press of Kansas, 1995).

Key sources on the changing scale of American social organization are Robert Wiebe, *The Search for Order, 1877-1920* (New York: Hill and Wang, 1967) and *The Segmented Society: An Introduction to the Meaning of America* (New York: Oxford University Press, 1975); Kenneth Boulding, *The Organizational Revolution* (New York: Harper, 1953); John Kenneth Galbraith, *American Capitalism* (Boston: Houghton Mifflin, 1952); Louis Galambos, "The Emerging Organizational Synthesis in American History," *Business History Review*, 44 (1970): 279-90; Robert Berkhofer, Jr., "The Organizational Interpretation of American History: A New Synthesis," *Prospects*, 4 (1979): 611-29.

Social theorists who have explored the distinction between local and cosmopolitan orientations include Robert Merton, *Social Theory and Social Structure* (Glencoe, IL: Free Press, 1957); Don Martindale and R. Galen Hanson, *Small Town and the Nation: The Conflict of Local and Translocal Forces* (Westport, CT: Greenwood Publishing Co., 1969); C. Wright Mills, *White Collar: The American Middle Classes* (New York: Oxford University Press, 1951); John Kenneth Galbraith, *The Affluent Society* (Boston: Houghton Mifflin, 1958) and *The New Industrial State* (Boston: Houghton Mifflin, 1967); B. Bruce-Biggs, ed., *The New Class?* (New Brunswick, NJ: Transaction Books, 1979). A recent attack on the rootless culture of the "talking classes" is Christopher Lasch, *The Revolt of the Elites and the Betrayal of Democracy* (New York: W. W. Norton, 1995).

A classic study of the capture of planning efforts by local economic and political interests is Philip Selznick, *TVA and the Grassroots* (Berkeley: University of California Press, 1949).

203

Notes

Introduction

page 1—*Francis Fuller Victor*: from *Atlantis Arisen, or Talks of a Tourist about Oregon and Washington* (1891), page 54.

page 1—*Commissioner H.J. Vandenberg*: Paul Koberstam and Jeannie Senior, "Bill Signing Brings Celebration, Shock," *The Oregonian*, November 18, 1986.

page 4—*Union Pacific Railway*: Henry T. Finck, *The Pacific Coast Scenic Tour* (New York: Charles Scribner's Sons, 1890), 189; *Wealth and Resources of Oregon and Washington; The Pacific Northwest: A Complete Guide over the Local Lines of the Union Pacific Railway* (Portland: Passenger Department, Union Pacific Railway, 1889), 248.

page 5—*curiosity, and admiration combine"*: Francis Fuller Victor, *Atlantis Arisen, or Talks of a Tourist about Oregon and Washington* (Philadelphia: J. B. Lippincott, 1891), 54.

page 6—*"resettle"*: The term is from Ed Marston, *Reopening the Western Frontier* (Washington: Island Press, 1989).

page 10—*the future of those communities"*: "Hatfield Makes Stops in Gorge," *Gorge Weekly*, June 9, 1995.

page 12—*Las Vegas or Disneyland*: The specific terminology and many of the concepts in this paragraph are drawn from several unpublished papers by Hal Rothman: "Tourism and Transformation: The Evolution of Tourism in the Twentieth-Century American West," "Tourism as Colonial Economy: The Distribution of Economic Power and the Significance of Place in Western Tourism," and "'East Goes West, West Goes East:' The Structure of Tourism and Its Impact on Place in the Development of the Modern American West."

page 14 (sidebar)—*local knowledge)*: Paul Niebanck, "The Shape of Environmental Planning Education," *Environment and Planning B: Planning and Design*, 20 (1993): 511-18.

page 19—*ethic of place*: Charles Wilkinson, "Toward an Ethic of Place," in *The Eagle Bird: Mapping a new West* (New York: Patheon, 1992).

pages 21, 22, table—Source: Columbia River Gorge Commission, *Final Draft Management Plan for General and Special Management Areas*, July 1991

Chapter 1

page 23—*"private Elysium"*: John Yeon to Tom McCall, September 12, 1967, copy reproduced by Oregon Roadside Council, in Governor's Committee for a Livable Oregon Papers, Oregon Historical Society.

page 25—*Trying to survive"*: Harold Walton, quoted in William G. Robbins, *Hard Times in Paradise: Coos Bay, Oregon, 1850-1986* (Seattle: University of Washington Press, 1988), 162.

page 27—*republished in 1916 and 1926*: Samuel C. Lancaster, *The Columbia: America's Great Highway through the Cascade Mountains to the Sea* (Portland: J. K. Gill Co., 1926).

page 27—*public rooms and cabins*: Henry T. Finck, *The Pacific Coast Scenic Tour* (New York: Charles Scribner's Sons, 1890), 189; *Wealth and Resources of Oregon and Washington, The Pacific Northwest, A Complete Guide over the Local Lines of the Union Pacific Railway* (Portland: Passenger Department of the Union Pacific Railway, 1889), 248; *Summer Saunterings over the Lines of the Oregon Railway and Navigation Company and the Northern Pacific Railroad* (Portland: George Himes, 1882).

page 27—*the wondering senses"*: Francis Fuller Victor, *Atlantis Arisen, or Talks of a Tourist about Oregon and Washington* (Philadelphia: J. B. Lippincott, 1891), 55.

page 27—*series of backdrops:* Sarah Hall Ladd: *Columbia River Scenery* (Portland, 1904); William D. Lyman, *The Columbia River: Its History, Its Myths, Its Scenery, Its Commerce, Including a Section on the River Today* (New York: G.P. Putnam's Sons, 1904).

page 29—*Portland's greatest assets: Oregon Journal,* Feb 21, 1915.

page 31—*and Mount Defiance for park use: Major Traffic Street Plan, Boulevard and Park System for Portland, Oregon* (Portland: City Planning Commission, 1921), 81-87.

page 32—*Columbia Scenic Highway": Tourist's Guide of Portland and Vicinity* (Portland: Portland Chamber of Commerce, 1922); *Portland, Oregon, Featuring the Columbia River Highway* (Portland: Broadway Auto Service, 1925); Edward S. Jordan, *A Tribute to Portland* (Portland: Portland Chamber of Commerce, n.d.).

page 33—*new state parks department:* C. P. Keyser to S. H. Boardman, April 7, 1947, in Portland Archives and Records Center, Correspondence-Parks Bureau Superintendent, RS 720G-01.

page 33—*to the markets of the world:* Bonneville Power Administration, *Columbia River Industrial Survey: Astoria to The Dalles* (Portland, 1940; reissued 1944).

page 33—*Columbia River power is distributed":* John H. Lewis, Commissioner, to Port of Portland Commission, Jan. 31, 1936, Box 35, Portland Chamber of Commerce Papers, University of Oregon [hereafter cited as Portland Chamber Papers].

page 34—*a truly regional resource: Tacoma Progress,* March 1938 [newsletter of Tacoma Chamber of Commerce], in Box 16, Portland Chamber Papers.

page 35—*direct cost of production:* W. D. B. Dodson to Arthur Farmer, Jan. 18, 1935, Box 16, Portland Chamber Papers.

page 35—*a 1937 report: Report on the Problem of Conservation and Development of Scenic and Recreational Resources of the Columbia Gorge in Washington and Oregon* (Portland: Pacific Northwest Regional Planning Commission, 1937).

page 36—*no place for factories":* Malcolm Bauer, "The Columbia Gorge: Scenery Versus Industry," *The Oregonian,* Nov. 27, 1938, magazine section, p. 8. Samuel C. Lancaster, dedication to F. M. Richards, Aug. 30, 1939, in *The Columbia* (copy in authors' possession).

page 36—*near the Sandy River:* Lewis Mumford, *Regional Planning in the Northwest: A Memorandum* (Portland: Northwest Regional Council, 1939); "Confidential Report to Hon. Harold Ickes, Secretary of the Interior, of a conference of engineers and economists on Bonneville Power, held at the University Club, Portland, Oregon, June 19, 1937, by the Oregon Commonwealth Federation," Box 15, Portland Chamber Papers; Oregon Planning Board, revised draft of "Report on Bonneville Power," April 1, 1936, p. 48, Box 35, Portland Chamber Papers; City Club of Portland, "Progress Report Frowns on Blanket Rates for Bonneville," *Portland City Club Bulletin* (May 22, 1936), 11; Joseph K. Carson, Jr., testimony to House Committee on Rivers and Harbors [1937], Box 15, Portland Chamber Papers.

page 37—*recreation, scenic and historic areas":* ORS 358-610-630.

page 38—*roads and basic facilities":* Quoted phrases from "Statement of J. Michael McCloskey on Preliminary Findings of the Columbia Gorge Recreation Study, Mount Hood National Forest, September 18, 1964," in Oregon Environmental Council Papers, Manuscript Collection 2386, Oregon Historical Society.

page 39—*"quiet recreational activities":* Vancouver *Columbian,* July 14, 1971; *Report of Mazama Study of Columbia Gorge Area* (Nov. 1969), in papers of Governor's Committee for a Livable Oregon, Oregon Historical Society; "Testimony of Oregon Environmental Council . . . May 16, 1972," Oregon Environmental Council Papers, Oregon Historical Society.

page 39—*cliff-faces of the gorge*": Douglas C. Couch, *Mid-Columbia Park and Open Space Plan* (The Dalles: Mid-Columbia Economic Development District, 1974), 44; "Report of the Committee on Recreation to the Columbia River Gorge Conference [1970], in Oregon Environmental Council Papers, Oregon Historical Society.

Chapter 2

page 42—*Now you have a choice*": Bev Rowland, Hood River County commissioner, in *Hood River News,* April 17, 1996

page 42—*make a go of it*": *Hood River News,* March 20, 1993, reprinting story from March 26, 1959.

page 44—*power within the gorge*: Joe Wrabek and Ed McLarney interviews.

page 48 (sidebar)—*to enforce their demands*": David Thompson, July 28, 1811, at the Cascades. David Thompson, *Columbia Journals,* ed. Barbara Belyea (Montreal and Kingston: McGill-Queen's University Press, 1994).

page 52—*timber-scarce eastern locales*: Fritz Timmen, *Blow for the Landing: A Hundred Years of Steam Navigation on the Waters of the West* (Caldwell, ID: Caxton Printers, 1973), 7.

page 54—*the orchardists here*: Ruth McClain Guppy, *Hood River News* supplement "Made in Hood River County," Fall 1992, p. 24.

page 55—*novel River Song*: Craig Lesley, *River Song* (Boston: Houghton Mifflin, 1989).

page 62—*less into the sailing part*": Blake Richards as quoted in *Hood River News,* "Made in Hood River County" supplement, fall 1991, p. 26.

page 67—*outside the county in 1992*: Melissa Carlson-Price interview (an argument supported by a position paper prepared by Skamania County staff in 1992).

Chapter 3

page 71—*in this section of the gorge*": U. S. Senate, Committee on Energy and Natural Resources, 1983, pp. 407, 411.

page 72—*part of an environmentalist conspiracy*": Tom Alkire, "Twilight for the Gorge," *Willamette Week,* April 21, 1980.

page 73—*significant population increases*": National Park Service, *Draft Study of Alternatives, Columbia River Gorge,* November, 1979, p. 51.

page 73—*protect threatened farmlands*": National Park Service, *Draft,* p. 54.

page 74—*Oregon cannot adopt*": John Yeon to Governor Thomas McCall, in Papers of the Governor's Committee for a Livable Oregon, Oregon Historical Society.

page 77—*agree on how to do it*": Pat Moser, "Everyone Agrees the Gorge is Beautiful, but..." *The Columbian* (Vancouver, WA), April 13, 1980.

page 79—*would be applied forcefully*": National Park Service, *Study of Alternatives, Columbia River Gorge,* April 1980, p. 173.

page 79—*would have made it infeasible*": National Park Service, *Study of Alternatives,* p. 181.

page 81—*or they will take it away from you*": Katy Tichenor, "Inholders Representative Tells Fate of Communities," *Skamania County Pioneer,* March 6, 1981.

206 page 81—*except for boundary defense*": U. S. Senate, Committee on Energy and Natural Resources, 1983, pp. 378-379.

page 82—*is at all a good idea*": U. S. Senate, Committee on Commerce, Science, and Transportation, *Hearing on the Columbia River Gorge,* 98th Congress, 1st Session, February 10, 1983, p. 96.

page 85—*where development already is*": *Hood River News,* April 17, 1996.

page 86—*variances upon request*": U. S. Senate, Subcommittee on Public Lands and Reserved Water of the Committee on Energy and Natural Resources, *Hearing on the Columbia River Gorge,* 98th Congress, 2nd Session, November 8, 1984, pp. 273-74.

Chapter 4

page 88—*Packwood noted*: U. S. Senate, Committee on Energy and Natural
   Resources, 1984, pp. 9-10.

page 90—*the provisions of the Act"*: U. S. Senate, Committee on Energy and
   Natural Resources, 1983, p. 31.

page 91—*is not substantially changed"*: U. S. Senate, Committee on Energy
   and Natural Resources, 1983, p. 35.

page 92—*two sitting Governors is historic"*: U. S. Senate, Committee on
   Energy and Natural Resources, 1983, p. 43.

page 92—*the support of both States"*: U. S. Senate, Committee on Energy and
   Natural Resources, 1983, pp. 49-50.

page 93—*by state and local agencies"*: U. S. Senate, Committee on Energy
   and Natural Resources, 1984, p. 626.

page 93—*will not protect the Gorge"*: U. S. Senate, Committee on Energy and
   Natural Resources, 1984, p. 257.

page 93—*requirements means shut-down"*: U. S. Senate, Committee on
   Energy and Natural Resources, 1984, p. 160.

page 94—*that are already dividing it"*: U. S. Senate, Committee on Energy and
   Natural Resources, 1983, p. 140.

page 99—*as necessary to ensure compliance"*: U. S. Senate, Committee on
   Energy and Natural Resources, 1986, p. 49.

page 102—*the use of private lands"*: U. S. Senate, Committee on Energy and
   Natural Resources, 1986, p. 132.

page 104—*zoning for non-federal lands"*: U. S. Senate, Committee on Energy
   and Natural Resources, 1986, p. 133.

page 107—*necessary to ensure compliance"*: *Columbia River Gorge National
   Scenic Area Act*, Public Law 99-663-November 17, 1986, p. 4297.

page 108—*management of the Columbia River Gorge"*: James Flanigan,
   "Hesitant Reagan Signs Columbia Gorge Bill," *The Oregonian*, November 18,
   1986.

page 109—*Daniel Mazmanian and Paul Sabatier. Implementation and Public
   Policy*, Glenview: Scott, Foresman and Company, 1983, p. 41.

page 109—*protecting the resources mentioned in (1)"*: *Columbia River Gorge
   National Scenic Area Act*, Public Law 99-663-November 17, 1986, p. 4276.

Chapter 5

page 114—*it's just how you go about it"*: Joyce Reinig, Columbia River gorge
   commissioner, in *Hood River News*, April 17, 1996.

page 114—*to assess whether it worked"*: Art Carroll, Forest Service manager
   for Columbia Gorge, in *Hood River News*, April 17, 1996.

page 118—*during the interim period*: Bowen Blair, Jr., to Dale Robertson, May
   8, 1987.

page 119—*ordinances are even adopted"*: Jeanie Senior, "Gorge Panel to Take
   Over Development Reviews in December," *The Oregonian*, October 28, 1987.

page 119—*financially in ruins"*: Columbia Gorge Coalition, "Columbia Gorge
   'Protection' Failing," *Gorge Winds*, Autumn, 1988.

page 120—*to stop the continuing destruction"*: Columbia Gorge Coalition,
   "Columbia Gorge 'Protection' Failing," *Gorge Winds*, Autumn, 1988.

page 122—*likely to acquire in a year"*: Larry Hilderbrand, "County Merits Best
   Gorge Panelist," (Editorial) *The Oregonian*, June 20, 1987.

page 133—*We assume this is an oversight"*: Friends of the Columbia Gorge,
   March 15, 1991, p. 2.

page 133—*to ignore statutory direction"*: Comments on Preliminary Draft
   Management Plan, in numbered binders at Gorge Commission office, White
   Salmon, Washington. The materials are identified by a letter-number code:
   Sierra Club, Northwest Office, L-636; Sierra Club, Columbia Group, L-665;
   Oregon Natural Resources Council, L-675; Friends of the Columbia Gorge,
   March 15, 1991, p. 25.

page 134—*That means endless litigation*": Jeanie Senior, "2 Washington Officials Criticize Gorge Plan," *The Oregonian*, February 23, 1991.

page 135—*in a disputed development review*": Kristine Olson Rogers, "Native American Collaboration in Cultural Resource Protection in the Columbia River Gorge National Scenic Area," *Vermont Law Review* 17(3): Spring 1993, p. 778.

page 136—*the vision for the future of the Gorge*": Columbia River Gorge Commission and USDA Forest Service, *Final Draft Management Plan for General and Special Management Areas*, July, 1991, p. vi.

page 137—*as much as possible*": Comments in Gorge Commission office: Friends of the Columbia Gorge, F-383, pp. 17-20.

page 138—*other provisions of this Plan*": Columbia River Gorge Commission, *GMA Gorge Planning Update*, June, 1991, p. 4; Columbia River Gorge Commission and U.S.D.A. Forest Service, *Final Draft Management Plan for General and Special Management Areas*, July, 1991, p. II-4.

page 138—*agriculture or forest practices*": Columbia River Gorge Commission and USDA Forest Service, *Final Draft Management Plan for General and Special Management Areas*, July, 1991, p. II-4.

page 140—*in favor of economic development*": Comments in Gorge Commission office: Friends of the Columbia Gorge, F-383, p. 1.

page 140—*and we lost*": Comments in Gorge Commission office: Columbia Gorge Coalition, F-209.

page 141—*well-being of Gorge people*": Skamania County Commissioners Position Statement, November 8, 1991, quote on p. 3. In binder with other Final Draft Plan comments.

page 141—*still much too specific*": Comments in Gorge Commission office: Booth Gardner, F-206, p. 2.

page 141—*to a much greater extent:* Comments in Gorge Commission office: Gardner, F-206, pp. 2-6.

page 141—*lessening the standards of the plan*": Columbia River Gorge Commission, *Minutes, Commission Meeting*, October 12, 1991, pp. 5-8.

page 142—*within the Department of Agriculture*": Rogers, "Native American Collaboration," p. 783.

page 144—*voted no*: Columbia River Gorge Commission, *Minutes of Commission Meeting*, October 15, 1991, pp. 17-21.

page 145—*ordinance the Commission adopted*": Skamania County Board of Commissioners to John Butruille, Regional Forester, November 15, 1991. In binder with other Final Draft Plan Comments.

Chapter 6

page 148—*who call this place our home*": Tom Koenninger, "A Storm in the Gorge," *The Vancouver Daily Columbian*, Feb. 14, 1993

page 150—*a necessary evil*": Austen Abrams interview; Joyce Reinig and Ray Matthew, quoted in Neita Cecil, "Four Original Members of the Gorge Panel Reflect on Last Seven Years," *Gorge Weekly*, April 22, 1994.

page 152—*more conciliatory styles:* This is particularly true of Tahoe and the Adirondacks.

page 152—*without imposing more regulation*": *Goldendale Sentinel*, February 11, 1993.

page 153—*changes in people's attitudes*": Carol York, letter to *Hood River News*, August 7, 1993; Cecil, "Four Original Members of Gorge Panel Reflect."

page 154—*on the people of the gorge*": Mary Lou Braden, letter to *Hood River News*, April 1, 1995. Also see letters to *The Oregonian* by Doug Holleston, April 8, 1994, and Stanley and Catherine Anderson, April 16, 1994.

page 154—*cooperation runs out*": *Skamania County Pioneer*, March 13, 1993.

page 155—*champagne and brie crowd*": Chuck Williams, Dan Spatz interviews: Stanley and Catherine Anderson of Stevenson used similar language in a letter to *The Oregonian*, April 16, 1994.

page 159—*approved by the federal government*": "Only a Beginning," *Hood River News*, Dec. 31, 1994; *Hood River News*, Dec. 21, 1994 and April 16, 1995; *Gorge Weekly*, Dec. 23, 1994.

page 160—*environmental and scenic concepts*": Jeanie Senior, "Gorge Plan Still Subject of Debate," *The Oregonian*, Sept. 9, 1991.

page 165—*in the Management Plan*": Columbia River Gorge Commission, "Briefing Paper: Land Acquisition in the Columbia River Gorge National Scenic Area" (October 20, 1993) and Minutes, October 26, 1993. Also *The Oregonian*, Nov. 25, 1992; Vancouver *Daily Columbian*, Nov. 29,1992; *The Dalles Chronicle*, March 22, 1993.

page 165—*for a VW*": Steve Mayes, "Environmental Activists Criticize the Gorge Act," *The Oregonian*, March 22, 1993.

page 172—*than is probably the case*": Paul Sabatier, Susan Hunter and Susan McLaughlin, "The Devil Shift: Perceptions and Misperceptions of Opponents," *Western Political Quarterly*, 40 (September 1986): 449-76.

page 172—*powerful forces of change:* "Gorge Partnership" (editorial), *Hood River News*, April 19, 1995; letter from Mary Lou Braden to *Hood River News*, April 19, 1995.

page 173—*barrier to exurban sprawl:* George Rohrbacher, quoted in *Hood River News*, April 17, 1996.

page 173—*the act passed when it did*": Sally Newell, letter to *Hood River News*, Dec. 28, 1994.

Chapter 7

page 174—*plowing of the pastures of heaven*": William Kittredge, *Who Owns the West?* (San Francisco: Mercury House, 1996), p. 143.

page 174—*angry citizen from the room:* Jesse Burkhardt, "Bingen Council Meeting Erupts with Controversy," *Hood River News*, May 18 1996.

page 174—*the question unresolved:*"Public Speaks Out: No Motel," *Hood River News*, April 23, 1994; "Tempers Flare at Port's First Hearing on Marina," *Hood River News*, May 14, 1994.

page 176—*character of subregions:* Jeanie Senior, "Gorge Plan Still Subject of Debate," *The Oregonian*, Sept. 9, 1991; Sourek interview.

page 177—*"You Own the Columbia River Gorge"*: Senior, "Gorge Plan Still Subject of Debate;" Julie Wilson, "You Own the Columbia River Gorge," *Town and Country*, 146 (September, 1992): 94-103; *The Oregonian*, March 29, 1994.

page 177—*professional calls "gorge creep"*: George Rohrbacher interview.

page 179—*"a lumber mill Disneyland"*: Jonathan Nicholas, "Chain Saws Roar, Bulldozers Growl . . . Tree Huggers Cheer?" *The Oregonian*, October 6, 1992; *The Oregonian*, March 29, 1994; John Yeon, testimony to Multnomah County Planning Commission, October 19, 1992; Nancy Russell, testimony to Multnomah County Planning Commission, October 19, 1992.

page 179—*opponent of the Scenic Area:* Stephen Kenney, Jr., letter to Multnomah County Planning Commission (received October 5, 1992).

page 181—*lucite over everything*": George Rohrbacher interview; Dan Spatz interview; Senior, "Gorge Plan Still Subject of Debate."

page 181—*"snapshot" that freezes change:* George Rohrbacher and Dan Spatz interview; Senior, "Gorge Plan Still Subject of Debate."

page 182—*complexity of institutions:* This understanding of United States history draws on historian Robert Wiebe's argument that the U.S. has moved from a nineteenth-century federation of "island communities" to a fully integrated national society in the twentieth century. It also draws on the work of historically minded social scientists such as Kenneth Boulding and John Kenneth Galbraith.

page 183—*national commitments and connections*: Academic readers may recognize that the distinction between Columbians and Cascadians (and part of the terminology) is adapted from the work of several sociologists who tried to pinpoint the nature of social change in mid-century America. Most basic is Robert Merton's description of a shift of community economic leadership from "locals" to "cosmopolitans." Increases in the scale of economic and social life, he argued, have tended to divide communities between members whose interests are confined to local problems and concerns and those who regard themselves as "integral parts" of the larger world. Cosmopolitans are likely to have lived in a series of cities around the country and are unlikely to feel rooted their current place of residence. They may enjoy their present community, but they do not depend on its future for their own.

In his book *White Collar* (1951), C. Wright Mills drew a related contrast between the "old middle class" of small business proprietors and skilled artisans and a rapidly growing "new middle class" of salaried white-collar workers whose careers and status are based on their levels of knowledge and expertise rather than their direct ownership of property or involvement the processes of production. In *The Affluent Society* (1958), John Kenneth Galbraith amplified Mills by talking about a "New Class" whose entry ticket is education. A decade later, in *The New Industrial State* (1967), he subdivided the group into the corporate and government managers and the "educational and scientific estate" (or what we might call knowledge workers) but argued that their similarities outweighed their differences.

page 190—*devil's bargain*: Hal K. Rothman, "Tourism and Transformation: The Evolution of Tourism in the Twentieth Century West," unpublished paper.

page 190—*inevitable in a dynamic society:* Charles F. Wilkinson, "Toward an Ethic of Place," in Charles F. Wilkinson, *The Eagle Bird: Mapping a New West* (New York: Pantheon, 1992), 145.

page 192—*protect us from them!":* George Rohrbacher, "Opponents May Need Gorge Act," *The Oregonian*, Dec. 27, 1995.

page 193—*"and they are going to be"*: Kittredge, 133.

page 193—*while staying true to our own"*: Kittredge, 142.

Index

Adirondack Park (New York), 7, 20-22, 10, 69, 83, 98, 115, 151, 176, 187
Agriculture: 54-56; immigrant workers, 55; farm acreage, 56; in management plans, 138, 160
Ainsworth, John C., 30
Atiyeh, Victor, 74, 87, 92, 95
AuCoin, Les, 108
Audubon Society, 93, 131

Bailey, Barbara, 79, 120, 144
Benner, Richard, 107, 123-24, 142, 146, 151, 156
Benson, Simon, 28, 30, 31
Bingen, Washington, 59, 97, 174, 177
Blair, Bowen, 179
Bleakney, Pat, 122, 141, 144, 146, 168
Boardsailing. See Windsurfing
Bonker, Don, 108
Bonneville Power Administration, 33, 38, 60
Bonneville Dam, 4, 33-37, 49, 59
Bridal Veil, Oregon, 178-79
Burdoin Mountain [Washington], 162
Bureau of Land Management, 26
Butcher, Kathleen, 146, 166

Callahan, Ed, 79
Cannard, David, 120-21, 141, 146
Cape Cod National Seashore, 7, 20-22, 69, 83, 115, 176
Carlson-Price, Melissa, 151
Catherine Creek [Washington], 162
Celilo Falls, 2, 4, 48, 49, 185
Chapin, F. Stuart, 96, 120-21, 141, 144, 146
Chenowith Table [Oregon], 158
Chesapeake Bay, 10

Clark County, Washington, planning, 13, 14-15; residential development, 72; and Scenic Area, 111, 186; implementing ordinance, 158-59
Clark, Don, 82, 120, 141, 144, 146
Columbia River Gorge National Scenic Area Act: evaluation, 109-13
Columbia Gorge Coalition, 72, 82, 84-85; and legislation, 89, 95, 101; and Scenic Area, 112, 119, 131, 132, 150, 154
Columbia River Gorge National Scenic Area: summarized, 6-10; land ownership, 8; population 8; evaluation, 17-19, 109-13, 153, 188-93; legal challenges, 135, 177, 188; as inter-governmental program, 186-87. See also Management Plan, Urban Areas, General Management Area, Special Management Area, Senate Bill 627, Senate Bill 2055
Columbia Gorge Development Bank, 94, 169-70
Columbia River Gorge Commission: in S. 2055, 98, 99-100; and Interim Guidelines, 118-19, 125; initial membership, 120-22; vision statement, 121, 188-90; relationship to Friends of Columbia Gorge, 122-23; executive director, 123-24, 146,152-53; early decisions, 125-29; development approvals, 128-29, 171; draft management plan, 129-31; approves final management plan, 142-46; new members, 146, 152; approach to enforcement, 152-53; in

federal system, 187; funding, 189
Columbia Gorge Boardsailors Association, 131, 137
Columbia Gorge United, 94, 146
Columbia River Gorge: physical features, 2; early exploration and settlement, 3-4, 48; description, 5-6; subareas, 17, 150
Columbia River Highway, 4, 27, 28-32, 103, 107, 176
Committee to Preserve Property Rights, 82, 84
Conference center. See Skamania Lodge
Corbett, Oregon, 65, 162-63
County implementing ordinances, 144, 156-60. See also Local control
Cultural resource management, 130-31, 134-35, 142, 171, 178-79
Cushman, Charles, 81, 85

Dallesport, Washington, 177
Dodson, W. D. B., 34
Doherty, Jonathan, 152-53, 166
Draft Management Plans: development, 129-31; public input, 130; public responses, 131-35; county opposition, 134-35; legal challenge, 135
DuFault, Art, 116, 181

Eagle Creek, 31
Economic development policy, in 1930s, 33-37; in 1960s, 38-39; in S. 2055, 102-103; in Management Plan, 137; Scenic Area incentives, 168-70
Economic transition, 6, 11-12, 42-47, 61-69, 84, 86, 94; in S. 2055, 102-3, 106-7, 170. See also Modernization
Employment, 46, 58, 59, 64, 66-67
Endangered Species Act, 26, 53

Rowena Plateau. Inset: Sign dedicating the Nature Conservancy's Governor Tom McCall Preserve at Rowena Plateau.
(Photos: Plateau: USDA Forest Service. Sign: authors)

ambitions with their local community and its region. Town and city economies revolved around the production, processing, trade, and management of regional resources. Three groups were mutually dependent on the future of their county and town—business owners, farm and factory workers who supplied their labor force, and locally oriented professionals such as school teachers, courthouse lawyers, and country doctors. Even the tycoons of Portland, with their investments in railroads, mills, and timber lands, shared a regional economic alliance with small business people and the working classes. Local communities were insulated from the world, making connections largely through long-distance trade.

Social dynamics have changed in the later decades of the century. Now living side by side with the Old Westerners are a growing group of city-centered people whose chief economic asset is often the ability to access and manipulate information. Their livelihood and sense of personal identity are based in national (or even international) professional networks and business corporations. They find themselves in Camas or Hood River out of personal choice and opportunity, but their commitments are to peers and careers as much as to particular places and regions. Loyalty to place of residence is in constant tension with their national commitments and connections.

183